MW00846111

Frank Kane's Taming Big Data with Apache Spark and Python

Real-world examples to help you analyze large datasets with Apache Spark

Frank Kane

BIRMINGHAM - MUMBAI

Frank Kane's Taming Big Data with Apache Spark and Python

Copyright © 2017 Packt Publishing

All rights reserved. No part of this book may be reproduced, stored in a retrieval system, or transmitted in any form or by any means, without the prior written permission of the publisher, except in the case of brief quotations embedded in critical articles or reviews.

Every effort has been made in the preparation of this book to ensure the accuracy of the information presented. However, the information contained in this book is sold without warranty, either express or implied. Neither the author, nor Packt Publishing, and its dealers and distributors will be held liable for any damages caused or alleged to be caused directly or indirectly by this book.

Packt Publishing has endeavored to provide trademark information about all of the companies and products mentioned in this book by the appropriate use of capitals. However, Packt Publishing cannot guarantee the accuracy of this information.

First published: June 2017

Production reference: 1290617

Published by Packt Publishing Ltd.
Livery Place
35 Livery Street
Birmingham
B3 2PB, UK.

ISBN 978-1-78728-794-5

www.packtpub.com

Credits

Author
Frank Kane

Commissioning Editor
Ben Renow-Clarke

Acquisition Editor
Ben Renow-Clarke

Content Development Editor
Monika Sangwan

Technical Editor
Nidhisha Shetty

Copy Editor
Tom Jacob

Project Coordinator
Suzanne Coutinho

Proofreader
Safis Editing

Indexer
Aishwarya Gangawane

Graphics
Kirk D'Penha

Production Coordinator
Arvindkumar Gupta

About the Author

My name is Frank Kane. I spent nine years at `amazon.com` and `imdb.com`, wrangling millions of customer ratings and customer transactions to produce things such as personalized recommendations for movies and products and "people who bought this also bought." I tell you, I wish we had Apache Spark back then, when I spent years trying to solve these problems there. I hold 17 issued patents in the fields of distributed computing, data mining, and machine learning. In 2012, I left to start my own successful company, Sundog Software, which focuses on virtual reality environment technology, and teaching others about big data analysis.

www.PacktPub.com

For support files and downloads related to your book, please visit www.PacktPub.com.

Did you know that Packt offers eBook versions of every book published, with PDF and ePub files available? You can upgrade to the eBook version at www.PacktPub.com and as a print book customer, you are entitled to a discount on the eBook copy. Get in touch with us at service@packtpub.com for more details.

At www.PacktPub.com, you can also read a collection of free technical articles, sign up for a range of free newsletters and receive exclusive discounts and offers on Packt books and eBooks.

https://www.packtpub.com/mapt

Get the most in-demand software skills with Mapt. Mapt gives you full access to all Packt books and video courses, as well as industry-leading tools to help you plan your personal development and advance your career.

Why subscribe?

- Fully searchable across every book published by Packt
- Copy and paste, print, and bookmark content
- On demand and accessible via a web browser

Customer Feedback

Thanks for purchasing this Packt book. At Packt, quality is at the heart of our editorial process. To help us improve, please leave us an honest review on this book's Amazon page at https://www.amazon.com/dp/1787287947.

If you'd like to join our team of regular reviewers, you can e-mail us at customerreviews@packtpub.com. We award our regular reviewers with free eBooks and videos in exchange for their valuable feedback. Help us be relentless in improving our products!

Table of Contents

Preface

We will do some really quick housekeeping here, just so you know where to put all the stuff for this book. First, I want you to go to your hard drive, create a new folder called `SparkCourse`, and put it in a place where you're going to remember it is:

Name	Date modified	Type	Size
Intel	8/18/2016 4:32 PM	File folder	
jdk	5/31/2017 5:06 PM	File folder	
PerfLogs	7/14/2009 8:50 AM	File folder	
Program Files	5/31/2017 5:09 PM	File folder	
Program Files (x86)	5/31/2017 1:18 PM	File folder	
spark	5/31/2017 6:24 PM	File folder	
SparkCourse	6/1/2017 12:27 PM	File folder	
Users	3/9/2017 3:10 PM	File folder	
Windows	3/10/2017 9:56 AM	File folder	
winutils	5/31/2017 2:16 PM	File folder	
FoxitReaderPrinterProfile	5/9/2017 4:16 PM	XML Document	0 KB

Computer ▸ Local Disk (C:) ▸

Open   Include in library ▾   Share with ▾   New folder

For me, I put that in my C drive in a folder called SparkCourse. This is where you're going to put everything for this book. As you go through the individual sections of this book, you'll see that there are resources provided for each one. There can be different kinds of resources, files, and downloads. When you download them, make sure you put them in this folder that you have created. This is the ultimate destination of everything you're going to download for this book, as you can see in my SparkCourse folder, shown in the following screenshot; you'll just accumulate all this stuff over time as you work your way through it:

Name	Date modified	Type	Size
ml-100k	6/2/2017 5:40 PM	File folder	
1800	6/8/2017 12:23 PM	Microsoft Excel C...	62 KB
book	6/8/2017 12:23 PM	Text Document	259 KB
customer-orders	6/8/2017 12:23 PM	Microsoft Excel C...	144 KB
degrees-of-separation	6/8/2017 12:23 PM	Canopy Document	4 KB
fakefriends	6/8/2017 11:59 AM	Microsoft Excel C...	9 KB
friends-by-age	6/8/2017 11:54 AM	Canopy Document	1 KB
Marvel-graph	6/8/2017 12:23 PM	Text Document	1,635 KB
Marvel-names	6/8/2017 12:23 PM	Text Document	344 KB
max-temperatures	6/8/2017 12:23 PM	Canopy Document	1 KB
min-temperatures	6/8/2017 12:23 PM	Canopy Document	1 KB

So, remember where you put it all, you might need to refer to these files by their path, in this case, C:\SparkCourse. Just make sure you download them to a consistent place and you should be good to go. Also, be cognizant of the differences in file paths between operating systems. If you're on Mac or Linux, you're not going to have a C drive; you'll just have a slash and the full path name. Capitalization might be important, while it's not in Windows. Using forward slashes instead of backslashes in paths is another difference between other operating systems and Windows. So if you are using something other than Windows, just remember these differences, don't let them trip you up. If you see a path to a file and a script, make sure you adjust it accordingly to make sense of where you put these files and what your operating system is.

What this book covers

Chapter 1, *Getting Started with Spark*, covers basic installation instructions for Spark and its related software. This chapter illustrates a simple example of data analysis of real movie ratings data provided by different sets of people.

Chapter 2, *Spark Basics and Simple Examples*, provides a brief overview of what Spark is all about, who uses it, how it helps in analyzing big data, and why it is so popular.

Chapter3, *Advanced Examples of Spark Programs*, illustrates some advanced and complicated examples with Spark.

Chapter 4, *Running Spark on a Cluster*, talks about Spark Core, covering the things you can do with Spark, such as running Spark in the cloud on a cluster, analyzing a real cluster in the cloud using Spark, and so on.

Chapter 5, *SparkSQL, DataFrames, and DataSets*, introduces SparkSQL, which is an important concept of Spark, and explains how to deal with structured data formats using this.

Chapter 6, *Other Spark Technologies and Libraries*, talks about MLlib (Machine Learning library), which is very helpful if you want to work on data mining or machine learning-related jobs with Spark. This chapter also covers Spark Streaming and GraphX; technologies built on top of Spark.

Chapter 7, *Where to Go From Here? - Learning More About Spark and Data Science*, talks about some books related to Spark if the readers want to know more on this topic.

What you need for this book

For this book you'll need a Python development environment (Python 3.5 or newer), a Canopy installer, Java Development Kit, and of course Spark itself (Spark 2.0 and beyond).

We'll show you how to install this software in first chapter of the book.

This book is based on the Windows operating system, so installations are provided according to it. If you have Mac or Linux, you can follow this URL http://media.sundog-soft.com/spark-python-install.pdf, which contains written instructions on getting everything set up on Mac OS and on Linux.

Who this book is for

I wrote this book for people who have at least some programming or scripting experience in their background. We're going to be using the Python programming language throughout this book, which is very easy to pick up, and I'm going to give you over 15 real hands-on examples of Spark Python scripts that you can run yourself, mess around with, and learn from. So, by the end of this book, you should have the skills needed to actually turn business problems into Spark problems, code up that Spark code on your own, and actually run it in the cluster on your own.

Conventions

In this book, you will find a number of text styles that distinguish between different kinds of information. Here are some examples of these styles and an explanation of their meaning. Code words in text, database table names, folder names, filenames, file extensions, path names, dummy URLs, user input, and Twitter handles are shown as follows: "Now, you'll need to remember the path that we installed the JDK into, which in our case was C:\jdk."
A block of code is set as follows:

```
from pyspark import SparkConf, SparkContext
import collections

conf = SparkConf().setMaster("local").setAppName("RatingsHistogram")
sc = SparkContext(conf = conf)

lines = sc.textFile("file:///SparkCourse/ml-100k/u.data")
ratings = lines.map(lambda x: x.split()[2])
result = ratings.countByValue()

sortedResults = collections.OrderedDict(sorted(result.items()))
```

```
for key, value in sortedResults.items():
    print("%s %i" % (key, value))
```

When we wish to draw your attention to a particular part of a code block, the relevant lines or items are set in bold:

```
from pyspark import SparkConf, SparkContext
import collections

conf = SparkConf().setMaster("local").setAppName("RatingsHistogram")
sc = SparkContext(conf = conf)

lines = sc.textFile("file:///SparkCourse/ml-100k/u.data")
ratings = lines.map(lambda x: x.split()[2])
result = ratings.countByValue()

sortedResults = collections.OrderedDict(sorted(result.items()))
for key, value in sortedResults.items():
    print("%s %i" % (key, value))
```

Any command-line input or output is written as follows:

```
spark-submit ratings-counter.py
```

New terms and **important words** are shown in bold. Words that you see on the screen, for example, in menus or dialog boxes, appear in the text like this: "Now, if you're on Windows, I want you to right-click on the Enthought Canopy icon, go to **Properties** and then to **Compatibility** (this is on Windows 10), and make sure **Run this program as an administrator** is checked"

 Warnings or important notes appear in a box like this.

 Tips and tricks appear like this.

Reader feedback

Feedback from our readers is always welcome. Let us know what you think about this book-what you liked or disliked. Reader feedback is important for us as it helps us develop titles that you will really get the most out of. To send us general feedback, simply e-mail feedback@packtpub.com, and mention the book's title in the subject of your message. If there is a topic that you have expertise in and you are interested in either writing or contributing to a book, see our author guide at www.packtpub.com/authors.

Customer support

Now that you are the proud owner of a Packt book, we have a number of things to help you to get the most from your purchase.

Downloading the example code

You can download the example code files for this book from your account at http://www.packtpub.com. If you purchased this book elsewhere, you can visit http://www.packtpub.com/support and register to have the files e-mailed directly to you. You can download the code files by following these steps:

1. Log in or register to our website using your e-mail address and password.
2. Hover the mouse pointer on the **SUPPORT** tab at the top.
3. Click on **Code Downloads & Errata**.
4. Enter the name of the book in the **Search** box.
5. Select the book for which you're looking to download the code files.
6. Choose from the drop-down menu where you purchased this book from.
7. Click on **Code Download**.

Once the file is downloaded, please make sure that you unzip or extract the folder using the latest version of:

- WinRAR / 7-Zip for Windows
- Zipeg / iZip / UnRarX for Mac
- 7-Zip / PeaZip for Linux

The code bundle for the book is also hosted on GitHub at https://github.com/PacktPubl ishing/Frank-Kanes-Taming-Big-Data-with-Apache-Spark-and-Python. We also have other code bundles from our rich catalog of books and videos available at https://github. com/PacktPublishing/. Check them out!

Downloading the color images of this book

We also provide you with a PDF file that has color images of the screenshots/diagrams used in this book. The color images will help you better understand the changes in the output. You can download this file from https://www.packtpub.com/sites/default/files/down loads/FrankKanesTamingBigDatawithApacheSparkandPython_ColorImages.pdf.

Errata

Although we have taken every care to ensure the accuracy of our content, mistakes do happen. If you find a mistake in one of our books-maybe a mistake in the text or the code-we would be grateful if you could report this to us. By doing so, you can save other readers from frustration and help us improve subsequent versions of this book. If you find any errata, please report them by visiting http://www.packtpub.com/submit-errata, selecting your book, clicking on the **Errata Submission Form** link, and entering the details of your errata. Once your errata are verified, your submission will be accepted and the errata will be uploaded to our website or added to any list of existing errata under the Errata section of that title. To view the previously submitted errata, go to https://www.packtpub.com/book s/content/supportand enter the name of the book in the search field. The required information will appear under the **Errata** section.

Piracy

Piracy of copyrighted material on the Internet is an ongoing problem across all media. At Packt, we take the protection of our copyright and licenses very seriously. If you come across any illegal copies of our works in any form on the Internet, please provide us with the location address or website name immediately so that we can pursue a remedy. Please contact us at copyright@packtpub.com with a link to the suspected pirated material. We appreciate your help in protecting our authors and our ability to bring you valuable content.

Questions

If you have a problem with any aspect of this book, you can contact us at questions@packtpub.com, and we will do our best to address the problem

1
Getting Started with Spark

Spark is one of the hottest technologies in big data analysis right now, and with good reason. If you work for, or you hope to work for, a company that has massive amounts of data to analyze, Spark offers a very fast and very easy way to analyze that data across an entire cluster of computers and spread that processing out. This is a very valuable skill to have right now.

My approach in this book is to start with some simple examples and work our way up to more complex ones. We'll have some fun along the way too. We will use movie ratings data and play around with similar movies and movie recommendations. I also found a social network of superheroes, if you can believe it; we can use this data to do things such as figure out who's the most popular superhero in the fictional superhero universe. Have you heard of the Kevin Bacon number, where everyone in Hollywood is supposedly connected to a Kevin Bacon to a certain extent? We can do the same thing with our superhero data and figure out the degrees of separation between any two superheroes in their fictional universe too. So, we'll have some fun along the way and use some real examples here and turn them into Spark problems. Using Apache Spark is easier than you might think and, with all the exercises and activities in this book, you'll get plenty of practice as we go along. I'll guide you through every line of code and every concept you need along the way. So let's get started and learn Apache Spark.

Getting set up - installing Python, a JDK, and Spark and its dependencies

Let's get you started. There is a lot of software we need to set up. Running Spark on Windows involves a lot of moving pieces, so make sure you follow along carefully, or else you'll have some trouble. I'll try to walk you through it as easily as I can. Now, this chapter is written for Windows users. This doesn't mean that you're out of luck if you're on Mac or Linux though. If you open up the download package for the book or go to this URL, `http://media.sundog-soft.com/spark-python-install.pdf`, you will find written instructions on getting everything set up on Windows, macOS, and Linux. So, again, you can read through the chapter here for Windows users, and I will call out things that are specific to Windows, so you'll find it useful in other platforms as well; however, either refer to that `spark-python-install.pdf` file or just follow the instructions here on Windows and let's dive in and get it done.

Installing Enthought Canopy

This book uses Python as its programming language, so the first thing you need is a Python development environment installed on your PC. If you don't have one already, just open up a web browser and head on to `https://www.enthought.com/`, and we'll install Enthought Canopy:

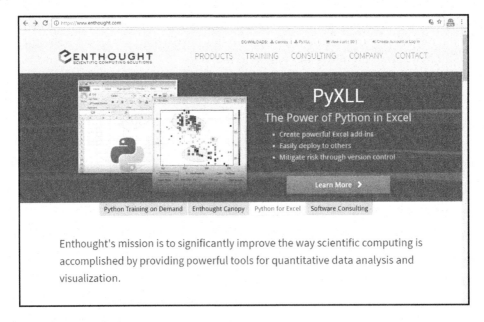

Enthought Canopy is just my development environment of choice; if you have a different one already that's probably okay. As long as it's Python 3 or a newer environment, you should be covered, but if you need to install a new Python environment or you just want to minimize confusion, I'd recommend that you install Canopy. So, head up to the big friendly download **Canopy** button here and select your operating system and architecture:

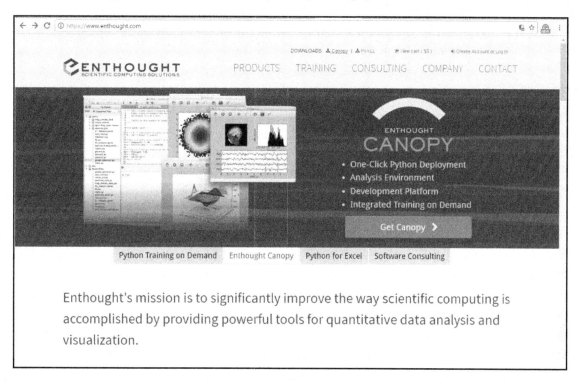

For me, the operating system is going to be Windows (64-bit). Make sure you choose Python 3.5 or a newer version of the package. I can't guarantee the scripts in this book will work with Python 2.7; they are built for Python 3, so select Python 3.5 for your OS and download the installer:

There's nothing special about it; it's just your standard Windows Installer, or whatever platform you're on. We'll just accept the defaults, go through it, and allow it to become our default Python environment. Then, when we launch it for the first time, it will spend a couple of minutes setting itself up and all the Python packages that we need. You might want to read the license agreement before you accept it; that's up to you. We'll go ahead, start the installation, and let it run.

Once Canopy installer has finished installing, we should have a nice little Enthought Canopy icon sitting on our desktop. Now, if you're on Windows, I want you to right-click on the Enthought Canopy icon, go to **Properties** and then to **Compatibility** (this is on Windows 10), and make sure **Run this program as an administrator** is checked:

This will make sure that we have all the permissions we need to run our scripts successfully. You can now double-click on the file to open it up:

The next thing we need is a Java Development Kit because Spark runs on top of Scala and Scala runs on top of the Java Runtime environment.

Installing the Java Development Kit

For installing the Java Development Kit, go back to the browser, open a new tab, and just search for `jdk` (short for Java Development Kit). This will bring you to the Oracle site, from where you can download Java:

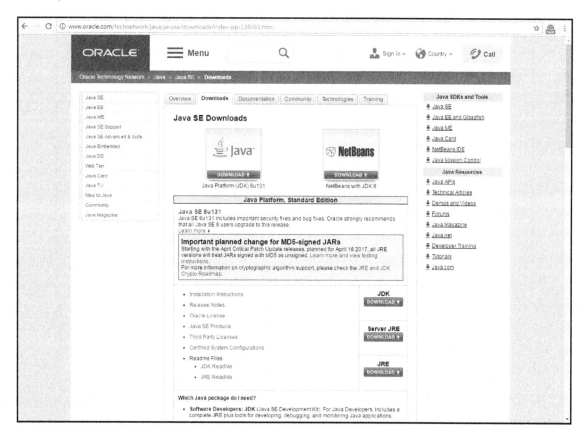

On the Oracle website, click on **JDK DOWNLOAD**. Now, click on **Accept License Agreement** and then you can select the download option for your operating system:

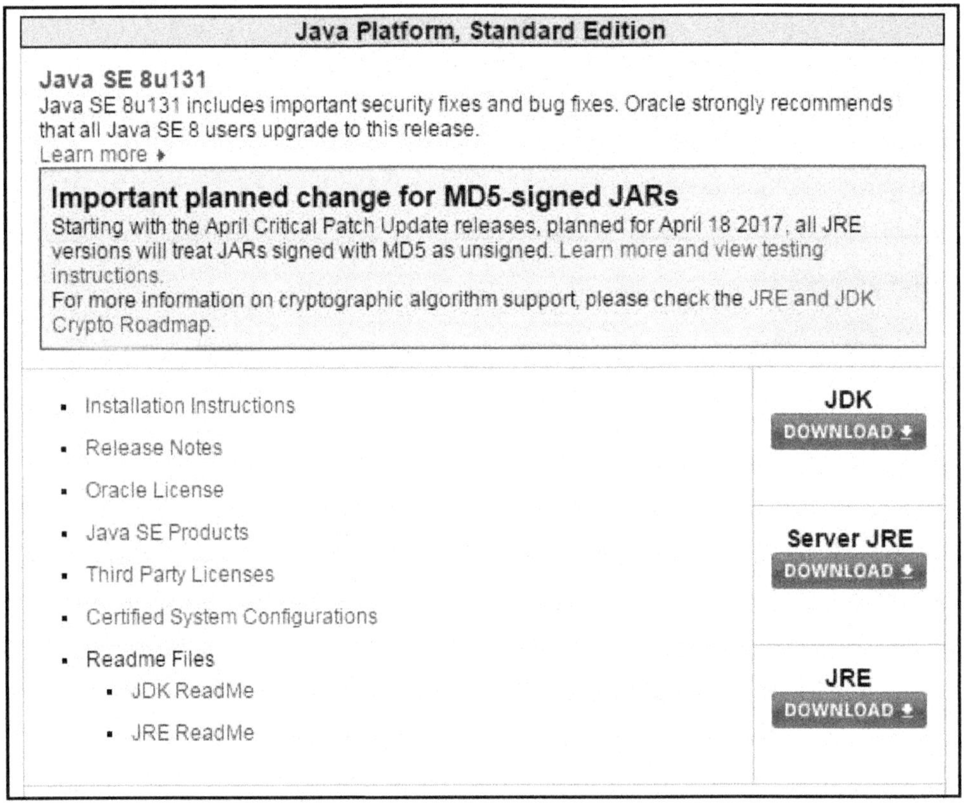

Java Platform, Standard Edition

Java SE 8u131
Java SE 8u131 includes important security fixes and bug fixes. Oracle strongly recommends that all Java SE 8 users upgrade to this release.
Learn more ▸

Important planned change for MD5-signed JARs
Starting with the April Critical Patch Update releases, planned for April 18 2017, all JRE versions will treat JARs signed with MD5 as unsigned. Learn more and view testing instructions.
For more information on cryptographic algorithm support, please check the JRE and JDK Crypto Roadmap.

- Installation Instructions
- Release Notes
- Oracle License
- Java SE Products
- Third Party Licenses
- Certified System Configurations
- Readme Files
    - JDK ReadMe
    - JRE ReadMe

JDK
DOWNLOAD ⬇

Server JRE
DOWNLOAD ⬇

JRE
DOWNLOAD ⬇

For me, that's going to be Windows 64-bit and a wait for 198 MB of goodness to download:

Java SE Development Kit 8u131

You must accept the Oracle Binary Code License Agreement for Java SE to download this software.
Thank you for accepting the Oracle Binary Code License Agreement for Java SE; you may now download this software.

Product / File Description	File Size	Download
Linux ARM 32 Hard Float ABI	77.87 MB	⬇jdk-8u131-linux-arm32-vfp-hflt.tar.gz
Linux ARM 64 Hard Float ABI	74.81 MB	⬇jdk-8u131-linux-arm64-vfp-hflt.tar.gz
Linux x86	164.66 MB	⬇jdk-8u131-linux-i586.rpm
Linux x86	179.39 MB	⬇jdk-8u131-linux-i586.tar.gz
Linux x64	162.11 MB	⬇jdk-8u131-linux-x64.rpm
Linux x64	176.95 MB	⬇jdk-8u131-linux-x64.tar.gz
Mac OS X	226.57 MB	⬇jdk-8u131-macosx-x64.dmg
Solaris SPARC 64-bit	139.79 MB	⬇jdk-8u131-solaris-sparcv9.tar.Z
Solaris SPARC 64-bit	99.13 MB	⬇jdk-8u131-solaris-sparcv9.tar.gz
Solaris x64	140.51 MB	⬇jdk-8u131-solaris-x64.tar.Z
Solaris x64	96.96 MB	⬇jdk-8u131-solaris-x64.tar.gz
Windows x86	191.22 MB	⬇jdk-8u131-windows-i586.exe
Windows x64	198.03 MB	⬇jdk-8u131-windows-x64.exe

Once the download is finished, we can't just accept the default settings in the installer on Windows here. So, this is a Windows-specific workaround, but as of the writing of this book, the current version of Spark is 2.1.1. It turns out there's an issue with Spark 2.1.1 with Java on Windows. The issue is that if you've installed Java to a path that has a space in it, it doesn't work, so we need to make sure that Java is installed to a path that does not have a space in it. This means that you can't skip this step even if you have Java installed already, so let me show you how to do that. On the installer, click on **Next**, and you will see, as in the following screen, that it wants to install by default to the `C:\Program Files\Java\jdk` path, whatever the version is:

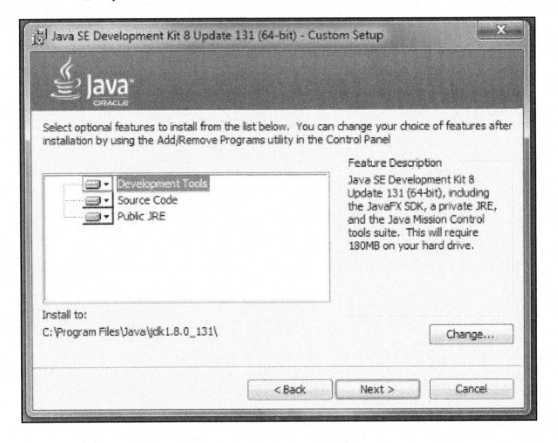

The space in the `Program Files` path is going to cause trouble, so let's click on the **Change...** button and install to `c:\jdk`, a nice simple path, easy to remember, and with no spaces in it:

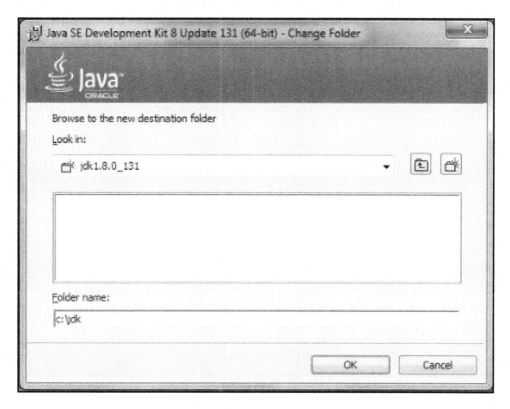

Now, it also wants to install the Java Runtime environment; so, just to be safe, I'm also going to install that to a path with no spaces.

At the second step of the JDK installation, we should have this showing on our screen:

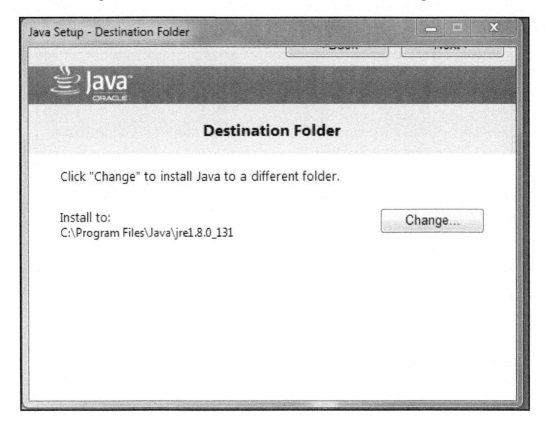

I will change that destination folder as well, and we will make a new folder called C:\jre for that:

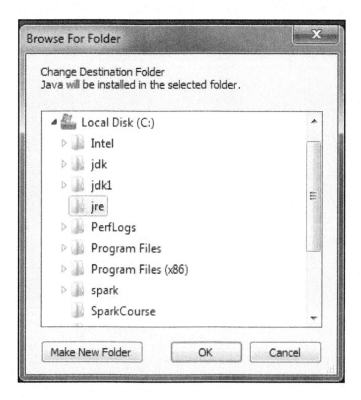

Alright; successfully installed. Woohoo!

Now, you'll need to remember the path that we installed the JDK into, which, in our case was C:\jdk. We still have a few more steps to go here. So far, we've installed Python and Java, and next we need to install Spark itself.

Installing Spark

Let's us get back to a new browser tab here; head to spark.apache.org, and click on the **Download Spark** button:

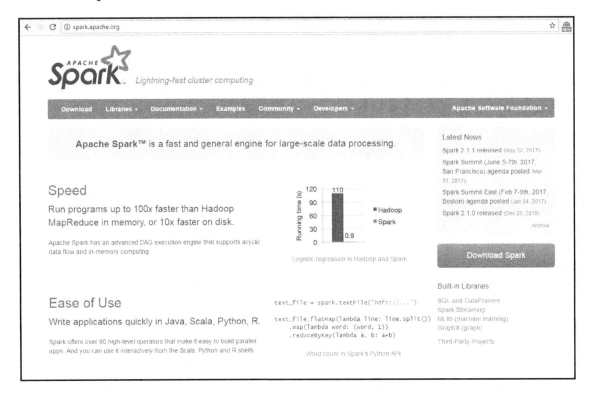

Now, we have used Spark 2.1.1 in this book. So, you know, if given the choice, anything beyond 2.0 should work just fine, but that's where we are today.

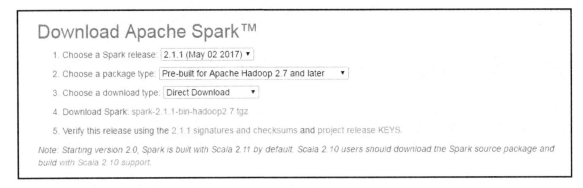

Make sure you get a pre-built version, and select a **Direct Download** option so all these defaults are perfectly fine. Go ahead and click on the link next to instruction number **4** to download that package.

Now, it downloads a **TGZ (Tar in GZip)** file, so, again, Windows is kind of an afterthought with Spark quite honestly because on Windows, you're not going to have a built-in utility for actually decompressing TGZ files. This means that you might need to install one, if you don't have one already. The one I use is called WinRAR, and you can pick that up from `www.rarlab.com`. Go to the **Downloads** page if you need it, and download the installer for WinRAR 32-bit or 64-bit, depending on your operating system. Install WinRAR as normal, and that will allow you to actually decompress TGZ files on Windows:

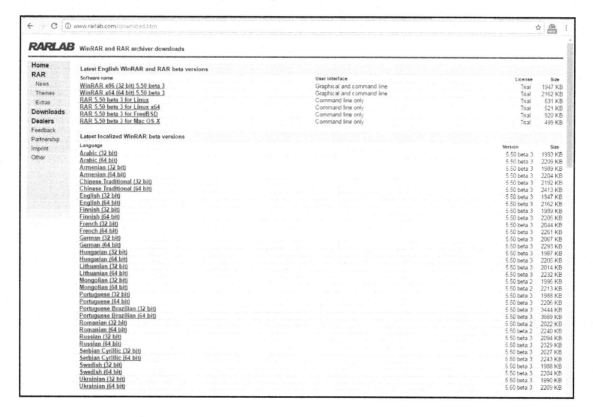

So, let's go ahead and decompress the TGZ files. I'm going to open up my `Downloads` folder to find the Spark archive that we downloaded, and let's go ahead and right-click on that archive and extract it to a folder of my choosing; just going to put it in my `Downloads` folder for now. Again, WinRAR is doing this for me at this point:

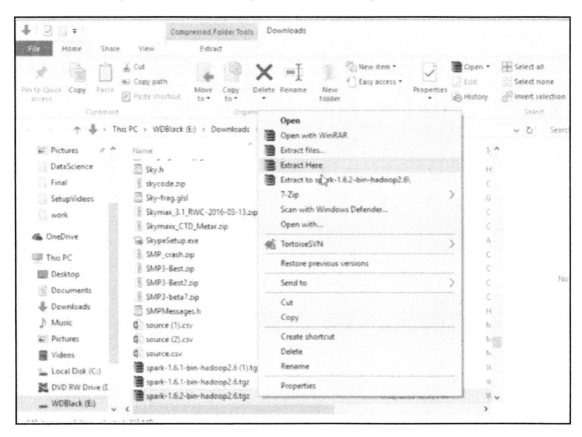

So I should now have a folder in my `Downloads` folder associated with that package. Let's open that up and there is Spark itself. So, you need to install that in some place where you will remember it:

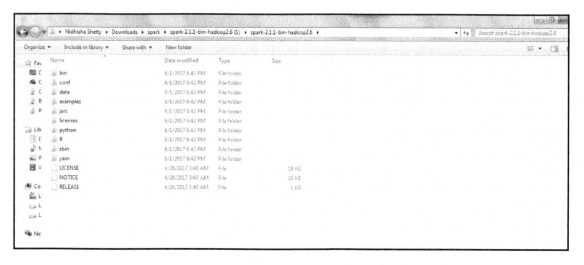

You don't want to leave it in your `Downloads` folder obviously, so let's go ahead and open up a new file explorer window here. I go to my `C` drive and create a new folder, and let's just call it `spark`. So, my Spark installation is going to live in `C:\spark`. Again, nice and easy to remember. Open that folder. Now, I go back to my downloaded `spark` folder and use *Ctrl + A* to select everything in the Spark distribution, *Ctrl + C* to copy it, and then go back to `C:\spark`, where I want to put it, and *Ctrl + V* to paste it in:

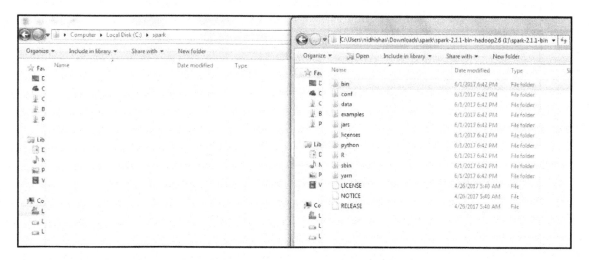

Remembering to paste the contents of the spark folder, not the spark folder itself is very important. So what I should have now is my C drive with a spark folder that contains all of the files and folders from the Spark distribution.

Well, there are yet a few things we need to configure. So while we're in C:\spark let's open up the conf folder, and in order to make sure that we don't get spammed to death by log messages, we're going to change the logging level setting here. So to do that, right-click on the log4j.properties.template file and select **Rename**:

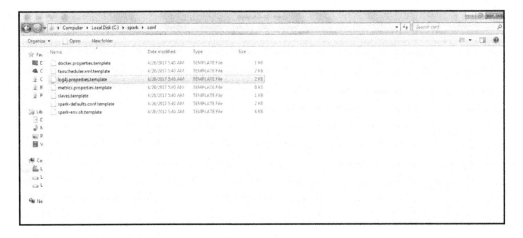

Delete the .template part of the filename to make it an actual log4j.properties file. Spark will use this to configure its logging:

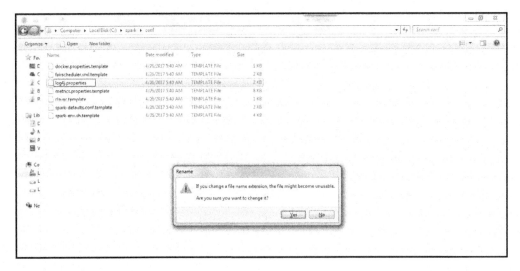

Now, open this file in a text editor of some sort. On Windows, you might need to right-click there and select **Open with** and then **WordPad**:

```
18  # Set everything to be logged to the console
19  log4j.rootCategory=INFO, console
20  log4j.appender.console=org.apache.log4j.ConsoleAppender
21  log4j.appender.console.target=System.err
22  log4j.appender.console.layout=org.apache.log4j.PatternLayout
23  log4j.appender.console.layout.ConversionPattern=%d{yy/MM/dd HH:mm:ss} %p %c{1}: %m%n
24
```

In the file, locate `log4j.rootCategory=INFO`. Let's change this to `log4j.rootCategory=ERROR` and this will just remove the clutter of all the log spam that gets printed out when we run stuff. Save the file, and exit your editor.

So far, we installed Python, Java, and Spark. Now the next thing we need to do is to install something that will trick your PC into thinking that Hadoop exists, and again this step is only necessary on Windows. So, you can skip this step if you're on Mac or Linux.

Let's go to `http://media.sundog-soft.com/winutils.exe`. Downloading `winutils.exe` will give you a copy of a little snippet of an executable, which can be used to trick Spark into thinking that you actually have Hadoop:

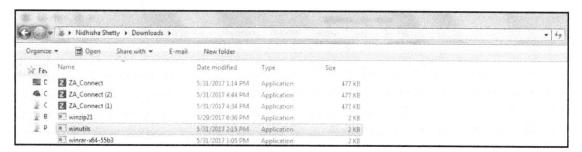

Now, since we're going to be running our scripts locally on our desktop, it's not a big deal, and we don't need to have Hadoop installed for real. This just gets around another quirk of running Spark on Windows. So, now that we have that, let's find it in the `Downloads` folder, click *Ctrl + C* to copy it, and let's go to our `C` drive and create a place for it to live:

So, I create a new folder again, and we will call it `winutils`:

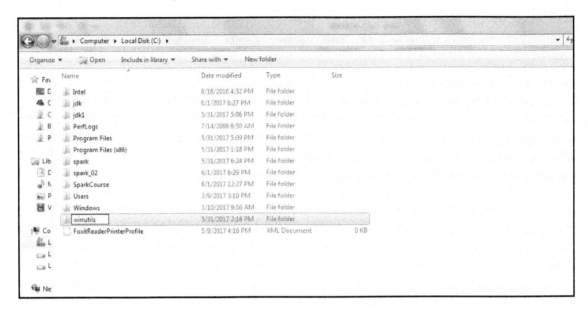

Now let's open this `winutils` folder and create a `bin` folder in it:

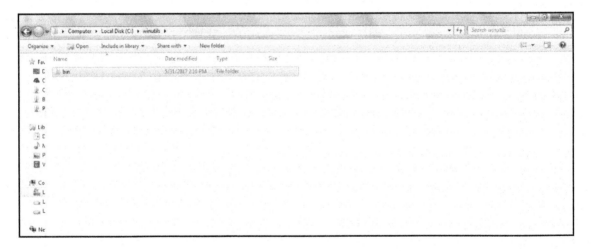

Now in this `bin` folder, I want you to paste the `winutils.exe` file we downloaded. So you should have `C:\winutils\bin` and then `winutils.exe`:

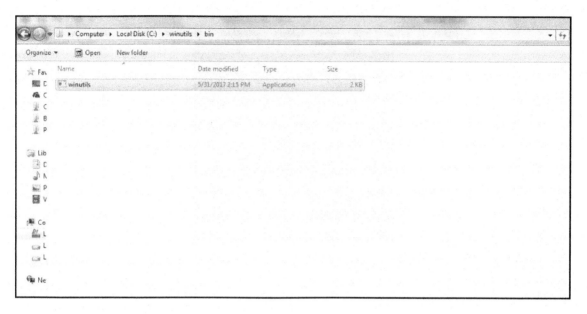

This next step is only required on some systems, but just to be safe, open Command Prompt on Windows. You can do that by going to your Start menu and going down to **Windows System**, and then clicking on **Command Prompt**. Here, I want you to type `cd c:\winutils\bin`, which is where we stuck our `winutils.exe` file. Now if you type `dir`, you should see that file there. Now type `winutils.exe chmod 777 \tmp\hive`. This just makes sure that all the file permissions you need to actually run Spark successfully are in place without any errors. You can close Command Prompt now that you're done with that step. Wow, we're almost done, believe it or not.

Now we need to set some environment variables for things to work. I'll show you how to do that on Windows. On Windows 10, you'll need to open up the Start menu and go to **Windows System | Control Panel** to open up **Control Panel**:

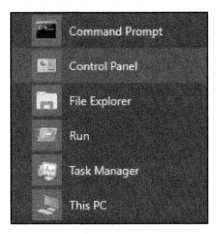

In Control Panel, click on **System and Security**:

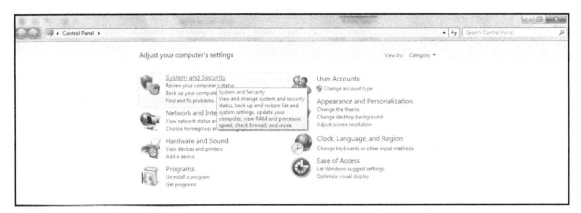

Then, click on **System**:

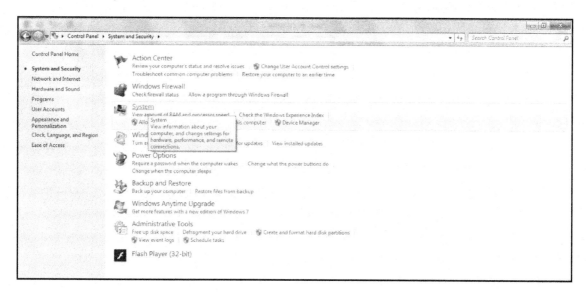

Then click on **Advanced system settings** from the list on the left-hand side:

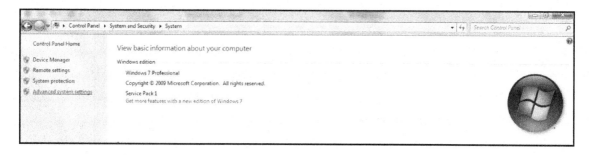

From here, click on **Environment Variables...**:

We will get these options:

Now, this is a very Windows-specific way of setting environment variables. On other operating systems, you'll use different processes, so you'll have to look at how to install Spark on them. Here, we're going to set up some new user variables. Click on the **New...** button for a new user variable and call it SPARK_HOME, as shown as follows, all uppercase. This is going to point to where we installed Spark, which for us is c:\spark, so type that in as the **Variable value** and click on **OK**:

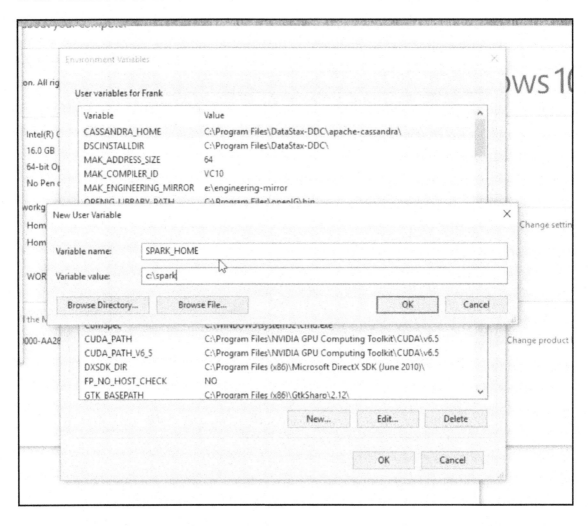

We also need to set up JAVA_HOME, so click on **New...** again and type in JAVA_HOME as **Variable name**. We need to point that to where we installed Java, which for us is c:\jdk:

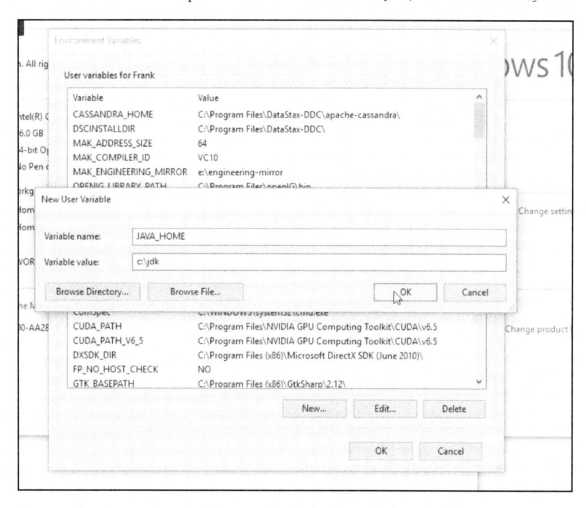

We also need to set up `HADOOP_HOME`, and that's where we installed the `winutils` package, so we'll point that to `c:\winutils`:

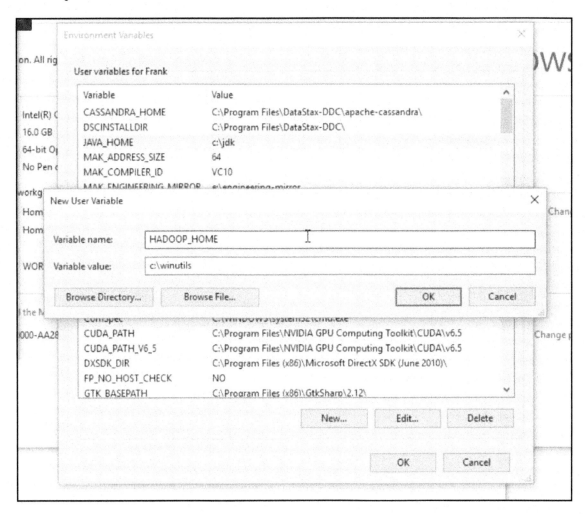

So far, so good. The last thing we need to do is to modify our path. You should have a **PATH** environment variable here:

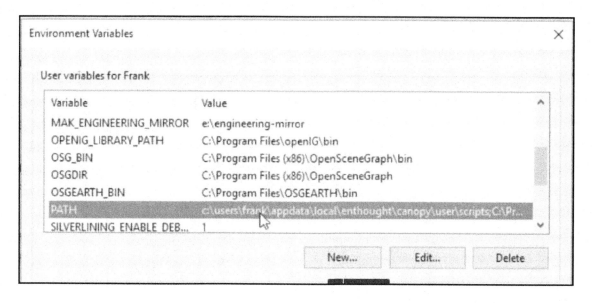

Click on the **PATH** environment variable, then on **Edit...**, and add a new path. This is going to be `%SPARK_HOME%\bin`, and I'm going to add another one, `%JAVA_HOME%\bin`:

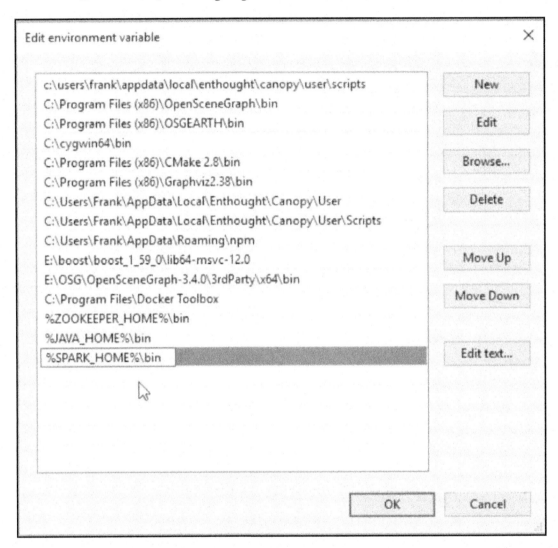

Basically, this makes all the binary executables of Spark available to Windows, wherever you're running it from. Click on **OK** on this menu and on the previous two menus. We finally have everything set up. So, let's go ahead and try it all out in our next step.

Running Spark code

Let's go ahead and start up Enthought Canopy. Once you get to the Welcome screen, go to the **Tools** menu and then to **Canopy Command Prompt**. This will give you a little Command Prompt you can use; it has all the right permissions and environment variables you need to actually run Python.

So type in `cd c:\spark`, as shown here, which is where we installed Spark in our previous steps:

We'll make sure that we have Spark in there, so you should see all the contents of the Spark distribution pre-built. Let's look at what's in here by typing `dir` and hitting *Enter*:

```
Canopy Command Prompt                                              _  □  X
(User) C:\Users\nidhishas>cd c:\spark

(User) c:\spark>dir
 Volume in drive C has no label.
 Volume Serial Number is B477-8D77

 Directory of c:\spark

05/31/2017  06:24 PM    <DIR>          .
05/31/2017  06:24 PM    <DIR>          ..
05/31/2017  01:25 PM    <DIR>          bin
05/31/2017  06:26 PM                23 CHANGES.txt
06/01/2017  06:59 PM    <DIR>          conf
05/31/2017  01:25 PM    <DIR>          data
05/31/2017  01:25 PM    <DIR>          examples
05/31/2017  01:25 PM    <DIR>          jars
04/26/2017  05:40 AM            17,811 LICENSE
05/31/2017  01:25 PM    <DIR>          licenses
04/26/2017  05:40 AM            24,645 NOTICE
05/31/2017  01:25 PM    <DIR>          python
05/31/2017  01:25 PM    <DIR>          R
04/26/2017  05:40 AM             3,817 README.md
04/26/2017  05:40 AM               128 RELEASE
05/31/2017  01:25 PM    <DIR>          sbin
05/31/2017  01:25 PM    <DIR>          yarn
               5 File(s)         46,424 bytes
              12 Dir(s)  181,354,946,560 bytes free

(User) c:\spark>
```

Now, depending on the distribution that you downloaded, there might be a README.md file or a CHANGES.txt file, so pick one or the other; whatever you see there, that's what we're going to use.

We will set up a little simple Spark program here that just counts the number of lines in that file, so let's type in `pyspark` to kick off the Python version of the Spark interpreter:

```
(User) c:\spark>pyspark
```

If everything is set up properly, you should see something like this:

```
(User) c:\spark>pyspark
Enthought Deployment Manager -- https://www.enthought.com
Python 2.7.13 |Enthought, Inc. (x86_64)| (default, Mar  2 2017, 16:05:12) [MSC v
.1500 64 bit (AMD64)] on win32
Type "help", "copyright", "credits" or "license" for more information.
Setting default log level to "WARN".
To adjust logging level use sc.setLogLevel(newLevel). For SparkR, use setLogLeve
l(newLevel).
17/06/07 15:01:46 WARN NativeCodeLoader: Unable to load native-hadoop library fo
r your platform... using builtin-java classes where applicable
17/06/07 15:01:50 WARN ObjectStore: Failed to get database global_temp, returnin
g NoSuchObjectException
Welcome to


                                 version 2.1.1


Using Python version 2.7.13 (default, Mar  2 2017 16:05:12)
SparkSession available as 'spark'.
```

If you're not seeing this and you're seeing some weird Windows error about not being able to find `pyspark`, go back and double-check all those environment variables. The odds are that there's something wrong with your path or with your SPARK_HOME environment variables. Sometimes you need to log out of Windows and log back in, in order to get environment variable changes to get picked up by the system; so, if all else fails, try this. Also, if you got cute and installed things to a different path than I recommended in the setup sections, make sure that your environment variables reflect those changes. If you put it in a folder that has spaces in the name, that can cause problems as well. You might run into trouble if your path is too long or if you have too much stuff in your path, so have a look at that if you're encountering problems at this stage. Another possibility is that you're running on a managed PC that doesn't actually allow you to change environment variables, so you might have thought you did it, but there might be some administrative policy preventing you from doing so. If so, try running the set up steps again under a new account that's an administrator if possible. However, assuming you've gotten this far, let's have some fun.

Let's write some Spark code, shall we? We should get some payoff for all this work that we have done, so follow along with me here. I'm going to type in `rdd = sc.textFile("README.md")`, with a capital `F` in `textFile` – case does matter. Again, if your version of Spark has a `changes.txt` instead, just use `changes.txt` there:

```
>>> rdd = sc.textFile("README.md")
```

Make sure you get that exactly right; remember those are parentheses, not brackets. What this is doing is creating something called a **Resilient Distributed Data store (rdd)**, which is constructed by each line of input text in that `README.md` file. We're going to talk about rdds a lot more shortly. Spark can actually distribute the processing of this object through an entire cluster. Now let's just find out how many lines are in it and how many lines did we import into that rdd. So type in `rdd.count()` as shown in the following screenshot, and we'll get our answer. It actually ran a full-blown Spark job just for that. The answer is `104` lines in that file:

```
>>> rdd = sc.textFile("README.md")
>>> rdd.count()
[Stage 0:>                                          (0 + 2) / 2]

104
>>>
```

Now your answer might be different depending on what version of Spark you installed, but the important thing is that you got a number there, and you actually ran a Spark program that could do that in a distributed manner if it was running on a real cluster, so congratulations! Everything's set up properly; you have run your first Spark program already on Windows, and now we can get into how it's all working and doing some more interesting stuff with Spark. So, to get out of this Command Prompt, just type in `quit()`, and once that's done, you can close this window and move on. So, congratulations, you got everything set up; it was a lot of work but I think it's worth it. You're now set up to learn Spark using Python, so let's do it.

Installing the MovieLens movie rating dataset

The last thing we have to do before we start actually writing some code and analyzing data using Spark is to get some data to analyze. There's some really cool movie ratings data out there from a site called `grouplens.org`. They actually make their data publicly available for researchers like us, so let's go grab some. I can't actually redistribute that myself because of the licensing agreements around it, so I have to walk you through actually going to the grouplens website and downloading its `MovieLens` dataset onto your computer, so let's go get that out of the way right now.

If you just go to `grouplens.org`, you should come to this web page:

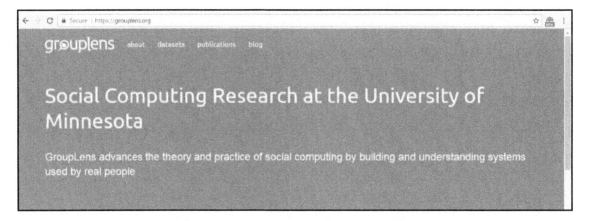

This is a collection of movie ratings data, which has over 40 million movie ratings available in the complete dataset, so this qualifies as big data. The way it works is that people go to MovieLens.org, shown as follows, and rate movies that they've seen. If you want, you can create an account there and play with it yourself; it's actually pretty good. I've had a go myself: Godfather, meh, not really my cup of tea. Casablanca - of course, great movie. Four and a half stars for that. Spirited Away - love that stuff:

The more you rate the better your recommendations become, and it's a good way to actually get some ideas for some new movies to watch, so go ahead and play with it. Enough people have done this; they've actually amassed, like I said, over 40 million ratings, and we can actually use that data for this book. At first, we will run this just on your desktop, as we're not going to be running Spark on a cluster until later on. For now, we will use a smaller dataset, so click on the **datasets** tab on `grouplens.org` and you'll see there are many different datasets you can get. The smallest one is 100,000 ratings:

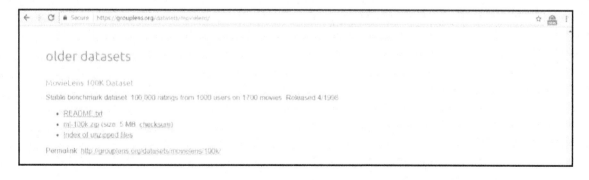

One thing to keep in mind is that this dataset was released in 1998, so you're not going to see any new movies in here. Movies such as Star Wars, some of the Star Trek movies, and some of the more popular classics, will all be in there, so you'll still recognize some of the movies that we're working with. Go ahead and click on the `ml-100k.zip` file to download that data, and once you have that, go to your `Downloads` folder, right-click on the folder that came down, and extract it:

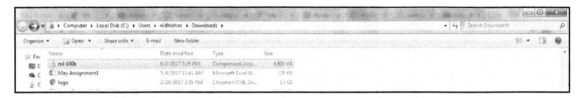

You should end up with a `ml-100k` folder as shown here:

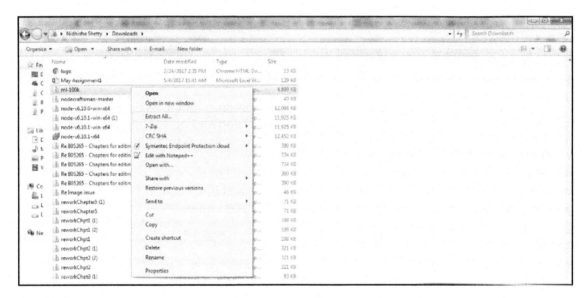

Now remember, at the beginning of this chapter we set up a home for all of your stuff for this book in the C folder in `SparkCourse`. So navigate to your `C:\SparkCourse` directory now, and copy the `ml-100k` folder into your `C:\SparkCourse` folder:

This will give you everything you need. Now, inside this `ml-100k` folder, you should see something like the screenshot shown as follows. There's a `u.data` file that contains all the actual movie ratings and a `u.item` file that contains the lookup table for all the movie IDs to movie names. We will use both of these files extensively in the chapters coming up:

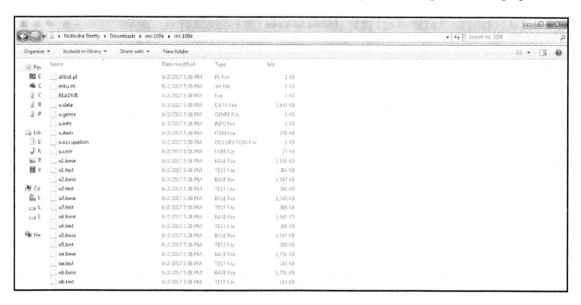

At this point, you should have an `ml-100k` folder inside your `SparkCourse` folder.

All the housekeeping is out of the way now. You've got Spark set up on your computer running on top of the JDK in a Python development environment, and we have some data to play with from `MovieLens`, so let's actually write some Spark code.

Run your first Spark program - the ratings histogram example

We just installed 100,000 movie ratings, and we now have everything we need to actually run some Spark code and get some results out of all this work that we've done so far, so let's go ahead and do that. We're going to construct a histogram of our ratings data. Of those 100,000 movie ratings that we just installed, we want to figure out how many are five star ratings, how many four stars, three stars, two stars, and one star, for example. It's really easy to do. The first thing you need to do though is to download the `ratings-counter.py` script from the download package for this book, so if you haven't done that already, take care of that right now. When we're ready to move on, let's walk through what to do with that script and we'll actually get a payoff out of all this work and then run some Spark code and see what it does.

Examining the ratings counter script

You should be able to get the `ratings-counter.py` file from the download package for this book. When you've downloaded the ratings counter script to your computer, copy it to your `SparkCourse` directory:

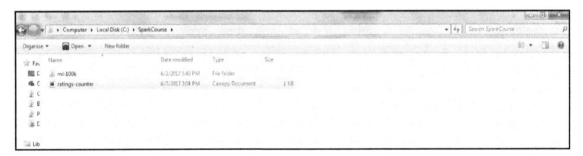

Once you have it there, if you've installed Enthought Canopy or your preferred Python development environment, you should be able to just double-click on that file, and up comes Canopy or your Python development environment:

```
from pyspark import SparkConf, SparkContext
import collections

conf = SparkConf().setMaster("local").setAppName("RatingsHistogram")
sc = SparkContext(conf = conf)

lines = sc.textFile("file:///SparkCourse/ml-100k/u.data")
```

```
ratings = lines.map(lambda x: x.split()[2])
result = ratings.countByValue()

sortedResults = collections.OrderedDict(sorted(result.items()))
for key, value in sortedResults.items():
    print("%s %i" % (key, value))
```

Now I don't want to get into too much detail as to what's actually going on in the script yet. I just want you to get a little bit of a payoff for all the work you've done so far. However, if you look at the script, it's actually not that hard to figure out. We're just importing the Spark stuff that we need for Python here:

```
from pyspark import SparkConf, SparkContext
import collections
```

Next, we're doing some configurations and some set up of Spark:

```
conf = SparkConf().setMaster("local").setAppName("RatingsHistogram")
sc = SparkContext(conf = conf)
```

In the next line, we're going to load the `u.data` file from the `MovieLens` dataset that we just installed, so that is the file that contains all of the 100,000 movie ratings:

```
lines = sc.textFile("file:////SparkCourse/ml-100k/u.data")
```

We then parse that data into different fields:

```
ratings = lines.map(lambda x: x.sploit()[2])
```

Then we call a little function in Spark called `countByValue` that will actually split up that data for us:

```
result = ratings.countByValue()
```

What we're trying to do is create a histogram of our ratings data. So we want to find out, of all those 100,000 ratings, how many five star ratings there are, how many four star, how many three star, how many two star and how many one star. Back at the time that they made this dataset, they didn't have half star ratings; there was only one, two, three, four, and five stars, so those are the choices. What we're going to do is count up how many of each ratings type exists in that dataset. When we're done, we're just going to sort the results and print them out in these lines of code:

```
sortedResults = collections.OrderedDict(sorted(result.items()))
for key, value in sortedResults.items():
    print("%s %i" % (key, value))
```

So that's all that's going on in this script. So let's go ahead and run that, and see if it works.

Running the ratings counter script

If you go to the **Tools** menu in Canopy, you have a shortcut there for Command Prompt that you can use, or you can open up Command Prompt anywhere. When you open that up, just make sure that you get into your `SparkCourse` directory where you actually downloaded the script that we're going to be using. So, type in `C:\SparkCourse` (or navigate to the directory if it's in a different location) and then type `dir` and you should see the contents of the directory. The `ratings-counter.py` and `ml-100k` folders should both be in there:

```
Administrator: Canopy Command Prompt

(User) C:\Users\nidhishas>cd c:\SparkCourse

(User) c:\SparkCourse>dir
 Volume in drive C has no label.
 Volume Serial Number is B477-8D77

 Directory of c:\SparkCourse

06/07/2017  03:04 PM    <DIR>          .
06/07/2017  03:04 PM    <DIR>          ..
06/02/2017  05:40 PM    <DIR>          ml-100k
06/07/2017  03:04 PM               452 ratings-counter.py
               1 File(s)            452 bytes
               3 Dir(s)  171,987,267,584 bytes free

(User) c:\SparkCourse>
```

All I need to do to run it, is type in `spark-submit ratings-counter.py`-follow along with me here:

```
(User) c:\SparkCourse>spark-submit ratings-counter.py_
```

I'm going to hit *Enter* and that will let me run this saved script that I wrote for Spark. Off it goes, and we soon get our results. So it made short work of those 100,000 ratings. 100,000 ratings doesn't constitute really big data but we're just playing around on our desktop for now:

```
(User) c:\SparkCourse>spark-submit ratings-counter.py
1 6110
2 11370
3 27145
4 34174
5 21201
```

The results are kind of interesting. It turns out that the most common rating is four star, so people are most generous with four star ratings, with 34,000 of them in the dataset, and people seem to reserve one stars for the worst of the worst, only about 6,000 one star ratings out of our 100,00 ratings. It might be fun to go and see what actually got rated one star if you want to find some really bad movies to watch.

Summary

You ran a Spark script on your desktop, doing some real data analysis of real movie ratings data from real people; how cool is that? We just analyzed a hundred thousand movie ratings data in just a couple of seconds really and got pretty nifty results. Let's move on and start to understand what's actually happening under the hood with Spark here, how it all works and how it fits together, and then we'll go back and study this example in a little bit more depth. In the next chapter, I'll review some of the basics of Spark, go over what it's used for, and give you some of that fundamental knowledge that you need to understand how this ratings counter script actually works.

2
Spark Basics and Spark Examples

The high-level introduction to Spark in this chapter will help you understand what Spark is all about, what's it for, who uses it, why is it so popular, and why is it so hot. Let's explore.

What is Spark?

According to Apache, Spark is *a fast and general engine for large-scale data processing*. This is actually a really good summary of what it's all about. If you have a really massive dataset that can represent anything - weblogs, genomics data, you name it - Spark can slice and dice that data up. It can distribute the processing among a huge cluster of computers, taking a data analysis problem that's just too big to run on one machine and divide and conquer it by splitting it up among multiple machines.

Spark is scalable

The way that Spark scales data analysis problems is, it runs on top of a cluster manager, so your actual Spark scripts are just everyday scripts written in Python, Java, or Scala; they behave just like any other script. Your "driver program" is what we call it, and it will run on your desktop or on one master node of your cluster. However, under the hood, when you run it, Spark knows how to take the work and actually farm it out to different computers on your cluster or even different CPUs on the same machine. Spark can actually run on top of different cluster managers. It has its own built-in cluster manager that you can use by default, but if you have access to a Hadoop cluster there's a component called YARN, that Spark can also run on top of to distribute work among a huge Hadoop cluster, if you have one available. For example, you can use Amazon's `Elastic MapReduce` service to get cheap and easy access to a Hadoop cluster, which we'll do later on in this course. As illustrated in the following diagram, the cluster manager will split up the work and coordinate it among various executors. Spark will split up and create multiple executors per machine – ideally you want one per CPU core. It can do all the coordination using the cluster manager, and also your driver program itself, to farm out work and distribute it to different nodes and give you fault tolerance. So, if one of your executors goes down, it can recover without actually stopping your entire job and making you start it all over again.

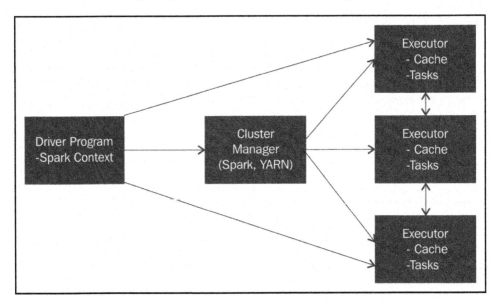

The beauty of it is that it scales out to an entire cluster of computers and it gives you horizontal partitioning and horizontal scalability; basically, the sky' is the limit. However, from a user's standpoint and from a developer's standpoint, it's all just one simple little program running on one computer that feels a lot like writing any other script. This is a really nice aspect of Spark.

Spark is fast

Why do people use Spark? Well, it has a lot in common with MapReduce, really, it solves the same sort of problems, so why are people using Spark instead of MapReduce? MapReduce has been around a lot longer and the ecosystems and the tools surrounding it are more mature at this point. Well, one of the main reasons is that Spark is really fast. On the Apache website, they claim that Spark can *Run Programs up to 100x faster than Hadoop MapReduce in memory, or 10x faster on disk*. Now, that's a little bit of hyperbole to be honest, I mean that's in a very contrived example. In my own experiments, if you compare some of the tasks that we run on Spark with the same tasks we run using MapReduce, it's not 100 times faster, it's definitely faster, but maybe two to three times faster. Spark definitely has that going for it.

The way that it achieves that performance is using what it calls the directed acyclic graph engine. The fancy thing about Spark is that it doesn't actually do anything until you ask it to deliver results, and at that point it creates a graph of all the different steps that it needs to put together to actually achieve the results you want. It does that in an optimal manner, so it can actually wait until it knows what you're asking for, and then figure out the optimal path to answering the question that you want.

Spark is hot

It's also very hot. If you go to this web page here, it will give you a list of some known people that are using Spark:
`https://cwiki.apache.org/confluence/display/SPARK/Powered+By+Spark`

A lot of big companies are kind of secretive about what they're doing inside, so I'm sure there are even more people using it than what are listed here, but we know a lot of the big players are already using Spark: Amazon, eBay, NASA's Jet Propulsion Laboratory, Yahoo, and many others. The list isn't as long as MapReduce because Spark hasn't been around as long as MapReduce, but it's definitely getting some big adoption quickly.

Spark is not that hard

The beautiful thing about Spark is it's not that hard. It allows you to code in Python, Java, or Scala, so if you're already familiar with Python, you don't have to learn a new language. From a developer's standpoint, it's built around one main concept, the **Resilient Distributed Dataset (RDD)**. There is one main kind of object that you'll encounter in Spark over and over and over again – the RDD. Various operations on that RDD will let you slice and dice and carve up that data and do what you want with it. So what would take many lines of code and different functions in a MapReduce job can often be done in just one line, much more quickly and efficiently using Spark.

If you actually took my MapReduce course, we're going to be doing a lot of the exact same problems in the Spark course. You might find it interesting how much simpler and how much easier those same problems are to solve in Spark compared to MapReduce in many cases.

Components of Spark

Spark is made up of many components. We're going to be focusing a lot on Spark Core, which means looking at what you can do with RDD objects and how you can use that to distribute the processing of data and the mapping and reducing of large datasets. But in addition to Spark Core, Spark also includes several libraries that run on top of it, as shown in the following diagram:

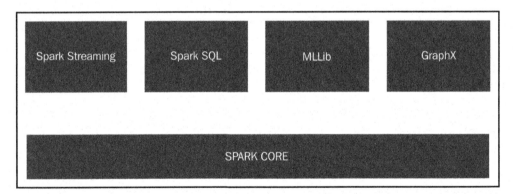

We have Spark Streaming, which actually gives you the ability to analyze real-time data streams – a set of web logs coming in from a fleet of web servers that need to be continually updated for instance. We'll talk about Spark Streaming later in the book. We have Spark SQL, which lets you run Spark on top of a Hive context, deal with structured data within Spark, and actually run SQL queries on top of it. So if you are familiar with SQL and you want to treat Spark as sort of a data warehouse, you can do that too. Spark also includes something called MLlib, which is a series of machine learning algorithms; if you're going to be doing any sort of machine learning or data mining with Spark, it contains many useful tools you can use to simplify a lot of common operations. For example, if you need to do a Pearson correlation or get statistical properties of your dataset, MLlib makes that very easy to do. Finally, we have GraphX: that's not the kind of graphs you draw on graph paper, it's actually managing graphs of information – network theory sort of stuff. So if you have a graph, for example, a social graph of people that are friends with each other or citations between documents and scholarly articles, or other things of that nature, GraphX can help you make sense of those sorts of networks and give you high-level information about the properties of those graphs. All these libraries run on top of Spark Core. Spark has a lot to offer and it's expanding all the time.

Using Python with Spark

Now, people who are already familiar with Spark might say why are you using Python in this book? Well, I'm using Python as the scripting language that I'm going to be working with, and there are some pretty good reasons, so I want to defend my choice here a little bit. For one thing, it's a lot easier to get up and running with Python under Spark. You don't have to deal with dependencies, running Maven, and figuring out how to get JAR files, where they need to be, and what not. With Python, if you just type your code, you don't have to compile it, it just runs and that makes life a lot simpler.

In this book, I really want to focus on the concepts behind Spark, how to deal with RDDs, what you can do with them, and how you can put these different things together; I don't really want to be focusing on things such as the mechanics of compiling and distributing JAR files and dealing with the Java and Scala stuff. Also, there's probably a better chance you are already familiar with Python as opposed to Scala, which is a newer language, and like I said, Java is just a little bit more complicated.

However, I will say that Scala is the more popular choice with Spark and that's because Spark is written in Scala. So if you write Scala code, it's native to Spark, it doesn't have to go through any sort of interpreter to convert your Python code and get it running in a Scala environment. I've never really run into problems with Python running on Spark, but you know, in theory, Scala should be a little bit faster and a little bit more reliable. The other thing to consider is that new features and libraries tend to come out in Scala before they come out in other languages in Spark. A good case in point is the GraphX library that we just talked about; today, as of writing this book, it is only available in Scala, but they're pretty far along in introducing support in Python and Java for graphics right now, and by the time you're reading this book, there's a good chance it will be available already. Similarly, with Spark Streaming, as of now, it is only partially implemented in Python, but again it's moving forward quickly and I believe that they will have feature parity among the three languages pretty quickly, so that shouldn't be too much of a concern going forward.

Another reason that Python isn't that bad of a choice for this book is that Python code in Spark looks a lot like Scala code in Spark. Even though they're very different languages, within Spark they look very much the same. They both use a lot of functional programming paradigms, as you can see here, we're using lambda functions in Python instead of the syntax in Scala for doing the same thing. Besides, having to qualify some of our variables as being `vals` in Scala, where they're just untyped in Python, the code looks very similar in most cases. In fact, the two bits of code shown here do exactly the same thing and you see that they look extremely similar to each other:

> **Python code to square number in a data set:**
>
> ```
> nums=sc.parallelize ([1, 2, 3, 4])
> squared=nums.map (lambda x: x * x). collect()
> ```
>
> **Scala code to square numbers in a data set:**
>
> ```
> val nums=sc.parallelize(List(1, 2, 3, 4))
> val squared=input.map(x= >x * x). collect()
> ```

So even if you learn Spark using Python, it's not going to be hard to transfer that knowledge to Scala, if you need to later.

So that's Spark at a very high level. What's the big deal about it, why is it so fast, and why are people using it? It's pretty cool stuff and it's very easy to use. So let's come down from the high level and get a little bit more technical. We're going to take a closer look at how Spark works under the hood and what the RDD object is.

The Resilient Distributed Dataset (RDD)

In this section, we'll stop being all high level and hand-wavy and go into a little bit more depth about how Spark works from a technical standpoint. In Spark, under the hood, there's something called the Resilient Distributed Dataset object, which is like a core object that everything in Spark revolves around. Even for the libraries built on top of Spark, such as Spark SQL or MLlib, you're also using RDDs under the hood or extensions to the RDD objects to make it look like something a little bit more structured. If you understand what an RDD is in Spark, you've come ninety per cent of the way to understanding Spark.

What is the RDD?

Let's talk about the RDD in a reverse order because I'm weird like that. So, fundamentally, the RDD is a dataset, and it is an abstraction for a giant set of data, which is the main thing you need to know as a developer. What you'll do is to set up RDD objects and the RDD will load them up with big datasets and then call various methods on the RDD objects to distribute the processing of that data. Now the beauty is that although RDDs are both "distributed" and "resilient," you don't really have to worry about those things. RDDs can be spread out across an entire cluster of computers that may or may not be running locally, they can also handle the failure of specific executor nodes in your cluster automatically, keep on going even if one node shuts down, and redistribute the work as needed when that occurs. You don't have to think about these things though, that's what Spark does for you and that's what your cluster manager does for you. So even though an RDD is distributed and resilient, which is a very powerful thing, you don't have to worry about the specifics about how that works because it's kind of magic. All you need to really know as a developer is that it represents a really big dataset and you can use the RDD object to transform that dataset from one set of data to another or to perform actions on that dataset to actually get the results you want from it.

The SparkContext object

From a programming standpoint, you're going to be given a `SparkContext` object. Now remember when we first tested out Spark just to see if it was running, we ran something called `Pyspark`, which gave us an interactive shell for Spark, and that gave us an `sc` object automatically, which we could use to run operations on. Once you have that `SparkContext` object, you can use that for creating RDDs; it's a little bit more useful, obviously, to have a script you can actually run over and over again. So, in a case where you're actually running a stand-alone script, you will create that `sc` object by hand and initialize it the way you want to. Either way, `sc` stands for `SparkContext`, and from a programming standpoint, it is sort of a starting point that you have. This `sc` object gives you methods you need to actually create an RDD.

Creating RDDs

One simple example of using `sc` is that you can use the `sc.parallelize` function to take a hardcoded set of data and make an RDD out of it. But that's not very interesting, it's not really going to be useful in a real production setting because if you could hardcode the data, then it's not really a big dataset to begin with now, is it? More often, we'll use something like `sc.txtFile` to create an RDD object. So, for example, if I have a giant text file full of, oh I don't know, movie ratings data for example, on my hard drive, we can use `sc.txtFile` to create an RDD object from `SparkContext` and then we can just use that RDD object going forward and process it:

```
sc.textFile("file:///c:/users/frank/gobs-o-text.txt")
```

Now, again, if I have a set of information that fits on my computer, that's not really big data either, you can also create a text file from an s3n location or from an HDFS URI. So these are both examples of distributed file systems that can handle much larger datasets, that we might be able to fit on one machine. You can just as easily use an s3n or an HDFS URI as well as the file URI to load up data from a cluster or from a distributed file system as well as from a simple file that might be running on the same machine as your driver script.

You can also create RDDs from Hive:

```
hiveCtx = HiveContext(sc) rows = hiveCtx.sql("SELECT name, age FROM users")
```

If you have a `HiveContext` object that's already been connected to an existing Hive repository, you can create an RDD from that. If you don't know what Hive is, don't worry about it: Hive is basically another thing that runs on top of Hadoop for data warehousing. You can also create RDDs from things, such as JDBC, you can tie it correctly to any SQL database that has a JDBC or ODBC interface. You can also use popular NoSQL databases such as Cassandra, and it has interfaces for things such as HBase and Elasticsearch and a lot of other things that are growing all the time. Basically, any data format that you can access from Python or from Java, depending on what language you're using, you can access through Spark as well, so you can load up JSON information and comma-separated value lists. You can also talk to things like sequence files and object files and load compressed formats directly. So there are a lot of ways to create an RDD; pretty much whatever format your source data might be in, the odds are that you can create an RDD from it in Spark pretty easily.

Transforming RDDs

One common thing you're going to do once you have an RDD is transform it in some way, shape, or form. The following list shows some of the basic operations you can do on RDDs. This is not a complete list, but these are all the most common operations you can do on an RDD:

- map
- flatmap
- filter
- distinct
- sample
- union, intersection, subtract, cartesian

There's not a whole lot to wrap your head around here. The thing is, although there aren't a lot of different operations you can do to transform an RDD, they're all very powerful. So let's start with the map function on an RDD. This allows you to take a set of data and transform it into some other set of data, given a function that operates on the RDD. So, for example, if I want to square all the numbers in an RDD, I might have a map that points to a function that just multiplies everything in that RDD by itself. The map function has a one-to-one relationship, so that every entry in your original RDD gets mapped to a new value in your new RDD. So your new RDD will have just as many entries as your original RDD.

Moving on to the `flatmap` function, which is very similar to `map` except it has the capability to produce multiple values for every input value that you have from the original RDD. So the RDD that you transform using `flatmap` may be larger or even smaller than `map` in the RDD you started with. But still, fundamentally, it transforms one RDD in to another using some function, it just has the ability to blow that out into multiple results, or even no results per original entry.

The `filter` function can be used to trim out information you don't need. So let's say, for example, you have an RDD filled with weblog data and you want to filter out everything but the error lines in that weblog. You could have a `filter` function that just looks for the word error in a line of text, and if it doesn't have error in it, it throws it away; that's what a filter would do in an RDD.

There are some other, less common operations such as `distinct`, which you would use if you just wanted to get the distinct values, the unique values that are in an RDD, and throw out all the duplicates. You could call sample on it if you just want to take a random sample from the RDD and get a smaller dataset to work with and experiment with. The sample operation can be very useful while you're testing a script on a large dataset and you just want to run it locally to work out the bugs. Finally, you can actually do intersections of various types between two RDDs. There are methods that can take two different RDDs as the input and output a single RDD. For this, we can call the `union`, `intersection`, or `subtraction` operations for subtracting one RDD's values from another. We also have the Cartesian product where you get every possible combination between every element in the RDD, and obviously, that fills up really quickly. So again, not a lot of different operations, but they are all very powerful and they allow you to input your own functions for transforming one dataset into another using RDDs.

Map example

Here's an example of a `map` operation, just to make these explanations a little more real. Let's say we have an RDD that's just, you know, hard-coded to contain the values 1, 2, 3, and 4:

```
rdd=sc.parallelize([1,2,3,4])
```

In Python, I could just say `rdd.map` and pass this `lambda` function of the x points to x times x:

```
rdd.map(lambda x:x*x)
```

This one line will go ahead and square every value of that original RDD and then will return a new RDD that contains the values 1, 4, 9, and 16, which are the squares of 1, 2, 3, and 4.

What was that lambda thing? Well, if you're new to Python, this might be a new concept for you. Basically, a lot of Spark is centered around this concept called functional programming; it sounds fancy, but it's really not that complicated. The only thing is, many of the methods in RDDs actually accept a function as a parameter, as opposed to a more typical parameter, such as a float or string or something like that. Instead, you're passing in some function, some operation that you want to perform on every value of the RDD. Lambda is just shorthand really, so it's exactly the same thing as passing in a function directly. So just like I could say `rdd.map`, lambda x gets transformed into x times x:

```
rdd.map(lambda x: x*x)
```

I can alternatively just define a function called `squareIt`, or whatever I want to call it. This takes x as a parameter and returns the square of that argument:

```
def squareIt (x) :
     return x*x
```

Then, I can say `rdd.map` and then the name of that function:

```
rdd.map(squareIt)
```

It does exactly the same thing as this line:

```
rdd.map(lambda x: x*x)
```

The lambda shorthand is just a little bit more compact. For simple functions that you want to use for your transformations on RDDs, it can save you a little bit of typing and give you a little bit more clarity. If you want to do something more complicated while you're mapping one RDD into another, you'll probably want to write a separate function for it and that's an option too. The basic concept is that you're passing in functions to your RDD methods instead of more traditional project parameters. That's all there is to that, I mean that's all there is to functional programming really, it wasn't that complicated, right? The more examples we look at, the more sense it makes.

RDD actions

In addition to transforming one RDD into another, you can also perform actions on to an RDD. So once you have the data that you want in an RDD dataset, you can then perform an action on it to actually get a result. This is a list of RDD actions:

- collect
- count
- countByValue
- take
- top
- reduce
- and more...

So you can call `collect`, to just dump out all the values that are in there right now and just print them all out or whatever you want to do with them. You can call `count` to get a count of all the values that are in it. Call `countByValue`, which will actually give you a breakdown by unique value of how many times each value occurs in your RDD. There are actions such as `take` and `top` that let you sample a few values from the RDD final results. More powerful is the `reduce` function, which lets you combine all the different values for a given key value and boils things down into a summation or aggregation of your RDD. This will make more sense when you look at more examples. There are more examples of actions you can do as well, but these are the more common ones.

Another thing to understand regarding RDDs is that nothing actually happens until you call an action. We talked earlier about how Spark is so fast because it constructs a directed acyclic graph as soon as you ask for an action to happen; at this point, it knows what actually needs to be done to get the results that you want, and it can compute the most optimal path to make that happen. So it's important that when you're writing your Spark driver scripts, your script isn't actually going to do anything until you call one of these action methods. At this point, it will actually start farming things out to your cluster or write it on your own computer, whatever you've told it to do, and actually start executing that program. You won't actually have any results or any processing whatsoever until one of these action methods are actually called within your script, so it's important to keep that in mind.

That's what an RDD is, it's sort of the foundation of Spark. Now that you understand how to use RDDs and what they're for, let's go back to that ratings histogram example and figure out what it's actually doing under the hood there.

Ratings histogram walk-through

Remember the RatingsHistogram code that we ran for your first Spark program? Well, let's take a closer look at that and figure out what's actually going on under the hood with it. Understanding concepts is all well and good, but nothing beats looking at some real examples. Let's go back to the RatingsHistogram example that we started off with in this book. We'll break it down and understand exactly what it's doing under the hood and how it's using our RDDs to actually get the results for the RatingsHistogram data.

Understanding the code

The first couple of lines are just boilerplate stuff. One thing you'll see in every Python Spark script is the import statement to import SparkConf and SparkContext from the pyspark library that Spark includes. You will, at a minimum, need those two objects:

```
from pyspark import SparkConf, SparkContext
import collections
```

SparkContext, as we talked about earlier, is the fundamental starting point that the Spark framework gives you to create RDDs from. You can't create SparkContext without SparkConf, which allows you to configure the SparkContext and tell it things such as, "do you want to run just some on computer or do you want to run on a cluster and if so, in what way?" The other bit of housekeeping at the beginning of our script is importing the collections package from Python. This is just because you want to sort the final results when we're done-that's just standard Python stuff.

Setting up the SparkContext object

Next, we actually create our SparkContext, and this is going to look very similar in every Spark script that we write in Python. We have these two lines:

```
conf = SparkConf().setMaster("local").setAppName("RatingsHistogram")
sc = SparkContext(conf = conf)
```

So let's look at what's going on here. In the first line, we have the SparkConf object that we imported earlier and we're telling it to set its master node as the local machine. Basically, it says we're going to be running on the local box only, not on the cluster, just on this one system. There are extensions to local that tell you to actually split it up among multiple CPU cores that you might have on your machine, but this is a very simple example, so we're just going to run it in a single thread on a single process, which is what local means. So we're not really doing any sort of distribution of the data: in this case, it's just sort of running on one process to keep it simple for now and get the concepts across. Later on, we'll run more complicated jobs that actually use every core of your computer, and ultimately, we'll run a job on a real cluster using Elastic MapReduce.

Finally, in that first line, we need to set the app name as part of this call by typing .setAppName. We're going to call this app "RatingsHistogram". This is just so if you actually look in the Spark Web UI to actually see what's going on while it's running, you'll be able to look up the job by its name there and understand and identify it. Now this job runs too quickly for you to even see it in the UI, so we're not going to worry about that, but it is good practice to give every app a name. In the second line, using that Spark configuration object, we create our SparkContext object and assign that to something called sc:

```
sc = SparkContext(conf = conf)
```

By convention, we will always call that sc for SparkContext.

Loading the data

Now we're going to load up our data file. If you remember from *Chapter 1, Getting Started With Spark*, a very common way of creating an RDD is through the sc.textFile method. So, as you can see in the line of code shown here, this is actually going to go out to our local file system, go to the ml-100k rating dataset from MovieLens, and then load up the data file that includes all of the movie ratings data:

```
lines = sc.textFile("file:///SparkCourse/ml-100k/u.data")
```

Now if you were to open up the u.data file in some sort of a text editor, it would look something like the following information, only with a hundred thousand lines:

```
196   242   3   881250949
186   302   3   891717742
22    377   1   878887116
244   51    2   880606923
166   346   1   886397596
```

What textFile does is it breaks up that input file line by line, so that every line of text corresponds to one value in your RDD. The first value of the lines RDD is going to be this entire line of text:

```
196    242    3    881250949
```

The second line will be this line of text:

```
186    302    3    891717742
```

The third value will be this line of text and so on and so forth.

```
22    377    1    878887116
```

So if this were my entire u.data file, my RDD would consist of five values where each value is a string that represents a line of text:

```
196    242    3    881250949
186    302    3    891717742
22     377    1    878887116
244    51     2    880606923
166    346    1    886397596
```

Later on, we'll actually break that up and look at what that string means.

Extract (MAP) the data we care about

This image demonstrates what our mapper function does:

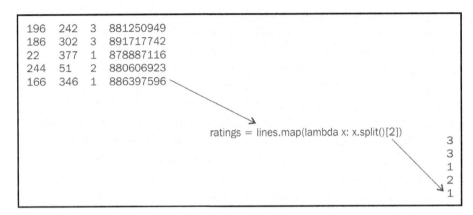

The Lambda sequence allows us to have a shorthand of passing a function that we want to pass into our `map`. So you can see, we have `lines.map` and then inside our parentheses, we have `lambda x`, where x gets passed into split, and we extract the 2 number field:

```
ratings = lines.map(lambda x: x.split()[2])
```

What this code is going to do, in every line, is take the line of input and split it based on whitespace individual fields. Running `split` on the first line, for example, is going to result in a list of values of 196 242 3 881250949. These numbers represent the user ID, 196, the movie ID, 242, the rating value, 3, and a timestamp, 881250949. So, the way to interpret the `u.data` file is: user ID 196 watched movie 242, gave it a rating of three out of five, and they did this at this particular timestamp. This can be translated into an actual human readable time; that's epoch seconds if you're curious. In computer programming, we start counting from 0. So the second field is actually the rating itself: 3. So what's this `map` function actually doing? Again, it's splitting up each line into its individual fields based on whitespaces, and then it's taking the field number two, which is the actual rating value. For every line of data, it sucks out the rating value and puts that into a new RDD that we're calling ratings.

Make sure you understand what's going on here, this is a very fundamental part in understanding Spark. If you need to stare at this some more, do what you have to do because it's very important that you get this concept. If you don't, you're going to have a hard time going forward. Understand this little one line of code:

```
ratings = lines.map(lambda x: x.split()[2])
```

This is going to take every individual input line from our lines RDD, which contains the raw input data, split it up into fields, in this case, a user ID field, movie ID field, ratings field, and timestamp, extract the ratings field which is field 2, and put that into a new RDD, called `ratings`. So we start with this:

```
196   242   3   881250949
186   302   3   891717742
22    377   1   878887116
244    51   2   880606923
166   346   1   886397596
```

After this `map` operation, the ratings RDD gets populated with these values:

```
3
3
1
2
1
```

Our new RDD, called `ratings`, will contain 3, 3, 1, 2, and 1 because these are the rating values extracted from the source data. It's also very important to remember that the `map` function and all the `action` functions don't transform the RDD in place. So your `lines` RDD remains untouched. What it's doing is creating a new RDD called `ratings`, and you need to remember to assign the result of that transformation to a new RDD or else it will just go nowhere. This is a very common mistake; you can't just call `lines.map` and expect it to change everything in your `lines` RDD. You need to assign that result to a new RDD, in this case, we've called it `ratings`. So, if you understand all of that, great, let's move forward. If not, again, take your time, do what you have to do to understand how we extract the ratings field in this instance, it's a very important concept.

Perform an action - count by value

Finally, we're going to perform an action on our RDD. So far we've transformed the RDD into the form that we want. We took our raw input data and created an RDD that contains nothing but ratings as its values. Now we can perform an action with this line of code:

```
result = ratings.countByValue()
```

What we're doing is calling our ratings RDD, which includes just the rating values in our example, 3, 3, 1, 2, and 1. Then we call an `action` method on that RDD, `countByValue`. This is a very easy way to cheat and quickly create something like a histogram:

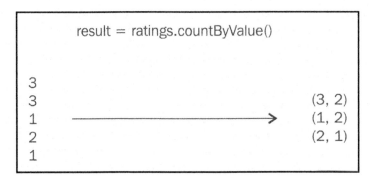

What it does is count up how many times each unique value in the RDD occurs. In this particular example, we know that the rating 3 occurs twice, the rating 1 occurs twice, and the rating 2 only occurs once-this is the output we'll get. We get these pair values, these tuples if you will, of rating and then the number of times that occurred:

```
(3, 2)
(1, 2)
(2, 1)
```

This is what will end up in our `result` object. All that's left to do at this point is to print that out. Now, `countByValue` is an action, so it's actually returning just a plain old Python object at this point, that's no longer an RDD. We can do what we want to do in order to sort those results, which is the final thing we do.

Sort and display the results

The code we use for sorting and displaying our results is all just straight-up Python code, there's nothing Sparkish about it:

```
sortedResults = collections.OrderedDict(sorted(result.items()))
for key, value in sortedResults.items():
    print("%s %i" % (key, value))
```

All it's doing is using the collections package from Python to create an ordered dictionary that sorts those results based on the key, which is the actual rating itself. Then it iterates through every key/value pair of those results and prints them out one at a time. So the output of this bit of code is going to be this:

```
12
21
32
```

Rating 1 occurred twice, rating 2 occurred once, and rating 3 occurred twice, that's all that's going on here. So we're taking those original key/value pairs that were returned by countByValue here:

```
result = ratings.countByValue()
```

We are sorting them just using this boilerplate Python code:

```
sortedResults = collections.OrderedDict(sorted(result.items()))
for key, value in sortedResults.items():
    print("%s %i" % (key, value))
```

I realize you may be new to Python, but if you look at this, it's pretty self-explanatory. As you go into more exercises in the future, you can use a lot of these examples that I'm giving you to actually create what you need and piece together the pieces that you need to actually construct your own program. So keep these snippets of code in your toolbox for future use.

There we have it, it's just that easy! We only had a handful of lines of code. Let's actually look at it as a whole again and take a look at that program all in one piece within Canopy. We'll run it one more time just to reiterate what's going on.

Looking at the ratings-counter script in Canopy

So now that we have a better idea of what's actually going on here, let's take another look at the `ratings-counter` script as a whole. Go back to your `SparkCourse` directory and open it back in Canopy:

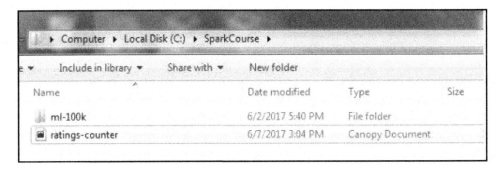

Here it is altogether, shown as follows. It looks a bit neater in here, so once again let's review what's going on here:

```
from pyspark import SparkConf, SparkContext
import collections

conf = SparkConf().setMaster("local").setAppName("RatingsHistogram")
sc = SparkContext(conf = conf)

lines = sc.textFile("file:///SparkCourse/ml-100k/u.data")
ratings = lines.map(lambda x: x.split()[2])
result = ratings.countByValue()

sortedResults = collections.OrderedDict(sorted(result.items()))
for key, value in sortedResults.items():
    print("%s %i" % (key, value))
```

We are importing the `SparkConf` and `SparkContext` objects from `pyspark`. You're going to have that at the beginning of pretty much every Spark Python script that we write:

```
from pyspark import SparkConf, SparkContext
```

We'll also use the collections object to sort our results so we import that next:

```
import collections
```

Next we create the `SparkContext` object using a `SparkConf` object that we create with the name `RatingsHistogram`, and we'll run it locally just on one process for now:

```
conf = SparkConf().setMaster("local").setAppName("RatingsHistogram")
sc = SparkContext(conf = conf)
```

Now the magic of Spark starts happening in these next lines, we create an RDD called `lines` by calling `sc.textFile` and we give it an absolute path to our data file for the MovieLens dataset. That data file contains 100,000 lines, and at this point, every one of those lines will be a value in this `lines` RDD:

```
lines = sc.textFile("file:///SparkCourse/ml-100k/u.data")
```

Now we'll apply a `map` function to that `lines` RDD, and pass in a `lambda` function that splits out that line, breaking it up with whitespace and taking field number 2 out of each line. And again, each line of the `u.data` file represents a user ID, a movie ID, a rating, and a timestamp, so field number 2, given that we start counting from 0, ends up being the rating value from each line:

```
ratings = lines.map(lambda x: x.split()[2])
```

What this line does is, it takes our `lines` RDD that contains raw lines of text from our raw input data, and creates a new RDD called `ratings`, which contains only the ratings values from that input data.

Now that we have our RDD transformed into the form we want, where every line and every value of the RDD is a rating value, in the next line we can call `countByValue` to get a count of how many times each unique rating value occurs:

```
result = ratings.countByValue()
```

This gets the output into a plain old Python object called `result`. We can then turn around and use the `collections` package to sort those key:value pairs of keys representing the ratings, and values representing the count of each rating:

```
sortedResults = collections.OrderedDict(sorted(result.items()))
```

We sort those, and then in the next lines, we iterate through each result and print them out on the screen:

```
for key, value in sortedResults.items():
    print("%s %i" % (key, value))
```

That's just plain old Python code there, given the result generated by our `ratings` RDD when we called `countByValue` on it.

Once more, let's run this just for good luck. Now that you know what's going on, it should make a little bit more sense. Let's open **Canopy Command Prompt** and type in `spark-submit`. This is a tool that's part of the Spark framework that allows you to submit Python scripts to the Spark framework; it does all the magic that needs to happen under the hood to make that actually run in the Scala environment for Spark. We also need to pass in the name of the script, `ratings-counter.py`. Then we can run our script using the following command:

```
spark-submit ratings-counter.py
```

You'll see some warnings every time we run on our local machine here, you can safely ignore them, by the way. These are our results:

```
(User) c:\SparkCourse>spark-submit ratings-counter.py
1 6110
2 11370
3 27145
4 34174
5 21201
```

So once again we have 34,000 4 star ratings, 21,000 5 stars, and so on and so forth. You can see now how that all happened:it was through the magic of RDDs. We started with one RDD that represented every line of our input data:

```
lines = sc.textFile("file:///SparkCourse/ml-100k/u.data")
```

We then created a new RDD that just extracted the ratings from each line:

```
ratings = lines.map(lambda x: x.split()[2])
```

Then, on that RDD, we used `countByValue` to produce these final counts for each rating type:

```
result = ratings.countByValue()
```

Then we just used some plain old standard Python code to sort and display those results when we were done, and that's all there is to it:

```
sortedResults = collections.OrderedDict(sorted(result.items()))
for key, value in sortedResults.items():
    print("%s %i" % (key, value))
```

Alright, now you've not only run your first Spark program, but hopefully you also understand how it works. So let's start building upon that and work our way up to some more complicated examples with Spark. Next, we'll take a look at how Spark handles key value data.

Key/value RDDs and the average friends by age example

A powerful thing to do with RDDs is to put more structured data into it. One thing we can do is put key/value pairs of information into Spark RDDs and then we can treat it like a very simple database, if you will. So let's walk through an example where we have a fabricated social network set of data, and we'll analyze that data to figure out the average number of friends, broken down by age of people in this fake social network. We'll use key/value pairs and RDDs to do that. Let's cover the concepts, and then we'll come back later and actually run the code.

Key/value concepts - RDDs can hold key/value pairs

RDDs can hold key/value pairs in addition to just single values. In our previous examples, we looked at RDDs that included lines of text for an input data file or that contained movie ratings. In those cases, every element of the RDD contained a single value, either a line of text or a movie rating, but you can also store more structured information in RDDs. There's a special case where you have a list of two items contained in an RDD and that is considered a key/value pair RDD. These are really useful things because once you start storing key/value pairs in an RDD, it looks a lot like a NoSQL database, it's just a giant key/value data store at that point. You can then do things where you can aggregate information by key/values for example, and that can come in handy for instance in this example we're about to do.

Creating a key/value RDD

Syntactically, there's nothing really special about key/value RDDs, it's all kind of magic in Python. If you are storing a list of two items as your values in the RDD, then it is a key/value RDD and you can treat it as such. Here's a simple example:

```
totalsByAge = rdd.mapValues(lambda x: (x, 1))
```

If I want to create a `totalsByAge` RDD out of an original RDD that contains a single value in each element, my lambda function here, x, can take each rating or each number, whatever happens to be x, and transform that into a pair of the original number and then the number 1. So the syntax with the parentheses indicates that this is a single entity as far as Python is concerned, but it consists of two elements; it's a list of two things and in this example, the first item will be the key and the second item will be the value. Again, the key is important because we can do things like aggregate by key.

That's all there is to creating a key/value RDD. It's also okay to have complex things in the value of the key/value RDD; so I could keep the key as being the original value here from the first RDD and make the value itself a list of however many elements I want to. I'm not limited to just storing one thing in the value of the key/value RDD, I can store a list of things there if I want to as well, and we're going to do that in this example too, just to illustrate how that works.

What Spark can do with key/value data?

As I mentioned earlier, one of the most useful things you can do with the key/value RDD is `reduceByKey`. What that does is to combine all the values that are found for the same key/value, using some function that you define. So, for example, if I want to add up all of the values for a given key, let's say all of the numbers of friends for a given age, something like this would do the job:

```
rdd.reduceByKey(lambda x, y: x + y)
```

When you call a `reduce` function in Spark, it will get not just an x value but also an x and a y value. You can actually call those values whatever you want, but what you need to do is define a function that defines how to combine things together that are found for the same key. In this case, our function is just x plus y, so it says we're going to keep adding things together to combine things together for a given key/value. For example, if I was doing `reduceByKey` on a key/value RDD where the keys were ages and the values were a number of friends, I could get the total number of friends found for that age with something like this, because every value that's found for that key will be added together using that function x plus y:

```
rdd.reduceByKey(lambda x, y: x + y)
```

There are other things you can do as well with key/value RDDs. You can call `groupByKey`, so if you don't actually want to combine them together quite yet, you can just get a list of all the values associated with each key using `groupByKey`. You can also use `sortByKey`, so if you want to sort your RDD by the key/values, `sortByKey` makes it easy to do. Third, you can split out the keys and the values into their own RDD using `keys()`, `values()`. You don't see that too often but it's good to know that it exists.

As I mentioned earlier, you've kind of created a NoSQL data store here. It's a giant key/value data store, so you can start to do SQLish sorts of things since we have keys and values in play here. We can use `join`, `rightOuterJoin`, `leftOuterJoin`, `cogroup` and `subtractByKey`, all ways to combine two key/value RDDs together to create some joined RDD as a result. Later on, when we look at making similar movie recommendations, we'll have an example of doing that by joining one key/value RDD with another to get every possible permutation of movies that were rated together.

Mapping the values of a key/value RDD

Now this is a very important point with key/value RDDs: if you're not going to actually modify the keys from your transformations on the RDD, make sure you call `mapValues()` or `flatMapValues()` instead of just `map` or `flatMap`. This is important because it's more efficient; getting a little technical, it allows Spark to maintain the partitioning from your original RDD instead of having to shuffle the data around, which can be very expensive when you're running on a cluster.

So anytime you're calling `map` or `flatMap` on a key/value RDD, ask yourself, am I actually modifying the key values? If the answer is no, you should be calling `mapValues()` instead or `flatMapValues()`.

Just to review again, mapValues will have a one-to-one relationship, so every element in your original RDD will be transformed into one new element, using whatever function you define. flatMap on the other hand can actually blow that out into multiple elements per original elements, so you can end up with a new RDD that's actually longer or contains more values than the original one with flatMapValues. Now, one thing to keep in mind is that if you're calling mapValues or flatMapValues, all that will be passed into your function that you're using to transform the RDD will be the values themselves. Don't take that to mean that the keys are getting discarded, they're not, they're just not being modified and not being exposed to you. So even though mapValues and flatMapValues will only receive one value, which is the value of the key/value pair, keep in mind the key is still there, it's still present, you're just not allowed to touch it. I realize this is a lot to digest, it's going to make a lot more sense when we look at a real example, so bear with me whilst we look at a real example.

The friends by age example

Let's go through a key/value RDD example to illustrate these concepts. I've generated a fake dataset just completely at random, which represents a social network. On every line is a user ID, a username, the age of that user, and the number of friends that user has:

```
0, Will,33,385
1, Jean-Luc,33,2
2, Hugh,55,221
3, Deanna,40,465
4, QUARK,68,21
```

▷ Input Data: ID, name, age, number of friends

So for example, user ID 0 might be named Will and he's 33 years old and has 385 friends-these ages and numbers of friends are all completely assigned at random, so don't associate any sort of deep meaning to them. You might notice that I'm a Star Trek fan here. So that's our source data that we're going to work with and our task is to figure out the average number of friends by age. For example, what's the average number of friends for the average 33-year-old in our dataset? Well, let's figure that out.

Parsing (mapping) the input data

Our first step is just to parse our input data into what we need; nothing special here, we're going to start by creating a `lines` RDD as shown here. This is calling `textFile` on our `SparkContext` object with our source data, and that's just going to give us an RDD where every individual line of that comma-separated value list is an individual entry in our RDD:

```
lines = sc.textFile("file:///SparkCourse/fakefriends.csv")
```

Now things get interesting; I'm going to transform my `lines` RDD into an `rdd` RDD (very creatively named) by calling `map` on it. Also, I'm passing in the `parseLine` function to actually conduct that mapping:

```
rdd = lines.map(parseLine)
```

So every line from my `lines` RDD will be passed into `parseLine` one at a time, and I'm going to parse it out, as shown here:

```
def parseLine(line):
    fields = line.split(',')
    age = int(fields[2])
    numFriends = int(fields[3])
    return (age, numFriends)
```

The first thing we're going to do is split it based on commas and that'll bust out the different fields we need:

```
fields = line.split(',')
```

I will then extract the fields that I'm interested in. If I'm just trying to figure out the number of friends by age, all I care about is the number of friends and age information, the user IDs and the usernames are irrelevant, so I'm just going to discard those. I will extract the age from the field number 2, which is actually the third field because remember we start counting from zero. It is important to note that I'm actually casting it to an integer value because I want to treat this as a numerical value, and that allows me to do arithmetic operations on it later:

```
age = int(fields[2])
```

Now if I didn't do that, it would just keep treating it as a string, so I wouldn't be able to do things like add them up and divide them, which I'm going to have to do if I want to get averages at the end of the day. Similarly, in the next line, I'm going to cast the number of friends to an integer value as well, using the correct syntax, in between parentheses. Fields 3 will give me back a string value of some number, and `int` will actually make sure Python knows that it's a number, that I should treat it as such, and I can perform arithmetic on it:

```
numFriends = int(fields[3])
```

The next line is where we actually transform things into a key/value RDD. Instead of returning a single value, I'm returning a key/value pair of the age and the number of friends:

```
return (age, numFriends)
```

The RDD I'm creating with the `parseLine` mapper function creates a new RDD that is a key/value RDD, with a key of age and a value of `numFriends`.

Hope you are with me so far. For example, if we transform our original data:

```
0, Will,33,385
1, Jean-Luc,33,2
2, Hugh,55,221
3, Deanna,40,465
4, Quark,68,21
```

The output will be a key/value pair RDD that contains something like this:

```
33, 385
33, 2
55, 221
40, 465
...
```

The first user in our data had an age of 33 and 385 friends, the second user had an age of 33 and 2 friends, the third user was 55 years old and had 221 friends, and so on and so forth. This is an important concept to grasp, so go over this as many times as you need in order to let it sink in. Let's move on.

Counting up the sum of friends and number of entries per age

Alright, now I'm going to throw you into the deep end of the pool here, look at this big scary line:

```
totalsByAge = rdd.mapValues(lambda x: (x, 1)).reduceByKey(lambda x, y:
(x[0] + y[0], x[1] + y[1]))
```

However, if we break it down into its components, what's going on here is pretty straightforward. What we need to do next is to aggregate our RDD information somehow. So let's just break this `totalsByAge` line down, one component at a time. You can see, we have sort of a compound operation going on here; we're taking our RDD of age and number of friend key/value pairs and we're calling `mapValues` on it, and then we're taking the resulting RDD and calling `reduceByKey` on it. Let's take this one step at a time, we'll start with the `mapValues` piece of it.

This piece transforms every value in my key/value pair, because remember we're calling `mapValues`, so the x that's getting passed is only going to be the value piece of the original RDD:

```
rdd.mapValues(lambda x: (x, 1))
```

Let's take the first entry in our `rdd` RDD for example. This entry has a 33-year-old who had 385 friends:

$$(33, 385) => (33, (385, 1))$$

So the value 385 gets passed in through `mapValues` for every line. This value is our x in the lambda function. As you can see in the following line, our output is going to be a new value that is actually a pair, a list if you will, of 385 and the number 1:

```
rdd.mapValues(lambda x: (x, 1))
```

The method behind our madness here is that in order to get an average, we need to count up all the total number of friends seen for a given age and the number of times that age occurred. Later on, if we sum up all of these pairs of information, we will get the total number of friends for that age and the total number of times that age occurred when we look at the totals for a given age. So that's kind of our strategy here-to build up a running total of how many times 33-year-olds were seen and the total number of friends that they had.

Let's get back to the syntax of this lambda function:

```
rdd.mapValues(lambda x: (x, 1))
```

Just to review again, `mapValues` will receive each value, which in our case is the number of friends, and output a new value, which is actually a tuple-`(x,1)`. This tuple contains the original number of friends and the value `1`. This is an example of ending up with a key/value pair, where the value is not just a single value or a single number, it's actually a collection of numbers, a list, and that's perfectly okay:

$$(33, 385) => (33, (385, 1))$$

Our output is a new RDD that is still a key/value pair, but the keys are untouched because we called `mapValues` and the values are now transformed from just a number of friends to a pair value of `385` and the number `1`.

Now we need to add everything up together and that's where the `reduceByKey` part comes in. Let's have a look at the second part of our big scary `totalsByAge` line. `reduceByKey` just tells us how we combine things together for the same key:

```
reduceByKey(lambda x, y: (x[0] + y[0], x[1] + y[1]))
```

Again, going back to our example here, let's say that we are looking at every 33-year-old, so we're looking at keys of `33`:

$$(33, 385)=> (33, (385, 1))$$
$$(33, 2) => (33, (2, 1))$$
$$(55, 221)=> (55, (221, 1))$$

Our lambda function takes in two values, shown as x and y, and says how do we add them up? So for example, in our data shown here, we have x coming in as (385, 1), and y might be (2, 1):

```
(33, 385) => (33, (385, 1))
(33, 2)=> (33, (2, 1))
(55, 221)=> (55, (221, 1))
```

Then this part of the function shown here just says add up each component. We take the first element of each value and add them together, take the second element of each value and add them together:

```
(x[0] + y[0], x[1] + y[1]))
```

The output in this case would be 385 plus 2, that is 387, and 1 plus 1, that is 2, and we'll keep doing that repeatedly for every time we encounter values for the key 33 and add them all up together:

```
(33, (387, 2))
```

So you see what we have at this stage is the grand total of number of friends, and the number of times we saw that key for the given key, which in this case is the age of 33 years old. It will do that for every single key. That's what reduceByKey does, and with that we have the information we need to actually compute the averages we want. Before we do that, it might be a good idea to go back over what we just covered and make sure that you understand how we count up the sum of friends and number of entries per age; even I had a hard time wrapping my head around this at first. Once you're sure you've understood, let's move on.

Compute averages

The last step is to transform the pairs of total number of friends and the number of times that key was encountered to an actual average value:

```
(33, (387, 2))=> (33, 193.5)
```

That's what this final line does with `mapValues`:

```
averageByAge = totalsByAge.mapValues(lambda x: x[0] / x[1])
```

Again, we're just receiving the value part of our key/value pair into our lambda function because we're calling `mapValues` and leaving the keys untouched.

So the age in this example, 33, will remain untouched and not even shown to us in our lambda function:

$$(33, (387, 2)) => (33, 193.5)$$

However, our lambda function will receive the value, which is the `(387, 2)` pair(the total number of friends and number of times that age was encountered) and just divide the two to get an average value:

```
(lambda x: x[0] / x[1])
```

To get the output at this stage for the key 33, we would be transforming 33 and this pair of `(387, 2)`, which is the total number of friends and the number of times 33-year-olds were seen, to 33-year-olds who had an average number of friends to 193.5:

$$(33, (387, 2)) => (33, 193.5)$$

Collect and display the results

Now we have our final results, all we have to do is call `collect` to get them and print them out:

```
results = averagesByAge.collect()
for result in results:
    print(result)
```

One thing I want to mention is that remember nothing actually happens in Spark until the first action is called. If you go back to when we called `reduceByKey`, that's actually the first action in our code so nothing actually occurred in our script until `reduceByKey` was called, which is kind of interesting:

```
reduceByKey(lambda x, y: (x[0] + y[0], x[1] + y[1]))
```

The other action that we have in our script is this `collect` call:

```
results = averagesByAge.collect()
```

At both stages, Spark will go out and actually construct that directed acyclic graph and figure out the optimal way to compute the answer we want. That's the key to why Spark is so fast.

So there we have it! That's the overview of how we're going to use key/value pairs in our RDDs to actually analyze the dataset of our fake social network. Now that we've walked through how that code is going to work, let's make it real. In our next section, we'll actually run this code for real on an actual dataset.

Running the average friends by age example

Okay, let's make it real, let's actually get some real code and some real data and analyze the average number of friends by age in our fabricated dataset here, and see what we come up with.

At this point, you should go to the download package for this book, if you haven't already, and download two things: one is the `friends-by-age` Python script, and the other is the `fakefriends.csv` file, which is my randomly generated data that's completely fictitious, but useful for illustration. So go take care of that now. When you're done, move it into your `C:\SparkCourse` folder or wherever you're installing stuff for this course. At this point in the course, your `SparkCourse` folder should look like this:

Name	Date modified	Type	Size
ml-100k	6/29/2017 12:37 PM	File folder	
fakefriends	6/8/2017 11:59 AM	Microsoft Excel C...	9 KB
friends-by-age	6/8/2017 11:54 AM	Canopy Document	1 KB
ratings-counter	6/7/2017 3:04 PM	Canopy Document	1 KB

At this moment, we need `friends-by-age.py` and `fakefriends.csv`, so let's double-click on the `friends-by-age.py` script, and Enthought Canopy or your Python environment of choice should come up. Here we have it:

```
friends-by-age.py

 1 from pyspark import SparkConf, SparkContext
 2
 3 conf = SparkConf().setMaster("local").setAppName("FriendsByAge")
 4 sc = SparkContext(conf = conf)
 5
 6 def parseLine(line):
 7     fields = line.split(',')
 8     age = int(fields[2])
 9     numFriends = int(fields[3])
10     return (age, numFriends)
11
12 lines = sc.textFile("file:///SparkCourse/fakefriends.csv")
13 rdd = lines.map(parseLine)
14 totalsByAge = rdd.mapValues(lambda x: (x, 1)).reduceByKey(lambda x, y: (x[0] + y[0], x[1] + y[1]))
15 averagesByAge = totalsByAge.mapValues(lambda x: x[0] / x[1])
16 results = averagesByAge.collect()
17 for result in results:
18     print(result)
19
```

Examining the script

So let's just review again what's going on here. We start off with the usual boilerplate stuff. We import what we need from `pyspark` for Spark:

```
from pyspark import SparkConf, SparkContext
```

We then set up a `SparkContext` object that's just going to run locally on our own computer on one process and we're going to call it `FriendsByAge`:

```
conf = SparkConf().setMaster("local").setAppName("FriendsByAge")
sc = SparkContext(conf = conf)
```

Alright, so the first thing we do is pretty typical. We call `textFile` on the `SparkContext` object to parse our input data, our `fakefriends.csv` file, and if you do have that in some other folder, make sure you modify that here first:

```
lines = sc.textFile("file:///SparkCourse/fakefriends.csv")
```

We will use that and put it into our lines RDD and then we call our `map` function, `parseLine` to transform our input data, one line at a time, into a new key/value RDD:

```
rdd = lines.map(parseLine)
```

We can see what it's doing if we look at these earlier lines of code:

```
def parseLine(line):
    fields = line.split(',')
    age = int(fields[2])
    numFriends = int(fields[3])
    return (age, numFriends)
```

It's splitting up the source data by the commas that are in it.

```
fields = line.split(',')
```

The `parseLine` function extracts the age and number of friends from each line and casts them as integer values so we can perform arithmetic operations on them later:

```
age = int(fields[2])
numFriends = int(fields[3])
```

The `parseLine` function then returns key/value pairs, where the key is the age and the value is the number of friends seen for this individual:

```
return (age, numFriends)
```

So at this point, we have a new RDD that contains key/value pairs of ages and number of friends for each person in our dataset:

```
rdd = lines.map(parseLine)
```

Next, we get to that big, long scary line that does a bunch of stuff at once. Get used to this because you will see a lot of this in Spark, people kind of do chain operations together like this:

```
totalsByAge = rdd.mapValues(lambda x: (x, 1)).reduceByKey(lambda x, y:
(x[0] + y[0], x[1] + y[1]))
```

Just break it down one bit at a time, left to right, to figure out what's going on. The first thing we're doing is this `mapValues` call:

```
rdd.mapValues(lambda x: (x, 1))
```

The `mapValues` function leaves the keys untouched; so our keys, which are ages, will still remain and only the values, which are the numbers of friends, get passed into our `lamda` function. So x in our lambda function is the number of friends for each individual in our RDD. We then transform that into compound objects, these tuples of number of friends and the `1 - (x, 1)` value, so we can add those all up together later:

```
rdd.mapValues(lambda x: (x, 1))
```

Again, we have a new RDD under the hood, where the key is still the ages, but the values are now these compound values of number of friends and the number 1. Then, in the other half of this long line of code, we need to aggregate everything together for each age; `reduceByKey` does that:

```
reduceByKey(lambda x, y: (x[0] + y[0], x[1] + y[1]))
```

The `reduceByKey` function will gather all the values found for each age, which is our key/value, and combine them together using the function that we provide. So again, x and y are two things we're combining together for a given key, for a given age, and we're just saying by this `lambda` function, all I want to do is add up each component. It takes the first element of each value and adds them together, takes the second element of each value and adds them together:

```
reduceByKey(lambda x, y: (x[0] + y[0], x[1] + y[1]))
```

What we end up with is a new RDD, where the key is still the age because we're not messing with the keys, but the values are the total number of friends seen for each age and the total number of times that age was encountered. With that, we have everything we need in the `totalsByAge` RDD to compute the averages.

In the next line, we have our final transformation. We're going to call `mapValues`. So again, our value at this point is a tuple, a composite value of total number of friends and the total number of times that age was encountered, and it just takes the tuple and divides it up to get our average number. That's our final result:

```
averagesByAge = totalsByAge.mapValues(lambda x: x[0] / x[1])
```

Finally, we call the `collect` action on the resulting RDD averages by age and we just print them out:

```
results = averagesByAge.collect()
for result in results:
    print(result)
```

Running the code

So let's see if it works. Go up to the **Tools** menu and go to **Canopy Command Prompt**, or do whatever you do to get your Command Prompt, and we'll type in `spark-submit friends-by-age.py`, and get our code running.

We'll get the usual warnings that we see whenever we run something locally, which are safe to ignore, and we should quickly get a result:

```
(47, 233)
(48, 281)
(49, 184)
(50, 254)
(51, 302)
(52, 340)
(53, 222)
(54, 278)
(55, 295)
(56, 306)
(57, 258)
(58, 116)
(59, 220)
(60, 202)
(61, 256)
(62, 220)
(63, 384)
(64, 281)
(65, 298)
(66, 276)
(67, 214)
(68, 269)
(69, 235)
(User) c:\SparkCourse>
```

This is all random data, there's really no meaning behind it that you can try to glean, but just through random luck of the draw it turns out that 63-year-olds are pretty popular, with 384 friends on average. So there you have it, our average number of friends by age script. It illustrates the use of key/value RDDs as well as the concept of storing more complex lists of information-composite values or tuples, whatever you want to call it-within the information that we're passing around. Both are very important concepts, feel free to play around with the script, make it do something different, experiment, get your hands dirty, it's the best way to learn.

This is our second example now of using some real hands-on code and using Spark on your own desktop. We've got some real results, we've covered the concept of using key/value pairs in RDDs and some of the special things you can do when you have key/value pair data in an RDD-a very important concept. So let's move on to our next examples.

Filtering RDDs and the minimum temperature by location example

Now we're going to introduce the concept of filters on RDDs, a way to strip down an RDD into the information we care about and create a smaller RDD from it. We'll do this in the context of another real example. We have some real weather data from the year 1800, and we're going to find out the minimum temperature observed at various weather stations in that year. While we're at it, we'll also use the concept of key/value RDDs as well as part of this exercise. So let's go through the concepts, walk through the code and get started.

What is filter()

Filter is just another function you can call on a mapper, which transforms it by removing information that you don't care about. In our example, the raw weather data actually includes things such as minimum temperatures observed and maximum temperatures for every day, and also the amount of precipitation observed for every day. However, all we care about for the problem we're trying to solve is the minimum temperature observed at a given station for the year. So we need to apply a filter that just looks for weather data types of TMIN and allows those to pass through our new RDD that we're calling minTemps as you can see in this line of code:

```
minTemps = parsedLines.filter(lambda x: "TMIN" in x[1])
```

Everything else like "TMAX" entries or precipitation entries will just get discarded. We can take our parseLines RDD, filter out anything that's not a "TMIN" entry and construct a new minTemps RDD out of it. So basically, filter takes a function that returns a Boolean value, true or false. If it comes back true then that value is passed on to your new RDD, if not, it just gets discarded, it's just that simple, and that's all there is to it.

Another common example of using filter might be if you're processing log data from a website and you only care about analyzing certain types of events or certain types of transactions or maybe certain types of error codes. Filter is the way to strip out all the other stuff in the log that you don't need, and then have a much smaller RDD that you can work on more quickly and more efficiently.

The source data for the minimum temperature by location example

So let's take a look at our actual source data that we're working with. This is real weather data from the year 1800:

```
ITE00100554,18000101,TMAX,-75,,,E,
ITE00100554,18000101,TMIN,-148,,,E,
GM000010962,18000101,PRCP,0,,,E,
EZE00100082,18000101,TMAX,-86,,,E,
EZE00100082,18000101,TMIN,-135,,,E,
```

The format of our data is a comma-separated list of values on each line, where each line indicates a given observation at a given day at a given weather station. Each line starts with the weather station ID. If I remember right, ITE00100554 corresponds to Paris and EZE00100082 to Prague. The weather station ID is followed by the date, 18000101, that's in year/month/day format, 1800 January 1 in this example. Then we get the observation type, so that's TMAX, TMIN, or PRCP. Then we get the temperature. So the maximum temperature observed on January 1, 1800 for the ITE00100554 weather station was -75, and that's actually in tenths of degrees Celsius, so that means -7.5° C:

```
ITE00100554,18000101,TMAX,-75,,,E,
ITE00100554,18000101,TMIN,-148,,,E,
GM000010962,18000101,PRCP,0,,,E,
EZE00100082,18000101,TMAX,-86,,,E,
EZE00100082,18000101,TMIN,-135,,,E,
```

I believe that station was in Paris-a pretty cold day! At the end of each line, we have a bunch of extra fields that are unused in this dataset and we can just discard those.

What we care about are the TMIN entries because we're trying to figure out the minimum temperature observed for each weather station for the entire year. So let's look at this line here:

```
ITE00100554,18000101,TMIN,-148,,,E,
```

We have the weather station ID, the date, min temperature is the type of observation, -14.8° C was the coldest temperature observed. This was the minimum temperature on that date at that weather station.

Parse (map) the input data

The first thing we need to do is load that data up into an RDD. So we'll call `textFile` on our `SparkContext` and load every line of that input into a `lines` RDD:

```
lines = sc.textFile("file:///SparkCourse/1800.csv")
```

We'll then take that RDD that we called `lines` and apply our `parseLine` mapper function to it to create a `parseLines` RDD:

```
parsedLines = lines.map(parseLine)
```

This is what we want that function to do:

```
def parseLine(line):
    fields = line.split(',')
    stationID = fields[0]
    entryType = fields[2]
    temperature = float(fields[3]) * 0.1 * (9.0 / 5.0) + 32.0
    return (stationID, entryType, temperature)
```

The function will split out our fields by commas:

```
fields = line.split(',')
```

Then it'll extract the station ID text field:

```
stationID = fields[0]
```

Then it'll extract the entry type, which is going to be `TMIN`, `TMAX`, or `PRECIP`:

```
entryType = fields[2]
```

After that, we will then convert the temperature to degrees Fahrenheit because I'm a Fahrenheit kind of guy as I live in the United States:

```
temperature = float(fields[3]) * 0.1 * (9.0 / 5.0) + 32.0
```

To convert it to Fahrenheit, we extract the numerical field of the temperature from this line:

```
(fields[3])
```

We need to tell Python that it's a floating-point numerical value, so we can actually perform arithmetic operations on it:

```
float(fields[3])
```

We convert it from tenths of degrees Celsius to degrees Celsius by adding `*` `0.1` `*` and finally apply a little bit of math to convert from Celsius to Fahrenheit:

```
* 0.1 * (9.0 / 5.0) + 32.0
```

Finally, in the next line, we'll return this composite value, this list that consists of the station ID, the entry type, TMIN, TMAX, or PRECIP, and the value of the actual temperature observed:

```
return (stationID, entryType, temperature)
```

Basically, I've parsed out my input data into something a little more structured, where the new values are these composite values that consist of the station ID, the entry type, and the temperature. Okay, so, that's what we do, our RDD contains one of these-(`stationID`, `entryType`, `temperature`)-for every observation seen for every weather station ID on every day of the year.

Filter out all but the TMIN entries

Alright, now we're going to call `filter` on our RDD. Now you remember that we stored the entry type in field number 1, we start counting at 0, so field 0 is the station ID, 1 is the entry type, and 2 is the temperature. If we see TMIN in field number 1 of our value, we're going to let that pass, otherwise we will discard it. So we're going to end up with here is a new RDD called `minTemps` that contains only TMIN entry type observations:

```
minTemps = parsedLines.filter(lambda x: "TMIN" in x[1])
```

The actual format of the RDD will be the same, we're still going to have station ID, entry type, and temperature-composite values, lists, if you will-but we're only going to have entry types that contain TMIN at this point.

Create (station ID, temperature) key/value pairs

Given that everything in our RDD consists of TMIN, we don't really need that TMIN any more, so we can strip those out now. We're going to apply a new map function to our RDD that does exactly that:

```
stationTemps = minTemps.map(lambda x: (x[0], x[2]))
```

So we're going to transform every composite value to a new one that just consists of two values, which is the station ID and the temperature:

```
(lambda x: (x[0], x[2]))
```

At this point, we have a key/value pair in our new `stationTemps` RDD. Since we're down to just two values, our key is the station ID and the value is the temperature observed, which again at this point is in Fahrenheit. So now for every day of the year, we have a minimum temperature observation for a given station ID.

Find minimum temperature by station ID

Given that, we want to find the minimum temperature for the entire year for every station, we can call `reduceByKey` to do that. The `reduceByKey` function is going to aggregate together every minimum temperature observed for every weather station ID, and then our `lambda` function will determine how we do that aggregation:

```
minTemps = stationTemps.reduceByKey(lambda x, y: min(x,y))
```

In that `lambda` function, we're saying that for whenever we try to combine two observations together for a minimum temperature for a given station, we're going to call the `min` function to actually only take the minimum value between those two. As we keep feeding more and more observations for each weather station in there, only the smallest value, the minimum value, will survive in the end. At the end, we have our final result: a `minTemps` RDD that's going to be reduced by key. All we have is one entry for every weather station ID that contains the minimum temperature observed throughout the entire year for each weather station.

Collect and print results

Finally, we need to call the `collect` action to actually kick it all off and make Spark go do something and collect the results into a regular Python list called `results`:

```
results = minTemps.collect();
```

We'll just iterate through that and print them out:

```
for result in results:
    print(result[0] + "\t{:.2f}F".format(result[1]))
```

We'll do a little bit of fancy formatting here. If you're new to Python, this is just saying that we're going to print the weather station identifier string, followed by a tab character, then by some formatting to ensure that the actual temperature is truncated to 2 decimal places to the right of the decimal point. We'll stick the letter F at the end just to indicate that the result is in Fahrenheit and not Celsius.

Alright, so that's how we're going to use filters to actually boil down the minimum temperature observed for each weather station. We'll use the key values and `reduceByKey` to actually boil down the final results just like before. Let's dive into the code, it's going to make a little bit more sense when we see it all together, so let's take a closer look and actually run it and see what the answer is.

Running the minimum temperature example and modifying it for maximums

Let's see this filter in action and find out the minimum temperature observed for each weather station in the year 1800. Go to the download package for this book and download two things: the `min-temperatures` Python script and the `1800.csv` data file, which contains our weather information. Go ahead and download these now. When you're done, place them into your `C:SparkCourse` folder or wherever you're storing all the stuff for this course:

Name	Date modified	Type	Size
ml-100k	6/2/2017 5:40 PM	File folder	
1800	6/8/2017 12:23 PM	Microsoft Excel C...	62 KB
fakefriends	6/8/2017 11:59 AM	Microsoft Excel C...	9 KB
friends-by-age	6/8/2017 11:54 AM	Canopy Document	1 KB
min-temperatures	6/8/2017 12:23 PM	Canopy Document	1 KB
ratings-counter	6/7/2017 3:04 PM	Canopy Document	1 KB

When you're ready, go ahead and double-click on `min-temperatures.py` and open that up in your editor. I think it makes a little bit more sense once you see this all together. Feel free to take some time to wrap your head around it and figure out what's going on here and then I'll walk you through it.

```
1 from pyspark import SparkConf, SparkContext
2
3 conf = SparkConf().setMaster("local").setAppName("MinTemperatures")
4 sc = SparkContext(conf = conf)
5
6 def parseLine(line):
7     fields = line.split(',')
8     stationID = fields[0]
9     entryType = fields[2]
10    temperature = float(fields[3]) * 0.1 * (9.0 / 5.0) + 32.0
11    return (stationID, entryType, temperature)
12
13 lines = sc.textFile("file:///SparkCourse/1800.csv")
14 parsedLines = lines.map(parseLine)
15 minTemps = parsedLines.filter(lambda x: "TMIN" in x[1])
16 stationTemps = minTemps.map(lambda x: (x[0], x[2]))
17 minTemps = stationTemps.reduceByKey(lambda x, y: min(x,y))
18 results = minTemps.collect();
19
20 for result in results:
21     print(result[0] + "\t{:.2f}F".format(result[1]))
22
```

Examining the min-temperatures script

We start off with the usual boilerplate stuff, importing what we need from `pyspark` and setting up a `SparkContext` object that we're going to call `MinTemperatures`:

```
from pyspark import SparkConf, SparkContext

conf = SparkConf().setMaster("local").setAppName("MinTemperatures")
sc = SparkContext(conf = conf)
```

If you skip down to line 13, you can see that we're loading up our source data file from `1800.csv` into a `lines` RDD:

```
lines = sc.textFile("file:///SparkCourse/1800.csv")
```

In line 14, we then parse that out using our `parseLine` mapper function:

```
parsedLines = lines.map(parseLine)
```

We defined that function here:

```
def parseLine(line):
    fields = line.split(',')
    stationID = fields[0]
    entryType = fields[2]
    temperature = float(fields[3]) * 0.1 * (9.0 / 5.0) + 32.0
    return (stationID, entryType, temperature)
```

What we're doing with these lines of code is, firstly, splitting out each line by commas:

```
fields = line.split(',')
```

We're then extracting the station ID from the first field and extracting the entry type, which is going to be `TMIN`, `TMAX`, or `PRECIP`, from field 2:

```
stationID = fields[0]
entryType = fields[2]
```

Next, we are extracting the actual temperature value from the third field and telling Python that this is actually a floating-point numerical value that we can do arithmetic operations on. We convert it from tenths of degrees Celsius to degrees Celsius and convert that to degrees Fahrenheit:

```
temperature = float(fields[3]) * 0.1 * (9.0 / 5.0) + 32.0
```

Our return value will be this composite value, this list of station ID, entry type, and temperature:

```
return (stationID, entryType, temperature)
```

So at this point in the script, we have every line of our input data converted into this structured data, where the first value is the station ID, the second value is the entry type, which is `TMIN`, `TMAX`, or `PRECIP`, and the third value is the temperature associated with that entry in degrees Fahrenheit.

Next, down in line 15, we filter out everything with the `TMIN` values with our `filter` function:

```
minTemps = parsedLines.filter(lambda x: "TMIN" in x[1])
```

We check that entry type field in field number 1; if it's TMIN, then it survives, if it doesn't, then it does not get passed on. The resulting minTemps RDD contains nothing but TMIN entries. So at this point, we have an RDD that has a station ID, TMIN, and the temperature. Next, we can transform that again to eliminate those redundant TMIN entries because everything is a TMIN, it's no longer an interesting piece of information:

```
stationTemps = minTemps.map(lambda x: (x[0], x[2]))
```

What we end up with now is a key/value RDD because we have these tuples that we're left with- (x[0], x[2]), where [0] represents the station ID and [2] is the temperature in Fahrenheit. So stationTemps is now a key/value RDD, where the key is station ID and the values are the minimum temperatures observed for every day of the year for each station.

We're now very close to what we want, all we need to do is call reduceByKey to combine together all of the minimum temperatures observed every day for each weather station ID, and find the minimum value as we go:

```
minTemps = stationTemps.reduceByKey(lambda x, y: min(x,y))
```

So what we're left with is a minTemps RDD that has only one entry per weather station ID and that contains the minimum temperature observed for the entire year. Finally, we just need to collect the results and print them out and make them look pretty. We format them to being two decimal points to the right of the decimal place:

```
results = minTemps.collect();

for result in results:
    print(result[0] + "\t{:.2f}F".format(result[1]))
```

Running the script

So let's go ahead and run this and see what it does. Go to **Canopy Command Prompt** in **Tools** and run spark-submit min-temperatures.py:

```
(User) c:\SparkCourse>spark-submit min-temperatures.py
```

The preceding command should chug through this pretty quickly. Here we have it:

```
(User) c:\SparkCourse>spark-submit min-temperatures.py
ITE00100554     5.36F
EZE00100082     7.70F
```

The minimum temperature observed in the year 1800 for this weather station ID, ITE00100554, which I think is Paris, was 5.36° F, and for this other place, which I think is Prague, was 7.7° F. There you have it, a minimum temperature script illustrating the use of filters and using key/value RDDs yet again.

In this section, we found out the minimum temperature observed in the year 1800 for two weather stations. We used the concept of filters, we used key/value RDDs, and we used the reduceByKey function to actually boil down the information we wanted for the whole year for each weather station ID. Pretty cool stuff! Now I want you to get your hands dirty, I want you to roll up your sleeves and actually dive in to that code and start messing with it. Get some confidence, especially, if you're new to Python. You can make changes to this code and actually make stuff happen yourself. So here's what I want you to do as a pretty simple task: take that code that we just wrote for the minimum temperature for the year and change it to actually find the maximum temperature observed for each weather station throughout the year 1800. It shouldn't be too hard, there are just a couple of things you have to change in there really. Give that a try and then we can compare what you came up with what I came up with.

Running the maximum temperature by location example

I hope you did your homework. You should have had a crack at finding the maximum temperature for the year for each weather station instead of a minimum temperature, using our min-temperatures Python script as a starting point. If you haven't, go give it a try! Really, the only way you're going to learn this stuff is by diving in there and messing with the code yourself. I very strongly encourage you to give this a try-it's not hard. If you have done that though, let's move forward and take a look at my results. We can compare that to yours and see if you got it right.

Hopefully, you didn't have too much of a hard time figuring out the maximum temperature observed at the each weather station for the year 1800; it just involved a few changes. If you go to the download package for this book, you can download my solution to it, which is the `max-temperatures` script. If you like, you can throw that into your `SparkCourse` directory and compare your results to mine:

Name	Date modified	Type	Size
ml-100k	6/2/2017 5:40 PM	File folder	
1800	6/8/2017 12:23 PM	Microsoft Excel C...	62 KB
fakefriends	6/8/2017 11:59 AM	Microsoft Excel C...	9 KB
friends-by-age	6/8/2017 11:54 AM	Canopy Document	1 KB
max-temperatures	6/8/2017 12:23 PM	Canopy Document	1 KB
min-temperatures	6/8/2017 12:23 PM	Canopy Document	1 KB
ratings-counter	6/7/2017 3:04 PM	Canopy Document	1 KB

Let's open that up. Alright, so you can see I didn't change the code a whole lot:

```python
from pyspark import SparkConf, SparkContext

conf = SparkConf().setMaster("local").setAppName("MaxTemperatures")
sc = SparkContext(conf = conf)

def parseLine(line):
    fields = line.split(',')
    stationID = fields[0]
    entryType = fields[2]
    temperature = float(fields[3]) * 0.1 * (9.0 / 5.0) + 32.0
    return (stationID, entryType, temperature)

lines = sc.textFile("file:///SparkCourse/1800.csv")
parsedLines = lines.map(parseLine)
maxTemps = parsedLines.filter(lambda x: "TMAX" in x[1])
stationTemps = maxTemps.map(lambda x: (x[0], x[2]))
maxTemps = stationTemps.reduceByKey(lambda x, y: max(x,y))
results = maxTemps.collect();

for result in results:
    print(result[0] + "\t{:.2f}F".format(result[1]))
```

```
1 from pyspark import SparkConf, SparkContext
2
3 conf = SparkConf().setMaster("local").setAppName("MaxTemperatures")
4 sc = SparkContext(conf = conf)
5
6 def parseLine(line):
7     fields = line.split(',')
8     stationID = fields[0]
9     entryType = fields[2]
10     temperature = float(fields[3]) * 0.1 * (9.0 / 5.0) + 32.0
11     return (stationID, entryType, temperature)
12
13 lines = sc.textFile("file:///SparkCourse/1800.csv")
14 parsedLines = lines.map(parseLine)
15 maxTemps = parsedLines.filter(lambda x: "TMAX" in x[1])
16 stationTemps = maxTemps.map(lambda x: (x[0], x[2]))
17 maxTemps = stationTemps.reduceByKey(lambda x, y: max(x,y))
18 results = maxTemps.collect();
19
20 for result in results:
21     print(result[0] + "\t{:.2f}F".format(result[1]))
22
```

The first thing I did though, if you look at line 15, was to extract and filter only the TMAX entries in my original data. Originally, we were pulling out the TMIN entry types from our source weather data, but this time I'm interested in the maximum temperatures observed on every day for each weather station. That's what this line will now do:

```
maxTemps = parsedLines.filter(lambda x: "TMAX" in x[1])
```

We are filtering out everything but TMAX and putting that into a maxTemps RDD. The rest is the same until we get to the reduction in line 17:

```
maxTemps = stationTemps.reduceByKey(lambda x, y: max(x,y))
```

Instead of trying to find the smallest temperature observed out of all the minimum temperatures, we're trying to find the maximum of the maximum-so out of every maximum temperature for every day of the year, what's the maximum temperature that we saw throughout the entire year for each weather station? So, instead of min(x, y), I now have a max (x, y) in this line. As I'm doing my reduction by key and boiling down all the TMAX entries for each weather station for the whole year, I am taking the max to find the largest value observed throughout the whole year. From there on, the script is same as before. We just collect the results and print them out.

So let's see what we end up with. Open up **Canopy Command Prompt** and type in `spark-submit max-temperatures.py`:

```
(User) c:\SparkCourse>spark-submit max-temperatures.py
ITE00100554     90.14F
EZE00100082     90.14F
```

You can see that exactly same temperature was observed for both weather stations throughout the year as the maximum. They're not that far apart geographically, so not too strange of a result. The final result was `90.14`° F. Obviously, that's more precision than the source data had, so if it seems like a coincidence, it really isn't.

If you ended up with `90.14`° F, great, you did it right! If not, go back and compare what you did with what I did in the script, and try to figure it out. Feel free to play around further too, there's more things you could do there. You could keep the answer in Celsius for example, instead of Fahrenheit, if you're more comfortable with that. So again, I encourage you to just roll up your sleeves get your hands dirty. The whole point here is just to get you comfortable with messing around with Spark code in Python, so hopefully, you've achieved that to some degree. At this point, you should have a script that also computes the maximum temperature found in the year 1800 for each weather station ID. You should have gained some experience in diving in and actually messing with some Spark code in Python yourself. Let's keep building upon what you learned and go to another example next.

Counting word occurrences using flatmap()

We'll do a really common Spark and MapReduce example of dealing with a book or text file. We'll count all the words in a text file and find out how many times each word occurs within that text. We'll put a little bit of twist on this task and work our way up to doing more and more complex twists later on. The first thing we need to do is go over the difference again between `map` and `flatMap`, because using `flatMap` and Spark is going to be the key to doing this quickly and easily. Let's talk about that and then jump into some code later on and see it in action.

Map versus flatmap

For the next few sections in this book, we'll look at your standard "count the words in a text file" sample that you see in a lot of these sorts of books, but we're going to do a little bit of a twist. We'll work our way up from a really simple implementation of counting the words, and keep adding more and more stuff to make that even better as we go along. So, to start off with, we need to review the concept of map versus flatMap. We talked about this a little bit in the past, but in our examples so far we've just been using map or mapValues to transform our RDDs.

Map ()

Just to review, a map function will transform each element of an RDD into one new element. There's always a one-to-one relationship between the RDD you started with and the transformed RDD that you end with. Look at the following figure. Let's say we have a text file that contains the sentence, "The quick red fox jumped over the lazy brown dogs", broken up on different lines as it's shown here. We could then write a mapper that has a lambda function that calls upper on each line that comes in, making everything uppercase. What we get back is exactly the same number of entries, just in uppercase:

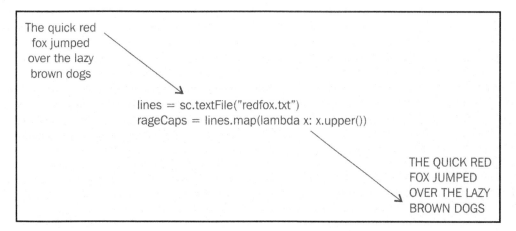

We would have started with four lines and ended up with four lines. The only difference is that they will be transformed in some way-in this case, they've been all changed to uppercase. If you're curious, that's a handy little sentence in the English language that actually includes every letter of the alphabet.

Flatmap ()

In contrast, `flatMap` has the ability to blow out an RDD into multiple entries. So you will end up with an RDD that has more elements than you started with when you use `flatMap`. As an example, let's see how that works. Look at the following figure. Let's say that we load up that same text file in the `lines` RDD and call `flatMap` on it. We have our mapping function as the split function:

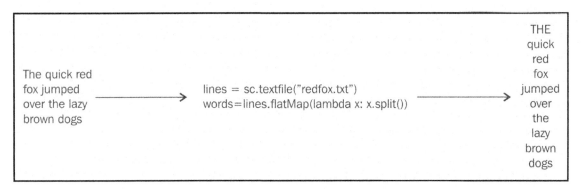

What this does is that it splits up every line into individual words based on whitespaces, and outputs multiple results, one for each word. So `x.split` returns a list of words, and each item returned in that list from the mapper function will become an entry of its own in the new RDD. The RDD ends up containing each individual word as its own entry in the RDD, whereas we only started with four entries in the original RDD, one for each line. Breaking up text by words is actually a pretty common thing to be doing with `flatMap`. With that, let's jump into the code and start with our simple example of counting words.

Code sample - count the words in a book

In order to make this more interesting and real, I'm going to actually use the text of a real book. It's one that I wrote, so I have the rights to include it here:

Go to the download package for this book at this point, and download both the `book.txt` file, which contains the text of the entire book, and the `word-count.py` script. Place them in your `SparkCourse` directory:

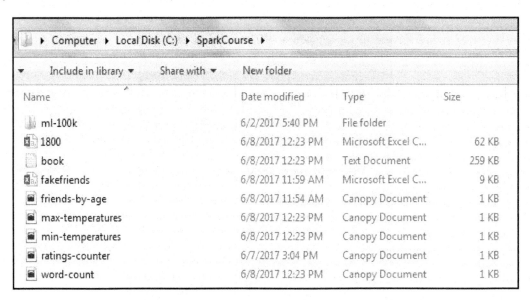

Double-click on the `word-count.py` script and we'll take a look at it:

```
1 from pyspark import SparkConf, SparkContext
2
3 conf = SparkConf().setMaster("local").setAppName("WordCount")
4 sc = SparkContext(conf = conf)
5
6 input = sc.textFile("file:///sparkcourse/book.txt")
7 words = input.flatMap(lambda x: x.split())
8 wordCounts = words.countByValue()
9
10 for word, count in wordCounts.items():
11     cleanWord = word.encode('ascii', 'ignore')
12     if (cleanWord):
13         print(cleanWord.decode() + " " + str(count))
14
```

This is very simple stuff, but the key point to note here is that we're using `flatMap` instead of `map`. Let's walk through the script.

We're going to do all the typical boilerplate stuff to set up our `WordCount` Spark application:

```
from pyspark import SparkConf, SparkContext

conf = SparkConf().setMaster("local").setAppName("WordCount")
sc = SparkContext(conf = conf)
```

We'll do our typical `textFile` call on the `SparkContext` to load up the text of the book, one line at a time. The way this is actually broken out, it ends up being about one paragraph per line-that's a lot of words on each line and not very useful:

```
input = sc.textFile("file:///sparkcourse/book.txt")
```

Next, since we want to count up how many times each word occurs in the book, we need to bust that out by word; this is where we're going to do our `flatMap` function. The `flatMap` function will take every individual line of text (a line represents a whole paragraph in our example) and our `lambda` function will then call `split`, which breaks the text up into individual words based on whitespaces. We then put that list of words into the `words` RDD, as shown here:

```
words = input.flatMap(lambda x: x.split())
```

In the next line, we can simply call `countByValue`, which is a way to very easily and very quickly get a count of how many times each unique value occurs. For every whitespace separated word in our book, we will get a count of how many times that word occurs. We will get the results in the `wordCounts` list here:

```
wordCounts = words.countByValue()
```

Next, we have just some standard Python code, there's nothing Spark-specific about it, we're just going to go through every single word in our list of words:

```
for word, count in wordCounts.items():
```

The next line takes care of some encoding issues. In case something was encoded as UTF-8 or Unicode in our original text, this makes sure that we can display it okay on our Terminal in our Command Prompt by converting it to the `ascii` format. This line also says we're going to ignore any conversion errors that might occur in the process of trying to convert from Unicode to ASCII. This is a way to make sure that we can display these words without errors, even though they might contain special characters-that's a little Python trick for you there:

```
cleanWord = word.encode('ascii', 'ignore')
```

If this comes back successfully, we will print out each word and the number of times it occurred:

```
if (cleanWord):
    print(cleanWord.decode() + " " + str(count))
```

Let's go ahead and run this. Go to **Canopy Command Prompt** and type:

```
spark-submit word-count.py:
```

The preceding command seems to handle that pretty quickly for an entire book! Here are some results:

```
DESIGNING 1
clients, 2
clients. 2
made 12
whether 21
this, 10
distract 1
this. 2
below 2
USING 1
this; 1
this: 2
intimidating 1
inadequate 1
meaningless 2
highlighted 1
kind. 1
avoided 1
improving 1
Sessions 1
other 71
incredibly 2
Banner 2
clicks 2
junk 1
kinds 3
webpage, 1
PLAN 3
S-corp 1
incurred 1
extort 1
click, 1
Company> 1
LEECHES 1
click" 1
Site 1
intentionally 2
entirely. 1

(User) c:\SparkCourse>
```

We can see the word `extort` only appeared once, the word `kinds` appeared three times, and the word `other` appeared 71 times in this book. If you look at these results carefully, they're not entirely helpful. Remember, we're only splitting based on whitespaces here, so we're not really just getting words counted up, we're getting all sorts of combinations of words with punctuation marks underneath them. Take the result for `webpage,`. When this word is followed by a comma, it counts as a different word from `webpage` without a comma following it. Also, `click` followed by a comma counts as a unique word as well. We also have `click` followed by a quotation mark, which also counts as its own unique word. This is not what we want; punctuation shouldn't count. Similarly, we also have uppercase and lowercase affecting things. We have all uppercase `LEECHES` counting as its own unique word, different from lowercase `leeches`. This is not very helpful. We want to combine all matching words together, regardless of punctuation or capitalization. We'll have to improve on this a little bit. The other thing too is that these aren't displayed in a very helpful manner, right? Ideally, we would get an ordered list, sorted by the most common words so we could quickly see what the least frequently and most frequently used words were without having to search through the entire thing. As I mentioned earlier, we're going to build on this and make this script even more useful. Let's take another round at it and try to improve on it in our next section.

Improving the word-count script with regular expressions

The main problem with the initial results from our `word-count` script is that we didn't account for things such as punctuation and capitalization. There are fancy ways to deal with that problem in text processing, but we're going to use a simple way for now. We'll use something called regular expressions in Python. So let's look at how that works, then run it and see it in action.

Text normalization

In the previous section, we had a first crack at counting the number of times each word occurred in our book, but the results weren't that great. We had each individual word that had different capitalization or punctuation surrounding it being counted as a word of its own, and that's not what we want. We want each word to be counted only once, no matter how it's capitalized or what punctuation might surround it. We don't want duplicate words showing up in there. There are toolkits you can get for Python such as **NLTK** (**Natural Language Toolkit**), that have fancy, very complicated ways of normalizing text data like this and automatically figuring out what words are the same. However, we can sort of do a more simplistic attack at it. We can use a regular expression in Python in order to convert words into some common format and strip out all the extra punctuation that we don't care about. This is not really a Spark-specific thing, but it's a very useful trick to have in your back pocket, especially, when you're doing text analysis. So let's take a look at the code and see how that works.

Examining the use of regular expressions in the word-count script

Okay, let's try and improve upon our word-count script. In the download package for this book, you should find a word-count-better.py script. Download that, save it into your SparkCourse folder, and as usual, let's double-click it and take a look:

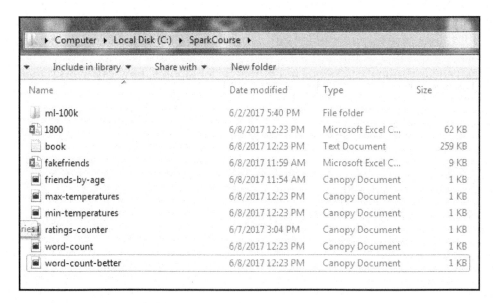

Alright, so you can see this is a little bit more complicated than what we had before:

```
 1 import re
 2 from pyspark import SparkConf, SparkContext
 3
 4 def normalizeWords(text):
 5     return re.compile(r'\W+', re.UNICODE).split(text.lower())
 6
 7 conf = SparkConf().setMaster("local").setAppName("WordCount")
 8 sc = SparkContext(conf = conf)
 9
10 input = sc.textFile("file:///sparkcourse/book.txt")
11 words = input.flatMap(normalizeWords)
12 wordCounts = words.countByValue()
13
14 for word, count in wordCounts.items():
15     cleanWord = word.encode('ascii', 'ignore')
16     if (cleanWord):
17         print(cleanWord.decode() + " " + str(count))
18
```

We have a lot of the same stuff as before in this script. The main difference is that when we're calling `flatMap`, instead of just using a `lambda` function that calls `split`, to just split up each word in the line based on whitespaces alone. We're going to pass in an actual function here called `normalizeWords`. The `normalizeWords` function does something a little bit fancy. We'll talk about that shortly.

```
words = input.flatMap(normalizeWords)
```

If you look at lines 4 and 5, you can see we're setting up a "regular expression". That's what `re` stands for:

```
def normalizeWords(text):
    return re.compile(r'\W+', re.UNICODE).split(text.lower())
```

You can see that we added `import re` to the top of the script:

```
import re
```

Regular expressions, if you're not familiar with them, are sort of a language of their own for text processing. They allow you to write little strings that define how to split up a string into other values or transform it. It's sort of a very shorthand way of doing some text processing. In our case, we're going to call `re.compile`; this is the magical string that means "I want you to break up this text based on words":

```
return re.compile(r'\W+',
```

The `W+` character tells it to break it up based on words. The regular expression engine knows how to do that on its own, it knows how to automatically strip out punctuation and other things that aren't really part of words. We'll also tell it in this line that this may have Unicode information in it:

```
re.UNICODE)
```

Then we will split it up based on what the regular expression identifies as individual words, and transform those all to lowercase:

```
.split(text.lower())
```

The regular expression will take care of breaking up the words, taking into account all the punctuation. Then we will force that to be lower case to make sure we don't get different results for different types of capitalization on each word. That should produce better results, so let's give it a try.

Running the code

Again, this is not really a Spark-specific exercise, but it's just a good tool to have when you're doing this sort of analysis. Run the following line:

```
spark-submit word-count-better.py:
```

This looks a lot prettier, doesn't it?

```
forgivable 1
details 5
normal 1
welcomes 1
mass 5
out 161
conversational 1
clicks 3
disposing 1
troll 1
junk 1
star 1
shown 4
variation 2
stay 7
chance 12
workaholic 1
spreadsheet 2
gap 2
friends 10
incurred 1
exposure 2
shock 1
ended 10
lasted 3
```

We don't have a whole lot of weird capitalization and punctuation going on, this looks like much more usable results. `clicks` shows up 3 times, the word `out` 161 times, and so on and so forth. `workaholic` only shows up once, I guess that's a good thing. You can scroll through this and eyeball what words tend to be popular.

The last thing we need to do is make this more usable by actually sorting it by what words are the most popular or the least popular. The main problem there is that if we were to just sort this list as is, it would sort it based on the word, right? What we really want to sort this list on is the count that's after the word. We're going to have to shuffle these results around a little bit before we can sort them the way we want. We'll go over how to do that in our next section.

Sorting the word count results

Okay, let's do one more round of improvements on our `word-count` script. We need to sort our results of `word-count` by something useful. Instead of just having a random list of words associated with how many times they appear, what we want is to see the least used words at the beginning of our list and the most used words at the end. This should give us some actually interesting information to look at. To do this, we're going to need to manipulate our results a little bit more directly-we can't just cheat and use `countByValue` and call it done.

Step 1 - Implement countByValue() the hard way to create a new RDD

So the first thing we're going to do is actually implement what `countByValue` does by hand, the hard way. This way we can actually play with the results more directly and stick the results in an RDD instead of just getting a Python object that we need to deal with at that point. The way we do that is we take our map of words-`words.map`-and we use a mapper that just converts each individual word into that word and the value of 1-(`lambda x: (x, 1)`):

```
wordCounts = words.map(lambda x: (x, 1)).reduceByKey(lambda x, y: x + y)
```

This is a very similar trick to what we did in the earlier script where we computed the average number of friends by age in a fake social network. There we also used that extra number 1 in our mapper as a way to count up how many times something occurs. We then call `reduceByKey`-our keys here are the individual words-and for every time that word occurred the number 1 will get added in as part of the reduction. So we're passing in a `lambda` function that just says, "add these two things together," and by doing so we'll end up getting values that just keep adding up, one plus one plus one plus one, for however many times that word occurs:

```
.reduceByKey(lambda x, y: x + y)
```

Let's walk through it one more time. We start off with a plain old RDD that contains words, every word that appears in the book:

```
wordCounts = words.map
```

We then map that so that every word is instead a key/value pair of the word and the number 1:

```
.map(lambda x: (x, 1))
```

We then reduce that by key, so we aggregate together every time that each individual word appeared:

```
.reduceByKey
```

We use this `lambda` function to add the values together for each individual key-that just keeps adding up one plus one plus one plus one for however many times that word appeared:

```
(lambda x, y: x + y)
```

So this entire line has the same effect as `countByValue`, except the result gets stored in a new RDD called `wordCounts` instead of a Python object that we need to then manipulate. Makes sense? If not, stare at this some more. As I mentioned earlier, it's a very similar trick to what we did in an earlier example, so hopefully that makes sense to you.

Step 2 - Sort the new RDD

What we have at this point is an RDD that contains words and the number of times they appear. We want to sort by the number of times each word appears. So before we sort, we need to flip that around and map things so that our keys become values and our values become keys. We start off with the keys being the words and the values being the number of times that the word occurred, then we flip that around in this mapper shown here. We now have the number of times the word occurred followed by the word itself:

```
wordCountsSorted = wordCounts.map(lambda x: (x[1], x[0])).sortByKey()
```

Then, we can chain together a call to `sortByKey` in order to sort the final RDD that we store in `wordCountSorted` by the number of times it occurred. Makes sense? It's pretty straightforward, we're just flipping things around so we can sort it the way that we want to. Let's go take a look at the code.

Examining the script

Usually, this is a really simple example in textbooks, but we're going to make it something a little bit more interesting. If you haven't already, go to the download package for this book, download `word-count-better-sorted.py`, and open that up in your favorite Python editor:

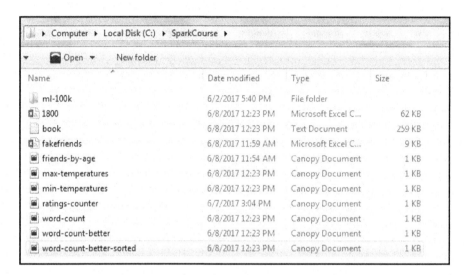

So what have we done differently here?

```
1 import re
2 from pyspark import SparkConf, SparkContext
3
4 def normalizeWords(text):
5     return re.compile(r'\W+', re.UNICODE).split(text.lower())
6
7 conf = SparkConf().setMaster("local").setAppName("WordCount")
8 sc = SparkContext(conf = conf)
9
10 input = sc.textFile("file:///sparkcourse/book.txt")
11 words = input.flatMap(normalizeWords)
12
13 wordCounts = words.map(lambda x: (x, 1)).reduceByKey(lambda x, y: x + y)
14 wordCountsSorted = wordCounts.map(lambda x: (x[1], x[0])).sortByKey()
15 results = wordCountsSorted.collect()
16
17 for result in results:
18     count = str(result[0])
19     word = result[1].encode('ascii', 'ignore')
20     if (word):
21         print(word.decode() + ":\t\t" + count)
22 |
```

Instead of just cheating and calling `countByValue`, we're actually implementing `countByValue` by hand. We have a mapper where we transform every word into a key/value pair of the word and the number 1. Then we use `reduceByKey` to add them all up. So for every unique word in our words map from our `words` RDD, we add up every instance using our addition `lambda` function, ending up with a key/value RDD where the keys are the words and the values are the number of times that word occurred:

```
wordCounts = words.map(lambda x: (x, 1)).reduceByKey(lambda x, y: x + y)
```

Then, in the next line, we flip that key/value pair around so that the key is the count and the value is the word. We can then use `sortByKey` to get a list sorted by the number of times each word occurs:

```
wordCountsSorted = wordCounts.map(lambda x: (x[1], x[0])).sortByKey()
```

Finally, we just grab the results through a `collect` action that'll kick everything off to actually execute:

```
results = wordCountsSorted.collect()
```

Then we go and print out in a slightly different format, just the word, followed by a colon, a couple of words, and the count:

```
print(word.decode() + ":\t\t" + count)
```

Running the code

So let's go ahead and run that and see it in action. Open up **Canopy Command Prompt** and run the following:

```
spark-submit word-count-better-sorted.py
```

These results should look a little bit better, a little bit more useful, a little more interesting:

```
with:            315
have:            321
as:              343
be:              369
can:             376
business:                    383
i:               387
s:               391
if:              411
are:             424
on:              428
for:             537
is:              560
in:              616
it:              649
that:            747
and:             934
of:              970
a:               1191
the:             1292
your:            1420
to:              1828
you:             1878

(User) c:\SparkCourse>
```

We have now sorted by the number of times each word occurred, and the most popular word in my book is the word you. Words, To, your, the, a, of, and, that are the most popular-all the words you'd expect to show up a lot in any book really. When we start looking at more interesting words, business turns out to be the most popular, which makes sense because it is a book about starting your own business. Now I do want to point out a couple of bad things here though, s is listed as a word, what's up with that? Well, our regular expression isn't perfect for breaking up words, it turns out that it was probably splitting out the s from contractions like it's or Frank's and other instances of an s being preceded by a possessive apostrophe. If you wanted possessive forms of words to be listed separately to non-possessive forms, this would be an issue. You want to make sure you account for weird results like this when you're analyzing your results. A more sophisticated natural text language processing toolkit such as NLTK would do a better job of that, but it's kind of overkill for what we're trying to do. These results are a good lesson though-your results in data mining or machine learning are often or always only as good as your input data, right? Getting good, meaningful, actionable results out of any data analysis you do is going to depend on your ability to clean the data that you're using beforehand into the form that you want. So always look at results skeptically, be on the lookout for weird things such as s and t just showing up, which are coming out of contractions. Anyway, a little bit of a digression there into machine learning and data mining in general. Always make sure you clean your data, it's just as important as everything else.

We now have a pretty good `word-counter` script. We got rid of at least the most egregious forms of splitting things incorrectly and we sorted the script to give us useful results. We got some real insights into the nature of this book by studying the words that are most frequently occurring in it. The results are not perfect, but good enough for my needs. You learned a lot as we've been working on the `word-count` script. You learned about `flatMap` versus `map`, some sorting tricks you can do with RDDs, and about different ways of dealing with regular expressions to cleanse text data. You now know a quick and dirty way to handle some text processing tasks you might run into in the future. We've worked on a pretty good collection of scripts now. Make sure you keep everything in your `SparkCourse` directory somewhere safe, there are going to be a lot of useful examples in there that you'll want to refer to again later on.

Find the total amount spent by customer

At this point in the book, I think you've seen enough examples and had enough concepts that I can finally set you loose and have you try to write your very own Spark script from scratch. I realize this might be your first Python script ever, so I'm going to keep it pretty easy and I'm going to give you a lot of tips on how to be successful with it. Don't be afraid! Let me introduce the problem at hand and give you some tips you need for success, and we'll set you loose.

Introducing the problem

I'm going to start you off with a pretty simple example here just to get your feet wet. What you're going to do is go to the download package for this book and find the `customerorders.csv` file. This just contains some random fake data that I generated. The input data in that file is going to look like this:

```
44,8602,37.19
35,5368,65.89
44,3391,40.64
47,6694,14.98
35,680,13.08
```

We have comma-separated fields of a customer ID, an item ID, and the amount spent on that item. What I want you to do is write a Spark script that consolidates that down to the total amount spent by customer ID. In the following example, we see the customer ID 44 appears twice and bought two items, one for $37.19 and one for $40.64. So our final output should tell us that customer ID 44 spent a total of $77.83. Similarly, customer ID 35 bought two items and spent $78.97. Customer ID 47 in this example only bought one thing for $14.98:

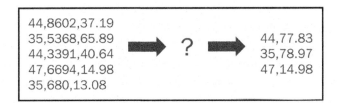

Strategy for solving the problem

So what should your general strategy be? I'll help you think through how to attack this problem. The first thing you want to do is write a map function that will read the input data and split it up based on comma-delimited fields. We've done that before, so go back and look at some of the other examples in your SparkCourse folder for a reminder on how that works. After doing that, you want to map each line to key/value pairs of customer IDs and amount spent per transaction. As we're going to structure this as a key/value RDD that allows us to then use reduceByKey to sum up all the amounts spent by customer ID. Finally, all you have to do is call collect() on the resulting RDD that reduceByKey gives you and print out the results. These are all things you've done before and seen through example. All you have to do is put it together and create a new script that does this.

Useful snippets of code

Now, here are a few useful snippets of code just to make it even easier for you. Again, I want you to be successful here, I recognize that this could be your first Python script ever, so I want to make this as simple as possible. Something you'll find useful in your mapper function is using `line.split (' , ')`, which will split up a comma-delimited line of text into a new RDD called `fields`, containing each individual field between the commas:

```
fields = line.split(',')
```

Of course, you can call `line` and `fields` whatever you want, those are just arbitrary names we're using for the RDDs in question.

One thing I want you to make sure of, since we're going to be doing some math on these results and adding up dollar amounts, is that when you're parsing these results in your mapper you are telling Python that these are numeric fields. So, look at the following line of code. If you're actually parsing this out and extracting the customer ID as field number 0, you might want to tell Python that's actually an integer value and not just a string. Even more important is that you tell it that field number 2, the dollar amount, is a floating-point decimal number, otherwise you won't be able to add them up later on:

```
return (int(fields[0]), float(fields[2]))
```

Keep all that in mind, and with that, I will set you loose! Let's see what you actually get done. I'll show you the solution next, but do give it a try yourself first. It's very important that you get hands on here and get the success of actually writing your own Spark script from scratch under your belt. Good luck, I'll see you when you've given it a try.

Check your results and sort them by the total amount spent

Did you do your homework? I hope so. Hopefully, you were able to draw on our previous examples and now have a running script that adds up the total amount spent by customer in my little fake dataset. Let's compare your implementation to my implementation and your results to mine and see if they match up. If they don't, hopefully you'll learn something from it.

Let's have a look at my solution. If you go to the download package for this book, you will see my `total-spent-by-customer` script, feel free to download that and put it into your `SparkCourse` folder alongside your own solution to this problem and the `book.txt` file that you should have from the previous section. Go ahead and open that up. When you're ready, here's my take at it:

```python
1 from pyspark import SparkConf, SparkContext
2
3 conf = SparkConf().setMaster("local").setAppName("SpendByCustomer")
4 sc = SparkContext(conf = conf)
5
6 def extractCustomerPricePairs(line):
7     fields = line.split(',')
8     return (int(fields[0]), float(fields[2]))
9
10 input = sc.textFile("file:///sparkcourse/customer-orders.csv")
11 mappedInput = input.map(extractCustomerPricePairs)
12 totalByCustomer = mappedInput.reduceByKey(lambda x, y: x + y)
13
14 results = totalByCustomer.collect();
15 for result in results:
16     print(result)
17
```

This is a very simple script, but the idea was just to get you into the practice of writing your own Spark programs. Even if it's a simple one, writing your first program is a big accomplishment. Let's go through how I did it and if you had any trouble with it yourself, you can compare your code with mine and see what might be different.

We have the usual boilerplate stuff at the top, hopefully, that didn't trip you up too much. The only thing I did differently was set a different name, which doesn't matter that much for what we're doing:

```python
from pyspark import SparkConf, SparkContext

conf = SparkConf().setMaster("local").setAppName("SpendByCustomer")
sc = SparkContext(conf = conf)
```

I then wrote a mapper function for the original input lines that uses those hints I gave you in the previous section. I called `split` with a comma to actually split up my comma-separated value data into individual fields. I then extracted them as key/value pairs. The key is the customer ID cast as an integer. The value is the amount spent for every line, cast as a floating-point numerical value so I can add them up later on:

```
def extractCustomerPricePairs(line):
    fields = line.split(',')
    return (int(fields[0]), float(fields[2]))
```

Getting into the meat of the program itself down at line 10, I started off by calling `sc.textFile` in our `SparkContext` to load up the `customer-orders.csv` data file that goes into the input RDD-you could call that whatever you want of course:

```
input = sc.textFile("file:///sparkcourse/customer-orders.csv")
```

Then, in the next line, I called `map`, using our `extractCustomerPricePairs` function that I described earlier, which just creates key/value pairs of customer IDs and the amounts spent. I saved that into a new RDD called `mappedInput`:

```
mappedInput = input.map(extractCustomerPricePairs)
```

A common error that I see people make is forgetting to assign that to a new RDD. You have to remember that if you call `map` on an RDD, it doesn't do it in place, it creates a new RDD that you need to assign to something. Make sure you do that.

So after I saved my `mappedInput` RDD, I was able to call `reduceByKey` with a `lambda` function that simply adds up all the values encountered for a given customer ID, like this:

```
totalByCustomer = mappedInput.reduceByKey(lambda x, y: x + y)
```

Again, our key is the customer ID, our value is the amount spent, and we're just going to add them all up using this `lambda` function. So hopefully the earlier examples you had of using `reduceByKey` helped you to figure out the syntax for doing that. We put our final results into the `totalByCustomer` RDD. To get that into a Python object that we can step through and print out, we call `collect`, which is an action on that RDD and forces Spark to go out and actually do it all. Then we just iterate through every result in the results object that was returned and print them out:

```
results = totalByCustomer.collect();
for result in results:
    print(result)
```

Let's go ahead and run that and see what it looks like. So open up **Canopy Command Prompt** and set off `spark-submit total-spent-by-customer.py` and you will see my results:

```
(77, 4327.729999999999)
(78, 4524.509999999999)
(79, 3790.5700000000001)
(80, 4727.860000000001)
(81, 5112.709999999999)
(82, 4812.489999999998)
(83, 4635.799999999997)
(84, 4652.939999999999)
(85, 5503.43)
(86, 4908.81)
(87, 5206.4)
(88, 4830.549999999999)
(89, 4851.479999999999)
(90, 5290.409999999998)
(91, 4642.259999999999)
(92, 5379.280000000002)
(93, 5265.750000000001)
(94, 4475.569999999999)
(95, 4876.840000000002)
(96, 3924.230000000001)
(97, 5977.189999999995)
(98, 4297.260000000001)
(99, 4172.289999999998)

(User) c:\SparkCourse>
```

I've tried to keep the code as simple as possible so there are some obvious things you could do to make it even better. If you actually did some fancy formatting in the output in order to contain the decimal places to two after the decimal point, bonus points for you, good job! I didn't do that here, just to keep it simple. Obviously, it's all random results, there's no real meaning here, but the way to interpret this is, for example, customer ID 84 spent $4,652 in total in our entire dataset here, and so on and so forth:

```
(84, 4652.939999999999)
```

What would be more useful from a pragmatic standpoint would be if I sorted these results based on the amount spent. This is your new challenge, you're not done yet! I want you to go back and actually add some more code to sort these results by the amount spent. This way we can easily see who's the most economic customer and who is the biggest spender in my database of fake order data. You can draw on some previous examples of when we did something similar. Remember, we flipped the orders around and called `sortByKey` in a previous example? See if you can do the same thing here. Your challenge is to extend the script even further to print out the results, sorted by the amount spent. So I'll let you have a crack at that, and next I'll show you how I did it.

Check your sorted implementation and results against mine

Let's take a look at my implementation of sorting the results for the total amount spent by customer and compare it with yours. If you got to this point and you haven't actually tried this yourself or you got stuck, let me give you one more hint before I show you my solution. If you look at the `word-count-better-sorted` script that we used in the previous example for doing word frequency counts sorted by word frequency, you'll see that we did something very similar in there. If you got stuck, have a look at that script and give it another try first before you peek at the answer here.

If you've given it a try, go ahead and download the `total-spent-by-customer-sorted` script from the download package for this book and compare your solution to mine. There's more than one way to do these things, so just because I did it one way it doesn't mean you can't do it another way. As long as it works, that's what matters:

```
1  from pyspark import SparkConf, SparkContext
2
3  conf = SparkConf().setMaster("local").setAppName("SpendByCustomerSorted")
4  sc = SparkContext(conf = conf)
5
6  def extractCustomerPricePairs(line):
7      fields = line.split(',')
8      return (int(fields[0]), float(fields[2]))
9
10 input = sc.textFile("file:///sparkcourse/customer-orders.csv")
11 mappedInput = input.map(extractCustomerPricePairs)
12 totalByCustomer = mappedInput.reduceByKey(lambda x, y: x + y)
13
14 #Changed for Python 3 compatibility:
15 #flipped = totalByCustomer.map(lambda (x,y):(y,x))
16 flipped = totalByCustomer.map(lambda x: (x[1], x[0]))
17
18 totalByCustomerSorted = flipped.sortByKey()
19
20 results = totalByCustomerSorted.collect();
21 for result in results:
22     print(result)
23
```

You can see all I really did was add a couple of different lines. Take a look at my `totalByCustomer` RDD here, which is just the key/value RDD of customer IDs to the total amount spent:

```
totalByCustomer = mappedInput.reduceByKey(lambda x, y: x + y)
```

If I want to sort that RDD by value, first I need to flip it around. So we call a mapper that has a `lambda` function of x and y for the key/value pair coming in, and it flips it around so we end up with y and x:

```
flipped = totalByCustomer.map(lambda x: (x[1], x[0]))
```

This makes our values our keys and our keys our values. Now we have this RDD named flipped that contains keys as the amount spent, and IDs as customer IDs as the values. It might seem a little weird to have an RDD, where you have multiple keys that are the same thing, but we're not doing any reduction so it turns out to be okay. Now that we have our RDD in that format, we can call sortByKey on it to actually sort by our new keys, which are the amount spent:

```
totalByCustomerSorted = flipped.sortByKey()
```

Then we can iterate through that RDD, collect the results and print them out:

```
results = totalByCustomerSorted.collect();
for result in results:
    print(result)
```

That's all there is to it, compare that to how you did it and let's go ahead and run the following:

```
spark-submit total-spent-by-customer-sorted.py
```

Here are the results:

```
(5368.249999999999, 70)
(5368.83, 43)
(5379.280000000002, 92)
(5397.879999999998, 6)
(5413.510000000001, 15)
(5415.150000000001, 63)
(5437.730000000005, 58)
(5496.050000000004, 32)
(5497.479999999998, 61)
(5503.43, 85)
(5517.240000000001, 8)
(5524.949999999998, 0)
(5637.62, 41)
(5642.89, 59)
(5696.840000000003, 42)
(5963.109999999999, 46)
(5977.189999999995, 97)
(5994.59, 2)
(5995.660000000003, 71)
(6065.389999999999, 54)
(6193.109999999999, 39)
(6206.199999999999, 73)
(6375.449999999997, 68)

(User) c:\SparkCourse>
```

It turns out that our biggest spender is customer ID 68, who spent $6,375 and some change.

There you have it, another example of doing an extra thing with an RDD there. We computed our results, flipped the RDD around, and sorted it the way we wanted to. If you got this far and you were able to code this up on your own, congratulations! This is a more advanced example, so you're far along the way to becoming a real Spark developer. You've actually written some real Spark code that does real data analysis, that's a big deal. But we're not done yet! We're going to keep on looking at some more examples and start building up to more and more complex problems.

Summary

We've covered a lot of ground in this chapter, and I hope it's given you an idea of the kinds of things that you can do with Spark and the power that it gives you. Please do continue to explore and experiment with these examples, altering things to see how they function and gaining familiarity with the workings of Spark. In the next chapter, we're going to turn our attention to the cloud and start working with really big data when we find out how to run Spark on a cluster.

3
Advanced Examples of Spark Programs

We'll now start working our way up to some more advanced and complicated examples with Spark. Like we did with the `word-count` example, we'll start off with something pretty simple and just build upon it. Let's take a look at our next example, in which we'll find the most popular movie in our MovieLens dataset.

Finding the most popular movie

Let's start by reviewing the data format of the `MovieLens` dataset, the `u.data` file.

As you might recall, the `u.data` file on each line, consists of a user ID, a movie ID, a rating, and a timestamp. Each line says, "this user watched this movie, gave it this rating, and did it at this time":

196	242	3	881250949
186	302	3	891717742
22	377	1	878887116
244	51	2	880606923
166	346	1	886397596
298	474	4	884182806

Our task is to just figure out which movie was watched most often or which movie ID appears most frequently in the entire dataset. This isn't a very hard thing to do; in fact, if you want to go give it a crack yourself, feel free. In this section we'll take a look at the implementation that I came up with, get that to run, and see what we come up with

Examining the popular-movies script

In the download package for this book, you'll find a popular-movies Python script. Download that, put it in your SparkCourse folder, and open it up. We will print out a list of all of the movies and the number of times they appear, and then sort them based on how often they appear. It's a pretty simple script here, there's nothing really new in this example, but there will be when we build upon it:

```
from pyspark import SparkConf, SparkContext

conf = SparkConf().setMaster("local").setAppName("PopularMovies")
sc = SparkContext(conf = conf)

lines = sc.textFile("file:///SparkCourse/ml-100k/u.data")
movies = lines.map(lambda x: (int(x.split()[1]), 1))
movieCounts = movies.reduceByKey(lambda x, y: x + y)

flipped = movieCounts.map( lambda (x, y) : (y, x) )
sortedMovies = flipped.sortByKey()

results = sortedMovies.collect()

for result in results:
    print(result)
```

Let's walk through it really quickly just to reinforce some of the stuff you've learned already. Your standard boilerplate stuff is up at the top:

```
from pyspark import SparkConf, SparkContext

conf = SparkConf().setMaster("local").setAppName("PopularMovies")
sc = SparkContext(conf = conf)
```

We will then open up the u.data file that contains the user ID, movie ID rating, and timestamp for every individual rating within that dataset:

```
lines = sc.textFile("file:///SparkCourse/ml-100k/u.data")
```

Then we'll call a mapper that simply splits it out and pulls out the movie ID from field number 1. What we end up with is just a movies RDD that is nothing but a list of movie IDs. Each movie ID may occur frequently; our task is to count them up. Notice that we're actually outputting a key/value pair in this line shown here, we have a movie ID and then the number 1:

```
movies = lines.map(lambda x: (int(x.split()[1]), 1))
```

What we can do now is use `reduceByKey` and add up all those `1` numbers together to get the count of how many times each movie appeared:

```
movieCounts = movies.reduceByKey(lambda x, y: x + y)
```

So let's go over that one more time, our mapper is going to extract the movie ID, put in a key/value pair where the key is the movie ID and the value is the number `1`:

```
movies = lines.map(lambda x: (int(x.split()[1]), 1))
```

We'll then call `reduceByKey`, which will group together and aggregate all of the values seen for each individual movie ID and add them all up. So all those `1` numbers get added up together and we end up with a final count of how many times each movie appears within our MovieLens dataset:

```
movieCounts = movies.reduceByKey(lambda x, y: x + y)
```

We're not done yet. At this point, we have a key/value RDD, where the keys are the movie IDs. However, we want to sort it by the value, so we're going to use that same trick we did before where we flip things around to make the values the keys and the keys the values. This is what this next line does. What we end up with in the flipped RDD shown here is now the count as the key and the movie ID as the value:

```
flipped = movieCounts.map( lambda (x, y) : (y, x) )
```

We will then use `sortByKey` in order to sort our RDD by the number of occurrences:

```
sortedMovies = flipped.sortByKey()
```

Next we'll collect the results and print them out:

```
results = sortedMovies.collect()

for result in results:
    print(result)
```

So let's see what we get. If that didn't make sense, stare at this for a while and it will. Do what you got to do to understand it.

Getting results

Open **Canopy Command Prompt** and run `spark-submit popular-movies.py`:

```
(User) c:\SparkCourse>spark-submit popular-movies.py
```

There we have it, sorted by the number of occurrences:

```
(336, 79)
(344, 405)
(350, 204)
(350, 313)
(365, 222)
(367, 172)
(378, 117)
(384, 237)
(390, 98)
(392, 7)
(394, 56)
(413, 127)
(420, 174)
(429, 121)
(431, 300)
(452, 1)
(470, 288)
(481, 286)
(485, 294)
(507, 181)
(508, 100)
(509, 258)
(583, 50)

(User) c:\SparkCourse>
```

You can see that the most popular movie was movie ID number 50, which was watched 583 times by people in that dataset. Well, that's all well and good but what is movie ID 50? That's not very helpful is it?

We can go look it up by hand and do it the hard way. Go into the `ml-100k` dataset and open up the `u.item` file-you might have to right-click that, select **Open with** and then **WordPad** so you can actually look at it:

Scroll through this file to find out what movie ID 50 actually is. It turns out that 50 is Star Wars, from 1977:

```
exact?Disclosure%20(1994)|0|0|0|0|0|0|0|0|1|0|0|0|0|0|0|0|1|0|
0
44|Dolores Claiborne (1994)|01-Jan-1994
||http://us.imdb.com/M/title-exact?Dolores%20Claiborne%20
(1994)|0|0|0|0|0|0|0|0|1|0|0|0|0|0|0|0|1|0|0
45|Eat Drink Man Woman (1994)|01-Jan-1994
||http://us.imdb.com/M/title-exact?Yinshi%20Nan%20Nu%20(1994)|
0|0|0|0|0|1|1|0|0|1|0|0|0|0|0|0|0|0|0|0
46|Exotica (1994)|01-Jan-1994||http://us.imdb.com/M/title-
exact?Exotica%20(1994)|0|0|0|0|0|0|0|0|1|1|0|0|0|0|0|0|0|0|0
47|Ed Wood (1994)|01-Jan-1994||http://us.imdb.com/M/title-
exact?Ed%20Wood%20(1994)|0|0|0|0|0|0|1|1|0|1|0|0|0|0|0|0|0|0|0
48|Hoop Dreams (1994)|01-Jan-1994||http://us.imdb.com/M/title-
exact?Hoop%20Dreams%20(1994)|0|0|0|0|0|0|0|1|1|0|0|0|0|0|0|0|0
|0|0
49|I.Q. (1994)|01-Jan-1994||http://us.imdb.com/M/title-exact?
I.Q.%20(1994)|0|0|0|0|1|1|0|0|0|0|0|0|0|1|0|0|0|0
50|Star Wars (1977)|01-Jan-1977||http://us.imdb.com/M/title-
exact?Star%20Wars%20(1977)|0|1|1|1|0|0|0|0|0|0|0|0|0|0|1|1|0|1
|0
51|Legends of the Fall (1994)|01-Jan-1994
||http://us.imdb.com/M/title-exact?Legends%20of%20the%20Fall%
20(1994)|0|0|0|0|0|0|0|0|0|1|1|0|0|0|0|0|1|0|0|1|1
52|Madness of King George, The (1994)|01-Jan-1994
||http://us.imdb.com/M/title-exact?Madness%20of%20King%
20George,%20The%20(1994)|0|0|0|0|0|0|0|0|1|1|0|0|0|0|0|0|0|0|0
53|Natural Born Killers (1994)|01-Jan-1994
||http://us.imdb.com/M/title-exact?Natural%20Born%20Killers%20
(1994)|0|0|1|0|0|0|0|0|0|0|0|0|0|0|0|0|1|0|0
54|Outbreak (1995)|01-Jan-1995||http://us.imdb.com/M/title-
exact?Outbreak%20(1995)|0|0|1|0|0|0|0|0|0|1|1|0|0|0|0|0|0|1|0|0
55|Professional, The (1994)|01-Jan-1994
```

Not too big of a surprise because when this dataset was created in 1998 this was definitely one of the most popular films. It would have certainly been popular with the people that tend to frequent websites about machine learning and movie recommendations on the internet.

So there you have it, *Star Wars* the most popular movie. This was a pretty simple example and the results we got kind of reflect the work that we put into it. Interpreting these results is not very easy; we have to search through the `ml-100k` dataset in order to find the name of each movie. We want to make this better. Wouldn't it be great if I could just automatically print out the name of each movie instead of the ID? In the next section, we'll go through how to actually build up a table of movie IDs to movie names and broadcast that table to every node that might be running your Spark job. That way we can actually display the names instead of the IDs, making these results more useful and human readable. So let's take care of that and we'll start to introduce some more advanced concepts in Spark in the process.

Using broadcast variables to display movie names instead of ID numbers

In this section, we'll figure out how to actually include information about the names of the movies in our MovieLens dataset with our Spark job. We'll include them in such a way that they'll get broadcast out to the entire cluster. I'm going to introduce a concept called broadcast variables to do that. There are a few ways we could go about identifying movie names; the most straightforward method would be to just read in the u.item file to look up what movie ID 50 was, see it means *Star Wars*, load up a giant table in Python, and reference that when we're printing out the results within our driver program at the end. That'd be fine, but what if our executors actually need access to that information? How do we get that information to the executors? What if one of our mappers, or one of our reduce functions or something, needed access to the movie names? Well, it turns out that Spark will sort of automatically and magically forward any Python objects that you might need for your mappers or reducers to complete. This can be very handy, but it can also be very inefficient. If that table was massive, you'd end up transferring that table across to all of your executor nodes every time it was needed. If you have a big table, it can add up quickly and cost you a lot of performance. However, Spark offers a way to transfer information once to every executor node in your Spark cluster and keep it there. So if you do know you're going to need some lookup data or some other data, or any kind of object on the various nodes of your Spark cluster, there is a way to do that efficiently. You can send it up there once and keep it there handy so it can be referenced whenever needed. This is called a broadcast variable.

Introducing broadcast variables

Spark offers something called as a broadcast object. The way it works is you take your SparkContext object and you call broadcast() on it as a parameter, you will then ship off whatever object you want to broadcast to every node:

```
sc.broadcast()
```

This will do all the work of serializing it and sending it across the wire and making it available to every executor node in your cluster. Then from your code, you can just call .value() to actually retrieve the object from the broadcasted object. It'll make a little more sense when we look at an example, so let's go off to the code and actually make that happen.

Examining the popular-movies-nicer.py script

So let's see how broadcast variables let us transmit the table of movie IDs to movie names to whatever nodes our job might be running on. In the download package for this book, look for the `popular-movies-nicer` Python script, save that to your `SparkCourse` folder, and open it up. You can see I've added a few things to our previous script here:

```
1 from pyspark import SparkConf, SparkContext
2
3 def loadMovieNames():
4     movieNames = {}
5     with open("ml-100k/u.ITEM") as f:
6         for line in f:
7             fields = line.split('|')
8             movieNames[int(fields[0])] = fields[1]
9     return movieNames
10
11 conf = SparkConf().setMaster("local").setAppName("PopularMovies")
12 sc = SparkContext(conf = conf)
13
14 nameDict = sc.broadcast(loadMovieNames())
15
16 lines = sc.textFile("file:///SparkCourse/ml-100k/u.data")
17 movies = lines.map(lambda x: (int(x.split()[1]), 1))
18 movieCounts = movies.reduceByKey(lambda x, y: x + y)
19
20 flipped = movieCounts.map( lambda (x, y) : (y, x))
21 sortedMovies = flipped.sortByKey()
22
23 sortedMoviesWithNames = sortedMovies.map(lambda (count, movie) : (nameDict.value[movie], count))
24
25 results = sortedMoviesWithNames.collect()
26
27 for result in results:
28     print(result)
29 |
```

The first new thing I've added is this `loadMovieNames` function:

```
def loadMovieNames():
```

This `loadMovieNames` function creates a dictionary in Python that maps movie IDs to movie names. If you're not familiar with dictionaries in Python, they're like hash tables, hash maps, or maps, depending on what language you might be coming from. The general idea, if you look at the following line, is that you can reference them in this fashion: basically, you have a dictionary and you have brackets in which you have a key value. This will let you either assign a value to that key, or retrieve a value from that key:

```
movieNames[int(fields[0])] = fields[1]
```

This is like a little mini key/value data store, which is not a new concept in this book, for sure, but it's a native way of doing it within Python. Let's walk through this. We initialize the `movieNames` dictionary as being empty, as shown here.

Those curly brackets signify an empty dictionary. This is so that we can set it off and kind of tell Python that `movieNames` is in fact a dictionary:

```
movieNames = {}
```

In the next line, we will then open up the `u.item` file:

```
with open("ml-100k/u.ITEM") as f:
```

We will go through every line in that file. Notice, we're actually doing this within Python itself, there's no Spark code going on here to do it. In the next lines, we'll just step through this file one line at a time, then split it up based on its pipe-delimiters. In line 8, we'll extract the movie ID cast as an integer and use that as the key for our dictionary. We will assign that to the movie name, which lives in field 1:

```
for line in f:
    fields = line.split('|')
    movieNames[int(fields[0])] = fields[1]
```

We then return the entire `movieNames` dictionary object to whoever called us:

```
return movieNames
```

Moving on, we have our usual boilerplate stuff here:

```
conf = SparkConf().setMaster("local").setAppName("PopularMovies")
sc = SparkContext(conf = conf)
```

The first thing we do now is to create a `nameDict` object that comes back from `SparkContext` broadcast:

```
nameDict = sc.broadcast(loadMovieNames())
```

This is going to call our `loadMovieNames` function, which returns a dictionary in Python that maps movie IDs to movie names. It's going to broadcast that to every node of our cluster so that it's available when needed. Everyone else on the cluster is going to refer to this as `nameDict` because that is the object that's been broadcast. So, from now on, we're not going to use that `movieNames` object, we'll use `nameDict`, alright? The next few lines are the same as in the previous section. In our driver script, we will load up the `u.data` file:

```
lines = sc.textFile("file:///SparkCourse/ml-100k/u.data")
```

We will then call a mapper that will split it up and create key/value pairs with movie IDs to the number 1:

```
movies = lines.map(lambda x: (int(x.split()[1]), 1))
```

Then we'll count them all up using `reduceByKey`, just like before:

```
movieCounts = movies.reduceByKey(lambda x, y: x + y)
```

Next, we'll flip them around because we want to sort by the number of times each one occurred, and the results end up in `sortedMovies`:

```
flipped = movieCounts.map( lambda (x, y) : (y, x))
sortedMovies = flipped.sortByKey()
```

Now we want to look up `sortedMovies` and replace the movie IDs with names. Here's where it gets interesting. Look at the next line of code shown here:

```
sortedMoviesWithNames = sortedMovies.map(lambda (count, movie) :
  (nameDict.value[movie], count))
```

Now we have a mapper that, as its `lambda` function, takes in each key/value pair, where the key is the count and the value is the movie ID at this point:

```
sortedMovies.map(lambda (count, movie)
```

Our mapper will then replace that with a new key/value pair. Where we're using the `nameDict` object that was broadcast to every node, we call value on it in order to retrieve the original dictionary object. We then use that to look up the name for that given movie ID:

```
: (nameDict.value[movie], count))
```

So our mapper is taking a key/value pair of count and movie ID and transforming that into a movie name and a count using our `nameDict` broadcast variable. We can do this within a mapper only because we broadcast that to every node ahead of time. If we don't use a broadcast variable, it would still work, but would end up transmitting that entire dictionary across the wire, possibly more times than it would need to. At this point, we can collect the results and print them out. This time our `sortedMoviesWithNames` RDD will actually contain movie names instead of movie IDs and be more readable:

```
results = sortedMoviesWithNames.collect()

for result in results:
    print(result)
```

Getting results

So let's now run that and see it in action:

```
(User) c:\SparkCourse>spark-submit popular-movies-nicer.py
```

These results are much easier to make sense of, aren't they?.

```
('Fugitive, The (1993)', 336)
('Mission: Impossible (1996)', 344)
('Back to the Future (1985)', 350)
('Titanic (1997)', 350)
('Star Trek: First Contact (1996)', 365)
('Empire Strikes Back, The (1980)', 367)
('Rock, The (1996)', 378)
('Jerry Maguire (1996)', 384)
('Silence of the Lambs, The (1991)', 390)
('Twelve Monkeys (1995)', 392)
('Pulp Fiction (1994)', 394)
('Godfather, The (1972)', 413)
('Raiders of the Lost Ark (1981)', 420)
('Independence Day (ID4) (1996)', 429)
('Air Force One (1997)', 431)
('Toy Story (1995)', 452)
('Scream (1996)', 478)
('English Patient, The (1996)', 481)
('Liar Liar (1997)', 485)
('Return of the Jedi (1983)', 507)
('Fargo (1996)', 508)
('Contact (1997)', 509)
('Star Wars (1977)', 583)

(User) c:\SparkCourse>
```

As we found out in the previous section, *Star Wars* is the most popular movie in this dataset. Now that we can actually see the names of movies, it's a lot easier to make sense of our results. So, in 1998, when this dataset was created, Contact was pretty hot - not too surprising because it had just come out the year before. The movie Fargo was still hot, that's a good movie. The movie Return of the Jedi was popular, Liar Liar was the 5th most popular, which is kind of a surprise. Later on we'll be looking at the similarities between movies and movie recommendations using the same dataset. So if you start to see some of the same titles appear again, don't think the results are too weird, remember these were hot movies back in 1998. If you see some movie being similar to English Patient or Liar Liar later on, that shouldn't surprise you, because in the context of 1998, it may have made perfect sense. Anyway, that's an example of using broadcast variables in Python and Spark. Now you can actually transmit information to every node on your cluster efficiently.

We are just running this example on one computer because we set the master to local when we created the Spark configuration. If you had run this on a cluster, which we'll do later on in this book, it would have transmitted things to every node. We did this example for the sake of illustration, to introduce you to the concept of broadcast variables because it is a useful concept in Spark and you will definitely be using it. Hopefully, you've discovered how a broadcast variable works and how you can use that to share information efficiently across all the nodes in a cluster.

Finding the most popular superhero in a social graph

Believe it or not, there's actually a publicly available dataset, where someone figured out all the appearances that Marvel superheroes had with each other in different comic books. We can use that to figure out relationships between superheroes in the Marvel Universe and other aspects of them that we might find interesting. Let's start off with a simple example, where we just try to find the most popular superhero in the Marvel dataset. Is Spider-Man or The Hulk the most commonly appearing superhero in Marvel Comics? Well, the answer might surprise you. Let's go dig in and find out.

Superhero social networks

We have a superhero social network that someone constructed, just by looking at what comic books characters appeared in together. So the idea is that if a comic book character appeared together with another comic book character in the same comic book, they're considered to be friends, they have a co-occurrence and they are therefore connected. You may have characters connected in complex patterns. This is really like a social graph that we're dealing with. Let's say the Hulk appeared in a comic book that had Thor in it and he also appeared in another comic book that had Iron Man in it. Maybe Iron Man and Thor appear together but all three of them never appear together in the same comic book. Maybe Spider-Man's off to the edge, appearing with the Hulk but never with Thor or Iron Man.

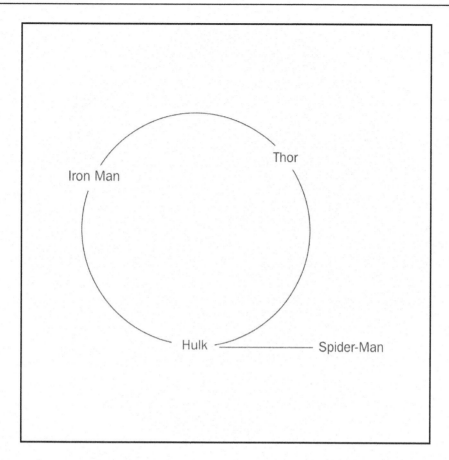

These are complex relationships going on that exist in these networks. We're going to start with a simple example and just try to figure out who is the most popular superhero. We'll define that by who is the superhero that appears with the most other characters.

Input data format

Let's take a look at our input data. Basically, there are two files that we're going to include. One is called `Marvel-graph.txt` and is something I prepared ahead of time. The format of this data is a given superhero ID, which in the case shown as follows is `4395`, followed by a list of all the superhero IDs that character `4395` appeared with in other comic books:

```
4395 2237 1767 472 4997 5931 6235 1478 1369 806 3994 6232
3519 4704 2460 763 1602 5306 5358 6121 6160 2459 3173 4963 6166
3518 5409
```

So, every line has the first entry as a given hero, followed by list of all the other heroes that they appeared with, and so on and so forth. It's important to note that a hero may span multiple lines, so in our source data they would actually break really long lines up into multiple lines, and that's been carried along here. You can't just count up the number of entries and be done with it, we actually need to aggregate things together, as we've seen so many times before in this book.

The second file we're going to use in this example is a `Marvel-names.txt` file that maps superhero IDs to actual human-readable names.

```
5300 "SPENCER, TRACY"
5301 "SPERZEL, ANTON"
5302 "SPETSBURO, GEN. YURI"
5303 "SPHINX"
5304 "SPHINX II"
5305 "SPHINX III"
5306 "SPIDER-MAN/PETER PAR"
5307 "SPIDER-MAN III/MARTH"
5308 "SPIDER CLONE/BEN"
5309 "SPIDER-WOMAN/JESSICA"
```

For example, hero ID `5306` is Spider-Man/Peter Parker, who you've probably heard of, but there's also a lot more obscure characters in there too. I don't know who General Yuri Spetsburo, is or Sphinx, or Anton Spertzel. The Marvel Universe is pretty huge it turns out.

So there's an introduction to your formatted data. We have a lookup table of IDs to hero names and then a graph file that maps each superhero ID to all the other superhero IDs that they appeared with.

Strategy

Let's outline our strategy for finding the most popular superhero, or more specifically, the one that had the most appearances with other superheroes or the most co-occurrences:

- Map input data to hero ID and number of co-occurrences per line:
    - We're going to start off by parsing out our file and map that input data to a key/value pair RDD of hero ID to number of co-occurrences per line. We can count up how many other heroes they appeared with per line.
- Add up co-occurrence by hero ID using `reduceBYKey()`:
    - Since we can actually have heroes that span multiple lines, we're going to need to add them up using `reduceByKey`. This'll give us the final count of how many occurrences by hero ID exist.
- Flip the (map) RDD to (number, hero ID):
    - Given, we want to find the most popular superhero, we're going to flip that around. Like we've done before in this book, we're just going to swap the keys with the values and end up with a key/value RDD, where the number of occurrences is the key and the hero ID is the value.
- Use `max()` on the RDD to find the hero with the most co-occurrences:
    - We then call `max` on that RDD to find the hero with the most co-occurrences.
- Look up the name of the winner and display the result.

We have our general strategy for finding out who the most popular superhero in the Marvel Universe is. Let's dive into some code and see how it all comes together. This is a little bit more of a complicated example than we've done in the past, but you should still be able to wrap your head around it pretty easily.

Running the script - discover who the most popular superhero is

Let's dive into the code for finding the most popular superhero in the Marvel Universe and get our answer. Who will it be? We'll find out soon. Go to the download package for this book and you're going to download three things: the `Marvel-graph.txt` data file, which contains our social network of superheroes, the `Marvel-names.txt` file, which maps superhero IDs to human-readable names, and finally, the `most-popular-superhero` script. Download all that into your `SparkCourse` folder and then open up `most-popular-superhero.py` in your Python environment:

```python
from pyspark import SparkConf, SparkContext

conf = SparkConf().setMaster("local").setAppName("PopularHero")
sc = SparkContext(conf = conf)

def countCoOccurences(line):
    elements = line.split()
    return (int(elements[0]), len(elements) - 1)

def parseNames(line):
    fields = line.split('\"')
    return (int(fields[0]), fields[1].encode("utf8"))

names = sc.textFile("file:///SparkCourse/marvel-names.txt")
namesRdd = names.map(parseNames)

lines = sc.textFile("file:///SparkCourse/marvel-graph.txt")

pairings = lines.map(countCoOccurences)
totalFriendsByCharacter = pairings.reduceByKey(lambda x, y : x + y)
flipped = totalFriendsByCharacter.map(lambda (x,y) : (y,x))

mostPopular = flipped.max()

mostPopularName = namesRdd.lookup(mostPopular[1])[0]

print(mostPopularName + " is the most popular superhero, with " + \
    str(mostPopular[0]) + " co-appearances.")
```

Alright, let's see what's going on here. We have the usual stuff at the top so let's get down to the meat of it

Mapping input data to (hero ID, number of co-occurrences) per line

The first thing we do, if you look at line 14, is load up our `names.txt` file into an RDD called `names` using `sc.textFile`:

```
names = sc.textFile("file:///SparkCourse/marvel-names.txt")
```

We're going to do this name lookup a little bit differently than we did in the previous example. Instead of using a broadcast variable, we'll store the superhero ID to name information as a key/value RDD. This too can be used across different nodes on your cluster if necessary. This is just another way to solve the same problem.

After we load up that text file, we use the `parseNames` function to map it from lines of input data to actual key/value pairs:

```
namesRdd = names.map(parseNames)
```

If we look at what `parseNames` does, it splits it based on the back-slash delimiter (`'\"'`), extracts the superhero ID, stores it as an integer as a key, and then after encoding things into UTF-8 format as a string, it stores the superhero name as the value:

```
def parseNames(line):
    fields = line.split('\"')
    return (int(fields[0]), fields[1].encode("utf8"))
```

At this point, the `names` RDD is a key/value RDD, where the key is a superhero ID, the value is the human-readable and displayable name of that superhero. We'll use that later.

Next, in line 17, we load up the social graph of superheroes itself into a `lines` RDD because it's just containing raw lines of input:

```
lines = sc.textFile("file:///SparkCourse/marvel-graph.txt")
```

Our mapper, in the next line, will turn that into something more useful with the `countCoOccurrences` function:

```
pairings = lines.map(countCoOccurences)
```

Look up at line 6 to see how we define that function. The CoOccurences function is going to split up each line based on whitespaces and return key/value pairs. This time these are of the superhero ID, which is the first ID in the list of each line, followed by the number of elements found in that line, subtracting 1 to account for that first entry-the hero ID that we're talking about:

```
def countCoOccurences(line):
    elements = line.split()
    return (int(elements[0]), len(elements) - 1)
```

So the output of this will be a key value RDD, where the key is the superhero ID:

```
(int(elements[0]),
```

The value is the number of times that hero occurred with other heroes within this line of data:

```
len(elements) - 1
```

Adding up co-occurrence by hero ID

Now remember, heroes can span multiple lines, so next we need to call reduceByKey in order to actually add them all up together. In the case where we have more than one line for a given hero, our standard lambda function for combining things together in a reduce operation will just add them all up:

```
totalFriendsByCharacter = pairings.reduceByKey(lambda x, y : x + y)
```

If we have two different entries for, say, superhero ID 5, it will get the counts for each, add them together, and reduce them into a single entry, here in line 20. So, we now we have totalFriendsByCharacter, which is itself a key/value RDD, where the key is the superhero ID and the values are the total number of co-occurrences seen for that character.

Flipping the (map) RDD to (number, hero ID)

We're now getting close to our answer. We have the information we need in that `totalFriendsByCharacter` RDD, but we need to find the maximum number of friends for all the people in it. When we want to sort things, we need to flip things around to get what we want. Since we want to get the maximum count of characters, we need to make that count the key. To do that, we just do our usual flippy trick here and have a mapper that swaps the keys with the values. You've seen that a few times before:

```
flipped = totalFriendsByCharacter.map(lambda (x,y) : (y,x))
```

What we have now is a key/value RDD where the key is the count and the value is the superhero ID.

Using max() and looking up the name of the winner

Next, we can just call max on that key/value ID, which will find the maximum key/value. This will basically give us back the entry for the superhero ID with the most co-occurrences:

```
mostPopular = flipped.max()
```

Finally, we need to look up a name so we can actually display who that is. As you can see in line 25, we're going to use that `names` RDD that we created earlier to look up the name for the character ID. This will give us back the value from that key/value pair – `[1]`. This value is simply a list that contains a single string, so we extract that value using the array operator `0`:

```
mostPopularName = namesRdd.lookup(mostPopular[1])[0]
```

This will give us back the actual name string itself into `mostPopularName`, which we can then print out. We also have the count that's still in the key/value from our original result that we can use to display as well. So we can say who is the most popular superhero and how many co-appearances that person had with other superheroes in our dataset:

```
print(mostPopularName + " is the most popular superhero, with " + \
    str(mostPopular[0]) + " co-appearances.")
```

Getting results

I'm itching to find this out; who do you think it's going to be, any guesses? My guess would be Spider-Man, but let's see if I'm correct:

```
(User) c:\SparkCourse>spark-submit most-popular-superhero.py
```

The answer is... Ooh! Isn't that a surprise? 1,933 co-appearances for CAPTAIN AMERICA, yay!

```
CAPTAIN AMERICA is the most popular superhero, with 1933 co-appearances.
(User) c:\SparkCourse>
```

He is the most popular superhero in our dataset. He seems like a pretty positive role model and his character seems like a nice guy. Personally, I prefer a more global perspective on the world, but there you have it, a little bit unexpected, I would have guessed someone else but Captain America. I guess the folks at Marvel like the guy, it turns out he shows up in a lot of comic books. There you have it, an example of using Spark in a little bit more of a complex manner. Let's keep on playing with that Marvel superhero data and do some more interesting stuff with it next.

Superhero degrees of separation - introducing the breadth-first search algorithm

You might have heard how everyone is connected through six degrees of separation. Somebody you know knows somebody else who knows somebody else and so on; eventually, you can be connected to pretty much everyone on the planet. Or maybe you've heard about how Kevin Bacon is within a few degrees of separation of pretty much everybody in Hollywood. Well, I used to work at imdb.com, and I can tell you that is true, Kevin Bacon is pretty well connected, but a lot of other actors are too. Kevin Bacon is actually not the most connected actor, but I digress! We want to bring this concept of degrees of separation to our superhero dataset, where we have this virtual social network of superheroes.

Let's figure out the degrees of separation between any two superheroes in that dataset. Is the Hulk connected to Spider-Man closely? How do you find how many connections there are between any two given superheroes that we have? To find the answer, we need to introduce an algorithm called breadth-first search. It's a "computer sciencey," "network theory" sort of thing, but it's not that hard to understand. Let me walk you through how breadth-first search works.

I'm going to take some problems that you might not think of as Spark problems initially, but they can be framed as Spark problems and they have some real-world analogues too. Let's say you're working at, for example, your favorite big social network company; you're going to have a lot of similar data to deal with there, it's going to be data on a such a scale that you can't do it on a single machine. You kind of have to use Spark or something like it to analyze data and pick relationships out of some of these larger social network datasets.

Degrees of separation

What we're going to be doing is play with superheroes and our superhero dataset. We're going to talk about an algorithm called breadth-first search, and use it to find the degrees of separation between superheroes. Along the way, we'll introduce a concept called accumulators. Accumulators, kind of like different executors, keep track of something together. Let's talk about how we're going to go about this. Remember, what we're trying to do is figure out the degrees of separation between superheroes. We want to find out which character is the Kevin Bacon of superheroes.

Look at the following figure. Let's say, we want to find out how far apart Iron Man is from Spider-Man, and these lines all indicate which superheroes appear together in the same comic books. In this example, Spider-Man is connected to the Hulk who is connected to Iron Man; therefore, Spider-Man and Iron Man are connected by two degrees of separation, whereas the Hulk and Thor are connected by one degree, the Hulk and Iron Man are connected by one degree and Thor and Spider-Man are connected by two degrees. Makes sense?

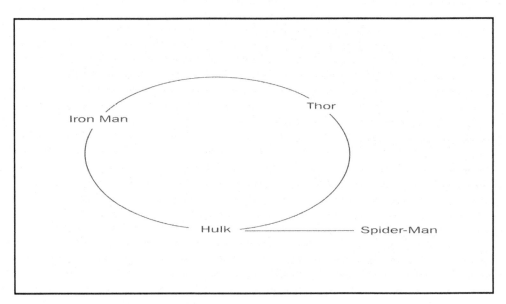

This is what we mean by degrees of separation. How many hops you need to go through some common acquaintance in order to find a connection with somebody else? To find this out, we're going to use an algorithm called breadth-first search. You're going to have to understand how breadth-first search works in order to understand how we're implementing it in Spark to solve this problem. It's basically a way to search through a graph like the preceding one and figure out what the distances are between any given two nodes within that graph. So we're going to pick someone to start with such as the Hulk, and search our way through the whole graph, keeping track of the distances from the Hulk to any other character.

How the breadth-first search algorithm works?

So here's how breadth-first search works. Look at the following diagram. Let's imagine that every one of these circles represents one of the superheroes in our social graph. The lines represent the connections between them:

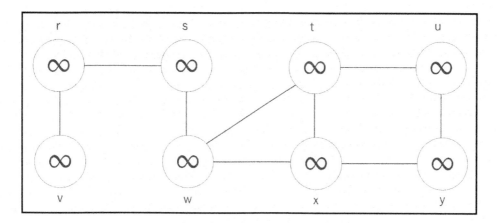

The line means that two superheroes appeared together in the same comic book at some point. You can see, you can have these kind of complicated relationships that go on. It's not really a straightforward problem; we need an algorithm to solve it. The idea is that we have associated each superhero with one of these circles in the diagram. Not only is there a superhero ID associated with each one of these nodes, there's also a distance to the node that we're interested in, as well as a color that we'll use to keep track of its processing state.

The initial condition of our social graph

So let's say that the **s** node represents the Hulk. We want to measure how many degrees of separation people are from the Hulk. Initially, we're going to color all the nodes white, this means that they are completely unprocessed. We're going to have an initial distance of infinity, this means that we just don't know the degrees of separation yet. They are infinitely far away from each other because we haven't computed anything yet:

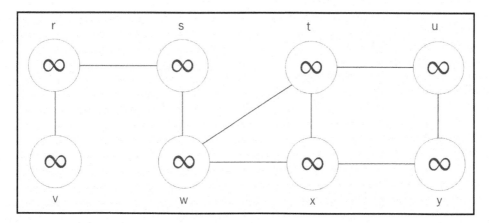

We know that we want to start with the Hulk who is in the **s** node. We're going to change the color of that node to gray. The color gray means that a node needs to be expanded upon, that we've just come across it, and we need to work our way out from there. We also add the number zero in the s circle. The number zero represents the degrees of separation from the Hulk. The Hulk is the Hulk, he has zero degrees of separation to himself:

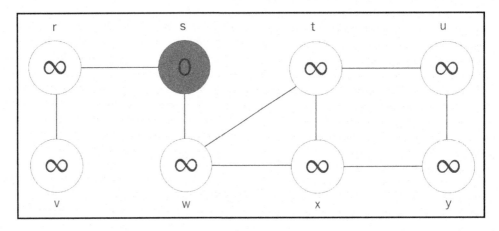

In our initial condition, everybody is white and infinitely far away. We then identify the person we're interested in measuring the distance from, color them gray, and give them an initial degree of separation of zero.

Now things get interesting. This is an iterative algorithm, so we're going to pass through the graph multiple times until we're finally done discovering every node in it.

First pass through the graph

So, in our next pass through the graph, we will take our gray node, which was the Hulk, and color it black. This means that we have processed it completely and that we don't have to look at it again. Then we go out to all of its connections and color those connections gray, this means that they need to be expanded upon next. We then increment the distance from the original node by 1:

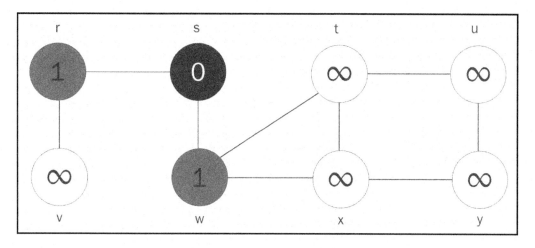

Zero plus one is one, so we now know that the **r** and **w** nodes, whoever they happen to represent, are one degree of separation from the Hulk, the **s** node.

Second pass through the graph

We then pass through it all again. We now have to then expand the **r** and **w** nodes. Let's start with **w**. Color it black, this means that we've processed it, color its connections gray, this means that they need to be explored next, and increment the distance one more time:

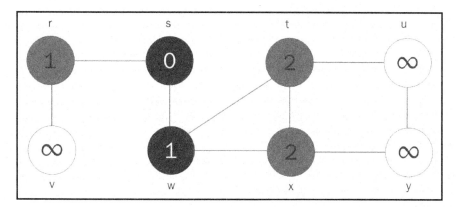

Now we know that the **x** and **t** nodes are two degrees of separation from the Hulk. We still have to handle the r circle, so color it black, increment the distance to 2 and color this new node that we just discovered, the **v** node, gray, meaning that we need to explore the **v** node further as well:

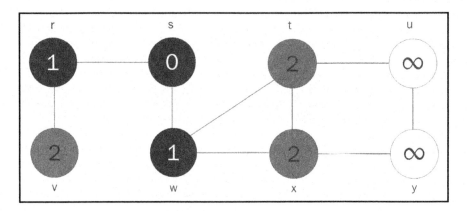

So this is the end of our second pass through the graph.

Third pass through the graph

Let's start our third pass, we'll start with this **t** node, color it black, this means that we've explored it. we've already come across the **x** node before, so we're going to leave it untouched and leave the previous minimum value there. The connection at the **u** node is new, so color that gray and increment its distance to 3. Now we're at a connection that has three degrees of separation from the Hulk:

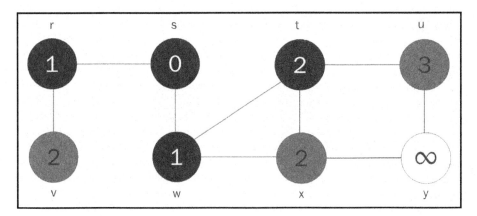

Then we'll explore the **x** node again, which will cause us to discover the **y** node, which is also three degrees of separation; color the **x** node black and the **y** node gray:

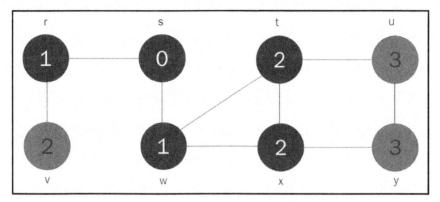

See what happened there?

Final pass through the graph

We still have to process the **v** node, which isn't connected to anybody. All we have to do is mark it black, this means that we're done with it. We just have the **u** and **y** nodes to go through; obviously, they're not connected to anybody new, so all we have to do is color them black to indicate they have been visited and processed. Finally, we are done:

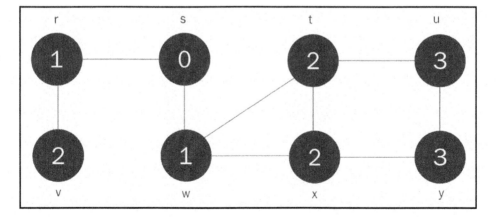

So, we covered breadth-first-search from a conceptual, algorithmic standpoint. If that didn't make sense, I encourage you to go back through this section to get your head around how the traversals work. It's important that you understand how we actually arrived at the degrees of separation from the **s** node as we worked our way through the graph. Next, let's talk about how we actually turn this into a Spark problem that we can run iteratively and get the results we want.

Accumulators and implementing BFS in Spark

Now that we have the concept of breadth-first-search under our belt and we understand how that can be used to find the degrees of separation between superheroes, let's apply that and actually write some Spark code to make it happen. So how do we turn breadth-first search into a Spark problem? This will make a lot more sense if that explanation of how BFS works is still fresh in your head. If it's not, it might be a good idea to go back and re-read the previous section; it will really help a lot if you understand the theory.

Convert the input file into structured data

The first thing we need to do is actually convert our data file or input file into something that looks like the nodes that we described in the BFS algorithm in the previous section, *Superhero degrees of separation - introducing breadth-first search.*

We're starting off, for example, with a line of input that looks like the one shown here that says hero ID 5983 appeared with heroes 1165, 3836, 4361, and 1282:

> 5983 1165 3836 4361 1282

We want to convert that to something a little bit more interesting and useful. We want to convert that to structured data, where we have for example, the hero ID in question, the list of their connections, a distance, and a color:

> (5983, (1165, 3836, 4361, 1282), 9999, WHITE)

Do you remember what we had in our nodes in the previous section? We had their connections to other nodes, a distance from the hero that we wanted to start from and a color that keeps track of what's been processed and what hasn't. So this line is kind of how we're going to represent one of those nodes within Spark and within Python:

```
(5983, (1165, 3836, 4361, 1282), 9999, WHITE)
```

Remember our initial condition is that nodes are all infinitely distant and we'll represent that as 9999-believe me, no one's going to be that far apart in a social network. The initial color will be white, which means that everything has been unprocessed. Let's now turn that into some code.

Writing code to convert Marvel-Graph.txt to BFS nodes

A big part of the code is just the conversion of our source data into something that looks like a node. Then what we're going to do is convert that to an actual key/value pair-a key of a hero ID and a value that's a composite value of the list of connections, the distance and the color:

```
return (heroID, (connections, distance, color))
```

This way, we can group things together by hero ID more easily later.

Let's look at what is going on in the rest of the code. It's pretty straightforward stuff:

```
def convertToBFS(line):
    fields = line.split()
    heroID = int(fields[0])
    connections = []
    for connection in fields[1:]:
        connections.append(int(connection))

    color = 'WHITE'
    distance = 9999

if (heroID == startCharacterID):
        color = 'GRAY'
        distance = 0
```

We split up the input line:

```
fields = line.split()
```

We extract the hero ID from the first field:

```
heroID = int(fields[0])
```

Next we have a little bit of Python syntax you might not have seen before. `[1:]` here means we are going to extract all the fields from number one forward. This lets us iterate through all of the "friends" of that hero ID that are in fields 1, going forward:

```
connections = []
for connection in fields[1:]:
```

In the next line, we append them into a list of connections:

```
connections.append(int(connection))
```

At this point, we have a hero ID that we've extracted and a list of all the connections for that hero ID. Finally, we set the initial conditions to white and an infinite distance that we represent with 9999:

```
color = 'WHITE'
distance = 9999
```

However, this shouldn't apply to our starting character. So if we're starting with the Hulk and the hero ID that we're encountering is the Hulk, we know that's the guy we want to start from. Let's say we want to measure degrees of separation from the Hulk, we would color his node gray and give him an initial distance of zero, meaning that the Hulk is the Hulk and therefore has zero degrees of separation from the Hulk. The color gray represents that this node needs to be processed and expanded upon through the next generation of breadth-first search:

```
if (heroID == startCharacterID):
        color = 'GRAY'
        distance = 0
```

Again, our final output will be the hero ID as the key, and the value will be a list of connections, the distance and the color. Remember that this is actually a list:

```
return (heroID, (connections, distance, color))
```

Iteratively process the RDD

Now we're going to go through the entire graph multiple times. We'll do this as many times as it takes to find the other character that we are interested in-we want to find the degrees of separation between two given characters. We will go through each time and we will look for gray nodes that need to be expanded. When we're done expanding them, we'll color them black. As we go along coloring new nodes gray, we'll update the distances to increment them, keeping track of the degrees of separation from our starting point, just like in the previous section.

Using a mapper and a reducer

Now, to do that, we're basically going to create a map function that will go through the data looking for gray nodes. If a node is gray, our function will create new nodes that have a distance incremented by one and a color of gray. These new nodes will have no connections, we'll combine them back together with their connection list in the reducer. Obviously, this is going to be a `flatMap` operation because we might be producing multiple nodes for each input node. We then color the processed node black, and we will copy the node itself into the results returned by the `flatMap` operation so we don't lose it.

We also use a `reduce` function. Our reducer recombines everything. It looks for nodes tied to the same hero ID-information associated with the same node. Remember, there's only one node per hero in our graph. Anything that comes together for that hero ID needs to be combined back together. The reducer will look for the shortest distance of all that information and preserve the darkest color for that node that we found. Then it will find the list of connections that we passed along originally when we copied the original node back in, and marry that back into the final node for this iteration:

How do we know when we're done?

We'll just go through this process over and over again until we encounter the character we're interested in. At that point, we can count how many iterations we had to go through to figure out the degrees of separation. But how do we know when we're done? I mean, this is running potentially on the cluster, and there's no set way of knowing when we've actually encountered the character we care about. Well, that's where accumulators come in.

Remember how broadcast variables let you share objects across all the nodes in your cluster? Well, an accumulator allows all the executors in your cluster to increment some shared variable. It's basically a counter that is maintained and synchronized across all of the different nodes in your cluster. Let's look at an example of usage. You can call the accumulator function on your `SparkContext` with an initial value of, say, zero, and call that accumulator object your hit counter:

```
hitCounter = sc.accumulator(0)
```

Then, when we'll go through our iterations. If any node that happens to be running this job encounters the character we're looking for, we can just increment that `hitCounter` accumulator. Then every other node and our driver script has access to that. So after each iteration, we can check that `hitCounter` to see if anybody incremented it, maybe even multiple people incremented it, and if it is greater than one, we're done. So we know that once `hitCounter` gets incremented by some value, we've found the guy we're looking for and we can declare victory. Okay, let's go look at this in action, let's run the code and actually make it happen.

Superhero degrees of separation - review the code and run it

Using breadth-first search, let's actually find the degrees of separation between two given superheroes in our Marvel superhero dataset. In the download package for this book, download the `degrees-of-separation` script into your `SparkCourse` folder. We'll work up a pretty good library here of different examples, so keep this handy. There's a good chance that some problem you face in the future will have a similar pattern to something we've already done here, and this might be a useful reference for you. Once you have downloaded that script, double-click it. We already have the `Marvel-graph` and `Marvel-names` text files for our input from previous sections.

Here is the `degrees-of-separation` script:

```
 1 #Boilerplate stuff:
 2 from pyspark import SparkConf, SparkContext
 3
 4 conf = SparkConf().setMaster("local").setAppName("DegreesOfSeparation")
 5 sc = SparkContext(conf = conf)
 6
 7 # The characters we wish to find the degree of separation between:
 8 startCharacterID = 5306 #SpiderMan
 9 targetCharacterID = 14   #ADAM 3,031 (who?)
10
11 # Our accumulator, used to signal when we find the target character during
12 # our BFS traversal.
13 hitCounter = sc.accumulator(0)
14
15 def convertToBFS(line):
16     fields = line.split()
17     heroID = int(fields[0])
18     connections = []
19     for connection in fields[1:]:
20         connections.append(int(connection))
21
22     color = 'WHITE'
23     distance = 9999
24
25     if (heroID == startCharacterID):
26         color = 'GRAY'
27         distance = 0
28
29     return (heroID, (connections, distance, color))
30
31
32 def createStartingRdd():
33     inputFile = sc.textFile("file:///sparkcourse/marvel-graph.txt")
34     return inputFile.map(convertToBFS)
35
36 def bfsMap(node):
37     characterID = node[0]
38     data = node[1]
39     connections = data[0]
```

The point here is just to illustrate how problems that may not seem like they lend themselves to Spark at first, actually can be incremented in Spark with a little bit of creative thinking. I also want to introduce the concept of accumulators here as we go. So let's look at our code. We have the usual boilerplate stuff at the top, nothing changed there:

```
#Boilerplate stuff:
from pyspark import SparkConf, SparkContext

conf = SparkConf().setMaster("local").setAppName("DegreesOfSeparation")
sc = SparkContext(conf = conf)
```

Setting up an accumulator and using the convert to BFS function

After our boilerplate lines, we're going to define two character IDs that we're interested in. We'll say we're interested in the degrees of separation from Spider-Man, who turns out to be character ID 5306. What we're interested in finding out is how many degrees of separation Adam 3031, whoever that is, is from Spider-Man:

```
# The characters we wish to find the degree of separation between:
startCharacterID = 5306 #SpiderMan
targetCharacterID = 14 #ADAM 3,031 (who?)
```

I intentionally picked some random character who I'd never heard of because it will be a little more interesting if it takes a few iterations to get a result.

We talked about using an accumulator to signal to the driver script when we found Adam 3,031. We're going to set up that accumulator, which all of our different executors can use, to signal once we've actually found that node that we're looking for. We'll set an initial value of zero in that accumulator and we'll call it hitCounter:

```
# Our accumulator, used to signal when we find the target character during
# our BFS traversal.
hitCounter = sc.accumulator(0)
```

We covered the convert to BFS function in the previous section. Here it is in our degrees-of-separation script:

```
def convertToBFS(line):
    fields = line.split()
    heroID = int(fields[0])
    connections = []
    for connection in fields[1:]:
        connections.append(int(connection))

    color = 'WHITE'
    distance = 9999

    if (heroID == startCharacterID):
        color = 'GRAY'
        distance = 0

    return (heroID, (connections, distance, color))
```

Just to recap quickly, this sets up the initial conditions of our graph and converts our input data into node structures, where each entry of our RDD is going to consist of the key/value pair. As you can see in the following line, in this key/value pair, the key is the superhero ID and the value is a composite value that consists of its list of connections, the distance, and the color:

```
return (heroID, (connections, distance, color))
```

Initially, distances will be 9,999, indicating infinity, and the color of white, except for Spider-Man, who will be colored gray to start with, with a distance of zero. Spider-Man is who we're starting with and gray indicates that we need to expand upon that node:

```
color = 'WHITE'
distance = 9999
if (heroID == startCharacterID):
    color = 'GRAY'
    distance = 0
```

Skipping down a bit to the meat of it, down to the main program at line 100, we start off by calling `createStartingRdd()`:

```
#Main program here:
iterationRdd = createStartingRdd()
```

Let's see what that does-we defined that up in line 32. The `createStartingRdd` function loads in our input file, the `Marvel-graph.txt`. Then it calls the convert to BFS map function that we described earlier, and converts that into something that looks like node IDs:

```
def createStartingRdd():
    inputFile = sc.textFile("file:///sparkcourse/marvel-graph.txt")
    return inputFile.map(convertToBFS)
```

So, nothing too complicated yet, we're just converting our input data into something that looks like nodes in a breadth-first search traversal.

Calling flatMap()

Okay, what happens next? Next, down in line 103, we're going to go through some upper bound of iteration. So we're going to assume that we're never going to be more than ten degrees of separation from anybody in this graph, if so, they're probably not connected at all. In this line, we're just picking some arbitrary upper bound, here, 10. We will iterate through the graph, doing the BFS traversal up to ten times. The first time we'll say we're running the BFS iteration number 10:

```
for iteration in range(0, 10):
    print("Running BFS iteration# " + str(iteration+1))
```

Then we will call our flatMap. This runs that first step, as we talked about in the previous section, of blowing out all the gray nodes. This is calling our bfsMap function:

```
mapped = iterationRdd.flatMap(bfsMap)
```

Let's see what that does, we've defined it up at line 36. As I mentioned earlier, it just extracts the information from each node:

```
def bfsMap(node):
    characterID = node[0]
    data = node[1]
    connections = data[0]
    distance = data[1]
    color = data[2]
```

After that, it looks for gray nodes and blows them out. It then colors them black and creates new gray nodes from their connections. This is flatMap operation, so we're returning a results list of nodes that get added into the new resulting RDD:

```
if (color == 'GRAY'):
    for connection in connections:
        newCharacterID = connection
        newDistance = distance + 1
        newColor = 'GRAY'
        if (targetCharacterID == connection):
            hitCounter.add(1)

        newEntry = (newCharacterID, ([], newDistance, newColor))
        results.append(newEntry)

    #We've processed this node, so color it black
    color = 'BLACK'
```

Finally, we put the original node back into the list as well so we can reconnect its connections back to that node in the reducer:

```
results.append( (characterID, (connections, distance, color)) )
return results
```

So this creates not only the original node we started with, but new nodes, colored gray, that need to be expanded upon, and for each new node we've incremented the distance to keep track of the degrees of separation. You're better served going back and looking at the previous two sections if that doesn't make sense to you. It's actually a little bit easier to understand graphically than by looking at the code.

Calling an action

To actually make all that happen, we have to call an action:

```
print("Processing " + str(mapped.count()) + " values.")
```

So remember, we have lazy evaluation in Spark-just calling `flatMap` doesn't actually make anything happen. A very key thing happened in the BFS map function-If we actually encountered the character that we were looking for, we incremented our `hitCounter`, our accumulator:

```
if (targetCharacterID == connection):
    hitCounter.add(1)
```

This is a very important point. The moment that we encounter Adam 3031, this `hitCounter` is going to get incremented, signaling back to our driver script that we have found the person we're looking for. The problem is, map functions are transforms. They don't actually cause to actually get run in Spark until you call an action. So what we're doing here is a little bit of a cheat, we're calling the count function on that RDD to force it to get evaluated. That way our accumulator will get set at this point:

```
print("Processing " + str(mapped.count()) + " values.")
```

Our accumulator also prints out some interesting information as a side effect. We can see how we're actually processing more and more nodes as we expand outward from our starting node. If we do in fact encounter Adam 3031 upon that mapping pass, we will check that hitCounter to see if it's greater than zero. If it is, we print it out and say hey, we found our guy, as shown in the following lines. We can actually print out how many times that hitCounter was hit because you can actually come at a given character from many different directions:

```
if (hitCounter.value > 0):
    print("Hit the target character! From " + str(hitCounter.value) \
        + " different direction(s).")
    break
```

Calling reduceByKey

If it's not greater than zero, we'll keep on processing. We will call the reduceByKey function to actually gather together all of the nodes that we might have generated in that flatMap operation and recombine them together for each given character ID. There can be only one node per character ID, and this enforces that:

```
iterationRdd = mapped.reduceByKey(bfsReduce)
```

The bfsReduce function, as you can see up at line 64, simply gathers the nodes back together:

```
def bfsReduce(data1, data2):
    edges1 = data1[0]
    edges2 = data2[0]
    distance1 = data1[1]
    distance2 = data2[1]
    color1 = data1[2]
    color2 = data2[2]

    distance = 9999
    color = 'WHITE'
    edges = []

# See if one is the original node with its connections.
# If so preserve them.
if (len(edges1) > 0):
    edges.extend(edges1)
if (len(edges2) > 0):
    edges.extend(edges2)
```

The `bfsReduce` function then preserves the minimum distance and the darkest color found and it reconnects the list of connections that were found for that original node:

```
# Preserve minimum distance
if (distance1 < distance):
    distance = distance1
if (distance2 < distance):
    distance = distance2
# Preserve darkest color
if (color1 == 'WHITE' and (color2 == 'GRAY' or color2 == 'BLACK')):
    color = color2
if (color1 == 'GRAY' and color2 == 'BLACK'):
    color = color2
if (color2 == 'WHITE' and (color1 == 'GRAY' or color1 == 'BLACK')):
    color = color1
if (color2 == 'GRAY' and color1 == 'BLACK'):
    color = color1
return (edges, distance, color)
```

If you want to stare at that code in a little more depth, you can get into the syntax of how it works, but conceptually that's what's going on.

That's it! We just keep on iterating through until we hit a maximum of ten iterations, but nothing's going to get that high. Let's go ahead and run it and see what happens.

Getting results

Open up **Canopy Command Prompt** and run this script:

```
(User) c:\SparkCourse>spark-submit degrees-of-separation.py
```

As you run that you should see it going through once, twice, and on the third iteration through our breadth-first search traversal we finally find who we're looking for:

```
Running BFS iteration# 1
Processing 8330 values.
Running BFS iteration# 2
Processing 220615 values.
Hit the target character! From 1 different direction(s).

(User) c:\SparkCourse>
```

He was only hit from one direction, so this guy is pretty obscure. Our answer is `Adam 3031`, whoever he is, is three degrees of separation from Spider-Man in our social graph. So there's your answer, and you can plug in different character IDs for anyone you want in here, if you're curious and want to play around with it. Notice how we started blowing out to more and more nodes than we were looking at originally. We started off with just 8330 connections to Spider-Man himself, but then we started looking at the connections of the connections and got into a very large number very quickly than we are processing through in each iteration.

You can see how these social graphs tend to branch out to a large number of people pretty quickly. People really have a small number of degrees of separation from each other in many cases. Granted, this is a fictitious dataset, but we had to pick a pretty obscure character to find someone who was even a little bit removed from Spider-Man. If you were trying to do this between any two well-known superheroes, you'd probably find that they're connected by just one degree. The whole point in this example was to illustrate how to do a more complex algorithm such as breadth-first search using Spark. You're not limited to just doing simple mapping and reducing functions with Spark. With a little creativity, you can take more complicated problems like this and frame them as Spark problems. That's really the skill that they're going to pay you the big bucks for. The more you can think about how to frame problems as distributed Spark problems, the more valuable you'll be as a data miner.

Item-based collaborative filtering in Spark, cache(), and persist()

We're now going to cover a topic that's near and dear to my heart-collaborative filtering. Have you ever been to some place like `amazon.com` and seen something like "people who bought this also bought," or have you seen "similar movies" suggested on `imdb.com`? I used to work on that. In this section, I'm going to show you some general algorithms on how that works under the hood. Now I can't tell you exactly how Amazon does it, because Jeff Bezos would hunt me down and probably do terrible things to me, but I can tell you some generally known techniques that you can build upon for doing something similar. Let's talk about a technique called item-based collaborative filtering and discuss how that works. We'll apply it to our MovieLens data to actually figure out similar movies to each other based on user ratings.

We're doing some pretty complicated and advanced stuff at this point in the book. The good news is this is probably the culmination of the book in terms of the difficulty level. Stay with me and bear with me, because after this section, things get easier, trust me. Predominantly, I just want to make sure that you understand that complex problems that may not appear to be a Spark problem can be framed as Spark problems. This is yet another example of taking something you might not think of as being distributable and actually making it into something that you can run on Spark with massive datasets. In addition to talking about finding similar movies using the MovieLens ratings dataset, we're also going to introduce a concept called caching and persisting RDDs, which is very important to know as well.

How does item-based collaborative filtering work?

Well, here's how we're going to do it; remember, this is only one way to do it, there are many techniques, this is just one which is easier to explain. What we do is we find every pair of movies that were watched by the same person. Then we find all the users that watched that pair of movies, and compare how similar their ratings were for each one. So the idea is that if you have two movies that were watched by a bunch of people and they all rated them similarly, those movies are probably similar to each other in some way, shape, or form. After we do that, we then compute the similarity of each movie pair, sort them by the movie and then by the strength of similarities. Then you can slice and dice the results and look up a specific movie and find the movies that are most similar to it.

Looking at an illustration makes more sense. Let's imagine that this good-looking little clipart woman in the following illustration watched *Star Wars* and *Star Wars: The Empire Strikes Back*. She rated them both similarly. Mr. Clipart Mohawk guy here comes along and also rates both movies, and rates them in a similar way to the first person. So with that information, we can establish a connection between these two movies, we know that there is some relationship between them:

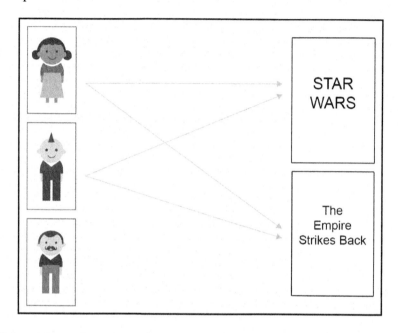

So, Mr. Handlebar Mustache comes along and he lives in some strange world, where he's never seen the first *Star Wars* movie, but he has seen The Empire Strikes Back. What we could do at this point if we were creating movie recommendations would be to take the fact that we discovered a connection between *The Empire Strikes Back* and *Star Wars* based on these other ratings, and recommend *Star Wars* to Mr. Handlebar Mustache. We can advise him that *Star Wars* is somehow connected to *The Empire Strikes Back*, and that maybe he should check that out too:

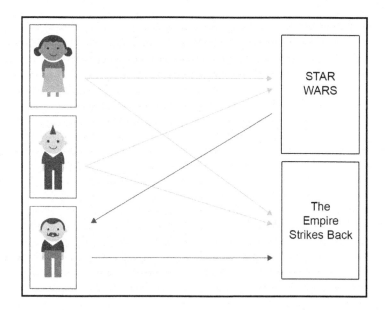

So that's it in a nutshell, that's item-based collaborative filtering, pretty simple concept with a fancy name, right? That tends to be the case in machine learning and data mining actually, you hear a lot of big fancy words and terms that sound very highfalutin and academic, but when it comes down to it, the concepts aren't that complicated. However, turning this into a Spark program is complicated.

Making item-based collaborative filtering a Spark problem

Turning item-based collaborative filtering into a Spark problem is complicated. I'm just going to kind of walk you through the approach that I used. The point here is just to illustrate how you can take something like this and turn it into a Spark problem. It's just an example to look at, so if you don't totally get everything that's going on here that's okay, the important thing is that you see that you can take a complex problem like this and make a Spark problem out of it and make it actually work. So here's our strategy:

- Map input ratings to (userID, (movieID, rating)):
    - We map the set of input ratings from the MovieLens dataset to key/value pairs, where the key is the user ID and the value is a composite movie ID and rating structure. So for every line of input, we're going to create a key/value, where the key is the user and the value is the rating for a given movie ID.

- Find every movie pair rated by the same user:
  - Next we need to find every movie pair that was rated by the same users. A while ago, I talked about some operations you can do on key/value RDDs that were very SQLish, and one of them was a join operation. It turns out if you join a database with itself you end up getting every possible permutation within that database. By doing a 'self-join' operation, I'll get back every single possible pair of movies that were rated like that same movie. What I end up with at this point is a huge list, structured like this:

```
(userID, ((movieID1, rating1), (movieID2, rating2)))
```

- This "self-joining" operation blows up quickly, it's like a Cartesian combination. We have this huge list of user IDs followed by every possible pair of movies that they watched together. We'll have a user ID watched movieID1 and rated it something, and they also watched this other movie and rated it something, and we will get that for every combination of movies that they have watched.
- Filter out duplicate pairs
  - We're going to get some duplicate pairs as part of the process of finding every movie pair rated by the same user. We're going to get some things that are in different orders, or maybe we'll get the same movie as movieID1 and movieID2. We're going to strip out all that duplicate, redundant information, just to boil things down a little bit more.

- Make the movie pairs the key
  - Next we're going to make the movie pairs the key because what we really care about is the similarity strength between pairs of movies, that's the end goal here. We're going to shuffle our data around, mapping it so that it looks like this composite value-(movieID1, movieID2)-ends up being the key and the value ends up being the ratings of those two movies-(movieID1, movieID2), (rating1, rating2). So movieID1 and movieID2 were watched together by some person and rated with these two values: rating1 and rating2. At this point, the user ID is irrelevant, we don't really care who the individual was, all we care about is that some person watched these movies together and gave them these ratings. With me so far?

- Use groupByKey() to get every rating pair found for each movie pair
  - Next we're going to use a `groupByKey`, we want to combine together all the ratings that individuals made for that given pair of movies. So what we had before this point was a given user's ratings for each individual movie pair that they watched. Now, with `groupByKey()`, we combine together all of the ratings that were made for that movie pair across the entire dataset.
- Compute similarity between ratings for each movie in the pair:
  - Once we have all of the ratings that were made for a movie pair across the entire dataset together, we can compute the similarity between those two movies just by looking at the similarity between the sets of ratings that different users gave to that movie. There are many ways to compute similarity, we'll pick one that's easy to do.
- Sort, save, and display the results:
  - Now we have what we need, we just need to sort, save, and display the results.

It's getting real

One thing I want to point out at this point is that we're doing some pretty heavy lifting here. That self-join is a huge operation that generates a huge RDD. It's time to start splitting this up across more than just one CPU. Odds are your PC at home has at least two cores on it. Do this following little trick here; instead of just saying `setMaster("local")`, do `setMaster("local[*]")`. This syntax means, go take advantage of every core you have available on this computer and run a separate executor:

```
conf = SparkConf().setMaster("local[*]").setAppName("MovieSimilarities")
sc = SparkContext(conf = conf)
```

So for the first time, we're going to be running a Spark program across multiple executors. It will still be just on your computer, but we're actually going to be running as many executors you have cores and combining the results back together later on. So again, let's go take a look.

Caching RDDs

I want to mention caching RDDs. I'll point this out as we go through the code in the next section. In our example, we're actually going to compute the RDD of movie similarities and query it a couple of times. The way Spark works is as soon as you call an action, it just discards that RDD, so if you actually want to use an RDD more than once and perform more than one action on it, you need to tell Spark explicitly to **cache** it and make it persistent. If you don't cache it, Spark might have to go back and reconstruct that RDD all over again and you might end up doubling the amount of work that you have to do. That would be bad because that self-join operation is very expensive in this example and we don't want to have to do that twice. What we do instead is, once we have that RDD of movie similarities, we call `.cache()` or `.persist()` on it in order to keep it around and prevent the need for recomputing. What's the difference between `.cache()` and `.persist()`? They're actually very similar, the only real difference is that `persist` gives you an optional argument that lets you cache it to disk instead of just memory. If you're really paranoid about losing that RDD and you don't want to lose it even if a node fails, you can use `persist` to make sure that it writes it to disk. Obviously, that's going to take more time and consume disk space, whereas `cache` will not.

There you have the concepts behind item-based collaborative filtering. It's a fancy word, but it's a pretty simple concept, right? Let's figure out how to take that and turn it into a Spark problem. This is an example of taking a more complex business problem and trying to frame it as a Spark problem that could be horizontally partitioned on a Spark cluster so you can take massive amounts of ratings data and process them with good results. Let's dive in next and turn this into some code.

Running the similar-movies script using Spark's cluster manager

Leading up to this point has been a lot of work, but we now have a Spark program that should give us similar movies to each other. We can figure out what movies are similar to each other, just based on similarities between user ratings. Let's turn this movie similarities problem into some real code, run it, and look at the results. Go to the download package for this book, you will find a `movie-similarities` script. Download that to your `SparkCourse` folder and open it up. We're going to keep on using the MovieLens 100,000 rating dataset for this example, so there's no new data to download, just the script. This is the most complicated thing we're going to do in this course, so let's just get through the script and walk through what it's doing. We described it at a high level in the previous section, but let's go through it again.

Examining the script

You can see we're importing the usual stuff at the top of the script. We do need to import the square root function from the `math` package in Python as well, so that we can do our similarity metric and compute similarities later on:

```
import sys
from pyspark import SparkConf, SparkContext
from math import sqrt
```

Let's get down to the meat of it; down in line 42 we create our `SparkContext`:

```
conf = SparkConf().setMaster("local[*]").setAppName("MovieSimilarities")
sc = SparkContext(conf = conf)
```

We're doing this with a `local[*]` master argument here, which means we're actually going to use Spark's built-in cluster manager and treat every core on your desktop as a node on a cluster. For the first time, we're going to be running on more than one process, and you actually kind of need it for this problem.

Next, we'll load up the dictionary of movie names:

```
print("\nLoading movie names...")
nameDict = loadMovieNames()
```

We've seen this before. If you look at the `loadMovieNames` script up at line 5, you can see it's just returning a Python dictionary that maps movie IDs to human-readable movie names so we can look at them more easily. We're using the usual decode trick, in line 10, to make sure that we can actually display them in our Terminal-that's all that decode stuff is doing:

```
def loadMovieNames():
    movieNames = {}
    with open("ml-100k/u.ITEM") as f:
        for line in f:
            fields = line.split('|')
            movieNames[int(fields[0])] = fields[1].decode('ascii',
'ignore')
    return movieNames
```

We're not going to muck around with broadcast variables in this particular example. We're just going to use that dictionary at the very end, when we're doing our final display. We're keeping that a little bit simpler.

Next, we load up our source data of movie ratings data. Again, the `u.data` format is user ID, movie ID, rating, timestamp, and that goes into a `data` RDD:

```
data = sc.textFile("file:///SparkCourse/ml-100k/u.data")
```

We then do this big long operation in the next line to map it into our initial pass.

We start off by splitting the data on whitespace into individual fields, and then we map it again into the format we want:

```
# Map ratings to key / value pairs: user ID => movie ID, rating
ratings = data.map(lambda l: l.split()).map(lambda l: (int(l[0]),
(int(l[1]), float(l[2]))))
```

This is going to give us back together an RDD that has `user ID` as the key and the values will be these composite values of movie ID and ratings. So we have a key/value RDD at this point, keys are user IDs and the values are movie-rating pairs.

Next, we do a self-join operation to find every possible combination of movies that were rated together by the same user:

```
# Emit every movie rated together by the same user.
# Self-join to find every combination.
joinedRatings = ratings.join(ratings)
```

That blows up really quickly. This is where most of the work is going to be happening in the script because when you start looking at every possible combination, you're looking at factorial relationships. It blows up like you wouldn't believe, but with Spark we can actually do it because it's scalable. At this point, we're going to end up with `user ID` still as the key, but then we're going to get lists of every movie ID rating pair that was viewed by that user ID. So we have this huge RDD now, where the keys are `user ID` and the values are every possible combination of movie rating pairs that user watched:

```
# At this point our RDD consists of userID => ((movieID, rating), (movieID,
rating))
```

Next, we need to eliminate duplicates because out of those possible permutations, we're probably going to get the same movie twice in a different order. We'll even get the same movie related to the same movie. We need to filter all that junk out because it's not helpful:

```
# Filter out duplicate pairs
uniqueJoinedRatings = joinedRatings.filter(filterDuplicates)
```

So our `filterDuplicates` map function, defined up in line 18, simply enforces that we only return pairs where movie 1 is less than movie 2; we enforce only one ordering of the movie pairs that are in sorted order, and we also eliminate pairs where movie 1 is the same thing as movie 2 because that's not helpful either:

```
def filterDuplicates( (userID, ratings) ):
    (movie1, rating1) = ratings[0]
    (movie2, rating2) = ratings[1]
    return movie1 < movie2
```

We've talked about filters before. This is another example of using filter to cut down a large RDD into a smaller one by throwing away information you don't want. So now we have a cleaned-up RDD that contains every movie rating pair, every movie pair for each user.

Next, now that we've filtered out the duplicates, we need to shuffle things around. What we care about in the end is the similarities between unique pairs of movies. So, we're just going to run another map operation on that to make the new key the movie pair itself. This is what the `makePairs` map function does:

```
# Now key by (movie1, movie2) pairs.
moviePairs = uniqueJoinedRatings.map(makePairs)
```

Go up to line 13 to see what it does. It extracts the movie and rating for each pair of the input RDD and outputs a new key/value RDD where the key is the movie pair and the value is the ratings for that movie pair:

```
def makePairs((user, ratings)):
    (movie1, rating1) = ratings[0]
    (movie2, rating2) = ratings[1]
    return ((movie1, movie2), (rating1, rating2))
```

Alright, we're almost done. Next, we're going to use `groupByKey` to actually get together all the rating pairs for each unique movie pair. For every pair of movies, we gather together all the pairs of ratings from every user that watched that pair of movies:

```
moviePairRatings = moviePairs.groupByKey()
```

Now that we have every set of ratings from every user that watched a given pair of movies, we can compute the similarity between those two movies by comparing the similarities between those two sets of ratings. This is what `computeCosineSimilarity` does:

```
# We now have (movie1, movie2) = > (rating1, rating2), (rating1, rating2)
...
# Can now compute similarities.
moviePairSimilarities =
moviePairRatings.mapValues(computeCosineSimilarity).cache()
```

I don't want to get too much into this from a mathematical standpoint, but it is basically a metric of how similar two vectors are, in this case, two vectors of ratings. It uses that to determine the similarity score between these two movies. Go up to line 23 to look at what it does:

```
def computeCosineSimilarity(ratingPairs):
    numPairs = 0
    sum_xx = sum_yy = sum_xy = 0
    for ratingX, ratingY in ratingPairs:
        sum_xx += ratingX * ratingX
        sum_yy += ratingY * ratingY
        sum_xy += ratingX * ratingY
        numPairs += 1
```

As it is sort of a cosine-like function, a strong similarity will be a rather high number close to 1.0, but less than 1.0. For example, 0.95 would be a good similarity. As we mentioned in the previous section, we're going to cache that result because we're going to need to use that movie pair of similarities RDD more than once:

```
moviePairSimilarities =
moviePairRatings.mapValues(computeCosineSimilarity).cache()
```

If we didn't do that and called more than one action on movie pair similarities, then we would be in trouble. We'd have to go back and recompute it all over again, which would be a shame. Now, if you want to, you can actually save the results to text files and go examine them offline later. If you want to do that, you can uncomment the following lines. This is just a little example of how you can use the `saveAsTextFile` method to actually output the results to text files:

```
# Save the results if desired
# moviePairSimilarities.sortByKey()
# moviePairSimilarities.saveAsTextFile("movie-sims")
```

Now, bear in mind, on my four-core computer, we would get four different output files, right? So each individual executor will end up writing out its own results. You would have to combine those together by hand at the end-just something to keep in mind.

Next, we'll introduce another concept. We're going to take in an input parameter on the script that indicates the movie that I care about, the one we want to get similarities for, and just extract the similarities for that one movie:

```
# Extract similarities for the movie we care about that are "good".
if (len(sys.argv) > 1):

    scoreThreshold = 0.97
    coOccurenceThreshold = 50
```

If we do provide an argument to the script, we're going to go look for that movie ID:

```
movieID = int(sys.argv[1])
```

Then we'll run the filter operation to filter out only movies that actually include the movie that I am interested in. Let's say we pass in movie ID 50, which is `Star Wars`. We run another filter on my similarities results to extract only the similarities that include *Star Wars* in the pair, okay?

```
# Filter for movies with this sim that are "good" as defined by
# our quality thresholds above
filteredResults =
moviePairSimilarities.filter(lambda((pair,sim)): \
(pair[0] == movieID or pair[1] == movieID) \
and sim[0] > scoreThreshold and sim[1] > coOccurenceThreshold)
```

Furthermore, we introduce a minimum threshold on the quality of the similarity:

```
and sim[0] > scoreThreshold and sim[1] > coOccurenceThreshold)
```

We do this by saying I only want results that have a score greater than 0.97 and have at least 50 different people that watch the same pair. This gives us more confidence in the quality of the results:

```
scoreThreshold = 0.97
coOccurenceThreshold = 50
```

If I were to allow similarities between movies that are only watched by one or two people, I'd get a lot of spurious results that didn't make sense. This is a very important thing to take into account.

Finally, we sort the final result by the quality score. We do the usual trick here of flipping the key and value to actually get the thing we want to sort by in the key and then `sortByKey`. We do it in the descending order and take the top 10:

```
# Sort by quality score.
results = filteredResults.map(lambda((pair,sim)): (sim,
pair)).sortByKey(ascending = False).take(10)
```

This is a one-line way of flipping the RDD to sort it by the similarity score in reverse order and take the top 10 results. Then we can print those results out. I'm going through this a little quickly, so if you're struggling just go back over things on your own, it's mostly self-explanatory if you think it through.

Getting results

Let's go ahead and do it! As I mentioned earlier, this is a very complicated example, the most complicated that we'll see in this book. If you need to go back and stare at it some more, please do. Open up **Canopy Command Prompt** and type movie-similarities.py, and remember, we need to take a parameter for the movie ID I care about, which is movie ID 50, Star Wars, run the following command:

```
<User> c:\SparkCourse>spark-submit movie-similarities.py 50
```

The movie names lookup table will be loaded and start running. You're going to see a bunch of stuff here that you haven't seen before because we're actually running this using Spark's built-in cluster manager this time. It's actually going to tell us how the cluster manager is progressing, where it's treating each core of my desktop computer as an individual executor node:

```
Loading movie names...
[Stage 0:>                                                          (0 + 0) / 4]
[Stage 0:>                                                          (0 + 4) / 4]
[Stage 0:==============================>                            (2 + 2) / 4]
[Stage 0:=============================================>             (3 + 1) / 4]
[Stage 1:>                                                          (0 + 4) / 4]
[Stage 1:=============>                                             (1 + 3) / 4]
[Stage 1:==============================>                            (2 + 2) / 4]
[Stage 1:=============================================>             (3 + 1) / 4]
[Stage 2:>                                                          (0 + 4) / 4]
[Stage 2:=============================================>             (3 + 1) / 4]

[Stage 5:>                                                          (0 + 4) / 4]
[Stage 5:==============================>                            (2 + 2) / 4]
[Stage 5:=============================================>             (3 + 1) / 4]

[Stage 8:>                                                          (0 + 4) / 4]
[Stage 8:=============>                                             (1 + 3) / 4]
[Stage 8:=============================================>             (3 + 1) / 4]
```

This is going to take a little bit of time. We have a hundred thousand ratings, and remember that self-join is going to create an entry for every possible combination of movies watched together by the same person. This ends up being a very large amount of data. Here are our results:

```
Top 10 similar movies for Star Wars (1977)
Empire Strikes Back, The (1980) score: 0.989552207839    strength: 345
Return of the Jedi (1983)    score: 0.985723086125    strength: 480
Raiders of the Lost Ark (1981)  score: 0.981760098873    strength: 380
20,000 Leagues Under the Sea (1954)    score: 0.97893856055    strength: 68
12 Angry Men (1957)    score: 0.977657612045    strength: 109
Close Shave, A (1995)    score: 0.977594829105    strength: 92
African Queen, The (1951)    score: 0.976469222267    strength: 138
Sting, The (1973)    score: 0.975151293774    strength: 204
Wrong Trousers, The (1993)    score: 0.974868135546    strength: 103
Wallace & Gromit: The Best of Aardman Animation (1996)   score: 0.97418161283
strength: 58

<User> c:\SparkCourse>
```

We have some real results here based on real data and real ratings. It turns out, in the top 10 similar movies for *Star Wars*, the first few results are exactly what I would expect, The Empire Strikes Back, Return of the Jedi, and Raiders Of The Lost Ark. 20,000 Leagues Under the Sea is fourth-I can go with that. Things start to get a little bit weird after that. I mean, to be honest though, I'm a *Star Wars* fan and I've seen a lot of these movies and I liked them. Remember, a lot of these results have to be taken within the context of 1998 when this dataset was published.

We got pretty good results, they're not awesome but they're pretty good. Let's talk about something you can do to try to make it better. This is an exercise for the reader and there's a lot you can do, there's a whole art and even a science to making good movie similarities data. This is just one technique and there are definitely better techniques out there. In our next section, we'll introduce a learning activity that let's you dive in and do just that.

Improving the quality of the similar movies example

Now it's time for your homework assignment. Your mission, should you choose to accept it, is to dive into this code and try to make the quality of our similarities better. It's really a subjective task; the objective here is to get you to roll up your sleeves, dive in, and start messing with this code to make sure that you understand it. You can modify it and get some tangible results out of your changes. Let me give you some pointers and some tips on what you might want to try here and we'll set you loose.

We used a very naive algorithm to find similar movies in the previous section with a cosine similarity metric. The results, as we saw, weren't that bad, but maybe they could be better. There are ways to actually measure the quality of a recommendation or similarity, but without getting it into that, just dive in there, try some different ideas and see what effect it has, and maybe they qualitatively will look better to you. At the end of the day, maybe that's all the matters. Here are some ideas and some simple things to try:

- Discard bad ratings:
    - Maybe you could just try throwing out any movie that has a bad rating. If someone rates something 1 star, is that really useful for your purposes? I mean, strictly speaking, it lets you see that bad movies are similar to each other, but at the end of the day, do you really want to be recommending bad movies to people? I don't think so. So if that's your intended use of this information, try just filtering out the bad ratings and see what that does.
- Try different similarity metrics:
    - You can try things such as the Pearson correlation coefficient or Jaccard coefficient that we could replace our cosine metric with and see what you get. Some of these might be better, might be worse, there's only one way to find out.
- Adjust the thresholds for the minimum co-raters or minimum score:
    - Maybe we're just not being picky enough with the final results.
- Invent a new similarity metric that takes the number of co-raters into account:
    - Maybe we don't really need that minimum threshold for minimum co-raters. Maybe we could just take that into account as part of the actual similarity itself, and automatically account for how much confidence we have in that relationship.
- Boost scores from movies in the same genre:
    - The u.items folder in the MovieLens dataset contains things such as genre information, so it might be interesting to extract that information and give a boost to movies that are in the same genre. For example, maybe similar movies to *Star Wars* that are science fiction films should count a little bit more, right?

Just dive in there, give it a try, see what you come up with. Have some fun with it. It's an interesting problem, it kept me occupied for a few years, so play around with it, get familiar with this script, it's a complicated one! There's no right or wrong answer here. As long as you have results that make sense and your script still works, consider yourself successful. We're not going to come back and compare your improvements to mine because there are infinite ways to actually approach this problem, I just want you to get in there and get some more familiarity with Spark in your development environment, that's the real goal here.

Summary

We've covered a lot of ground in this chapter, and I hope it's given you an idea of the kinds of things that you can do with Spark and the power that it gives you. Please do continue to explore and experiment with these examples, altering things to see how they function and gaining familiarity with the workings of Spark. In the next chapter, we're going to turn our attention to the cloud and start working with really big data when we find out how to run Spark on a cluster.

4
Running Spark on a Cluster

Now it's time to graduate off of your desktop computer and actually start running some Spark jobs in the cloud on an actual Spark cluster.

Introducing Elastic MapReduce

The easiest way to actually get up and running on a cluster, if you don't already have a Spark cluster, is using Amazon's Elastic MapReduce service. Even though it says MapReduce in the name, you can actually configure it to set up a Spark cluster for you and run that on top of Hadoop – it sets everything up for you automatically. Let's walk through what Elastic MapReduce is, how it interacts with Spark, and how to decide if it's really something you want to be messing with.

Why use Elastic MapReduce?

Using Amazon's Elastic MapReduce service is an easy way to rent the time you need on a cluster to actually run your Spark job. You don't have to just run MapReduce jobs, you can actually run Spark and use the underlying Hadoop environment to run as your cluster manager. It has something called Hadoop YARN. If you've taken my course on MapReduce and Hadoop you will have heard of this already. Basically, YARN is Hadoop's cluster manager and Spark is able to run on top of it-that is all installed as part of Elastic MapReduce for you.

Let's back up a little bit. This is a service offered by Amazon.com. Basically, what you're doing is renting time in their massive data centers of computers. You're saying you want to rent six or seven different instances of computers that you want to run your cluster across. Instead of actually buying those computers, you're just paying by the hour. Now, Spark also has its own built-in standalone cluster manager and you can actually use that to run on EC2. It has scripts to support that as well, but I find that if you're going to be using EC2 anyway you might as well just use the Amazon web services console application on the web to launch a Spark cluster that's already set up for you. Then all you have to do is SSH into the master node in your cluster, copy your script over, and run it from there directly. I think that's a lot more straightforward than trying to figure out how to use the EC2 scripts, especially, from Python where it gets a little bit tricky.

Warning - Spark on EMR is not cheap

Now, I do want to warn you that if you have been through my course on the MapReduce and Hadoop, we also used Elastic MapReduce during that and it was dirt cheap. The reason it was dirt cheap is because we were using dirt cheap instance types, which is basically the kind of computer that we're using in our cluster. But with Spark, by default, we're using something that's a little bit more expensive, actually a lot more expensive. We're using `m3.xlarge` instances. So even though we'll see that Spark runs a lot faster, bear in mind we're using much more powerful computers than we did in the previous course. Personally, I racked up about thirty dollars in Amazon web service charges developing this course. I had to run the jobs we're going to go through to do movie recommendations on the cluster four or five times, and I ended up running about thirty dollars. I racked that up while being very careful about only splitting up these clusters when I needed them and terminating them as soon as I was done with them-they add up quickly. So please, if you are going to follow along, remember to shut down your clusters when you're done or else you're going to rack up a very big bill very quickly and you're not going to be very happy about that. If that makes you nervous, if you don't think you have the discipline to actually remember to come back and shut down that cluster and terminate when you're done running it, maybe you shouldn't actually follow along with this, and just watch me do it. There is a very real risk here that you could accidentally run up a very large bill. If you do have a corporate account with Amazon web services and you're doing this on somebody else's time, maybe that's a different story. Perhaps, you already have a cluster for Spark that you have access to through your employer that's running all the time; by all means use that. I'm just going to walk through this as an alternative so you have a way of experimenting with Spark on a cluster from home if you want to play along. But again, please make sure that after your jobs are done, you manually terminate them in the console. I'll show you how to do that later.

There is another important thing you should do to keep your costs under control. Always run things locally on your desktop on a subset of your data first. Remember, we have operations on RDDs, such as `top` and `sample`, that you can use to create a smaller sample of a dataset. By doing that, you can create a subset that you can use to work the initial kinks out of your system at least. Then, when you're actually running on the cluster, hopefully, the only bugs you're dealing with will be things that are specific to running on a cluster; that will save you a lot of time and money.

So with all that said, let's take a look at Amazon web services, go through how to set up an Elastic MapReduce account, and then we'll move on from there. If it does seem like something you want to get down and dirty with and actually create an account for, I'll walk you through some of the basics on how to get started with that next and also how to connect to it using a Terminal for a Windows system.

Setting up our Amazon Web Services / Elastic MapReduce account and PuTTY

To get started with Amazon Web Services, first we're going to walk through how to create an account on AWS if you haven't one already. When we're done, we're going to figure out how to actually connect to the instances that we might be spinning up on Web Services. When we create a cluster for Spark, we need a way to log in to the master node on that cluster and actually run our script there. To do so, we need to get our credentials for logging in to any instances that our Spark cluster spins up. We'll also set up a Terminal, if you're on Windows, called PuTTY, and go through how to actually use that to connect to your instances.

Okay, let's go through how to set up an Amazon Web Services account and get started with Elastic MapReduce. We'll also figure out how to connect to our instances on Elastic MapReduce. Head over to `aws.amazon.com`:

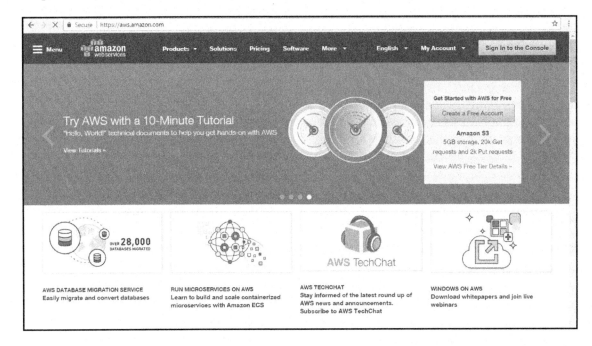

As I mentioned in the previous section, if you don't want to risk spending money, it might be best not to follow along on your computers at this point. You're going to need a credit card number to sign up for an account here, it's going to cost some real money and it can actually add up. To get a sense of the current pricing, you can click on the **Pricing** tab on Amazon Web Service homepage, click on Products and Services, and then click on **Amazon Elastic Compute Cloud (EC2)**. The primary cost of our clusters that we'll be spinning up will be for renting time on these computers:

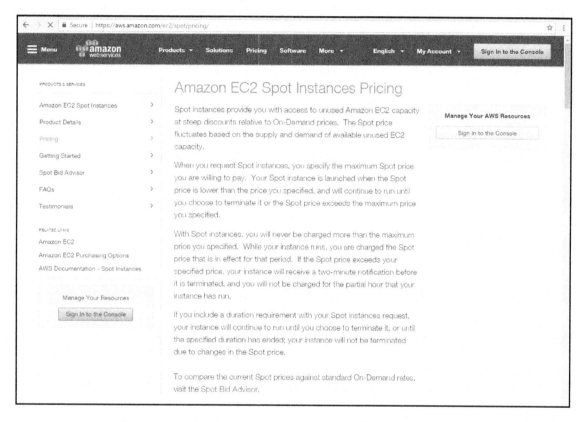

If you scroll down, you can see how much individual types of instances cost:

t2.small	1	Variable	2	EBS Only	$0.026 per Hour
t2.medium	2	Variable	4	EBS Only	$0.052 per Hour
t2.large	2	Variable	8	EBS Only	$0.104 per Hour
m4.large	2	6.5	8	EBS Only	$0.126 per Hour
m4.xlarge	4	13	16	EBS Only	$0.252 per Hour
m4.2xlarge	8	26	32	EBS Only	$0.504 per Hour
m4.4xlarge	16	53.5	64	EBS Only	$1.008 per Hour
m4.10xlarge	40	124.5	160	EBS Only	$2.52 per Hour
m3.medium	1	3	3.75	1 x 4 SSD	$0.067 per Hour
m3.large	2	6.5	7.5	1 x 32 SSD	$0.133 per Hour
m3.xlarge	4	13	15	2 x 40 SSD	$0.266 per Hour
m3.2xlarge	8	26	30	2 x 80 SSD	$0.532 per Hour

Compute Optimized - Current Generation

By default, an EMR cluster for Spark is going to spin up `m3.xlarge` instances; these are 4 CPU, 15 GB apiece instances, so these are very beefy:

m3.xlarge	4	13	15	2 x 40 SSD	$0.266 per Hour

Twenty-six cents per hour may not sound like much but it can add up! That's actually a very reasonable rate for a computer that is powerful, grant them that, but if you're running 10 of these things in a cluster, all of a sudden that's two dollars and sixty cents per hour, and if you're running 10 of these for 10 hours then you're now up to twenty-six dollars. If you were to run that for a whole month and not even realize it and just get the bill at the end, I don't want think about how much money that would be. So, do exercise caution if you're going to do this yourself. If you're confident in your ability to shut things down when you're done, and you have some extra money to spend, by all means sign up here and follow along with me, otherwise, let me incur the expense.

If you need an account, just click on the **Sign In to the Console** link in the top right-hand corner:

You will see a screen that allows you to either enter your username and password or create a new account. At this point, if you were to create a new account, it would ask you for all of your personal and credit card information, and it would phone you as part of a two-factor authentication process to make sure that you are who you say you are. After you get through all of that stuff, you should eventually arrive at a screen that looks like this, which is the AWS console:

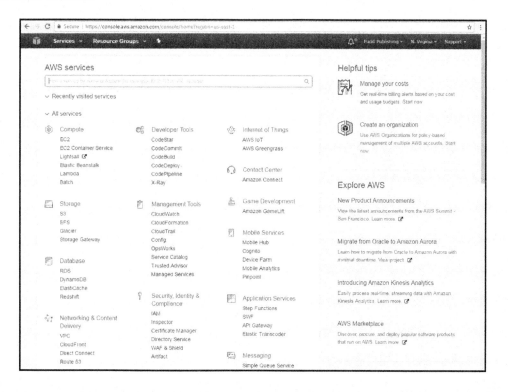

If you ever need to get to this screen, it's always available through the little cube icon at the left-hand corner:

We're going to be doing a lot of work with EMR, the Elastic MapReduce product from Amazon Web Services, which is under the **Analytics** section on this page:

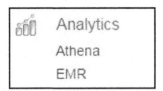

EMR is not just MapReduce, it's actually a managed Hadoop framework, so it spins up a Hadoop cluster for you, and that includes Spark as well. You can use the YARN component of Hadoop as a cluster manager that Spark runs on top of. By kicking off an EMR cluster in Amazon Web Services, you can very quickly get a master node and as many slave nodes as you want for the job that you have at hand-maybe one is all you need, given that you have four cores in a pretty powerful computer. It gives you everything you need, it deploys all the software you need automatically, all you have to do is log in to your master node on the cluster, copy your script there, make sure any data that it needs is accessible to it, and run it. That's it! It's very easy to use. First, however, you need a way to actually connect to those instances once you've spun them up. To do that, you're going to need login authentication credentials, which means you need to get a private/public key pair that you can use for signing in to your EMR cluster.

Let's click on the EC2 service under the **Compute** heading on this page:

EC2 (Elastic Compute Cloud) is the underlying service that EMR uses to actually spin up the different computers in the cluster. After you've clicked on the EC2 service, click on **Key Pairs** over in the side bar. Then you have to click on **Create Key Pair**:

Name it something you'll remember. I've already created one called `sparkkey`, so you might want to call the same thing. When you click on **create**, it will download a `sparkkey.pem` file to your `downloads` folder, which contains your public/private key pair. Make sure you actually download that file, keep it somewhere safe and back it up somewhere because once you've downloaded it here, you can never get it again. You can always create a new one if you need to, but for security reasons they make it impossible to actually redownload your public/private key. That's in case somebody breaks into your AWS console account; they don't want them to be able to gain the credentials to actually get into all the computers on your cluster and rack up a big bill for you. I've downloaded `sparkkey.pem` into my `SparkCourse` folder.

If you're on Windows, you're also going to need some sort of Terminal application so you can log in to your master node on the cloud, get your scripts and run them. I recommend a program called PuTTY if you need a Terminal for Windows and don't have one already. Search for PuTTY online and it will bring you to a website that looks like the following screenshot, not very fancy, and PuTTY itself isn't very fancy either, but it works:

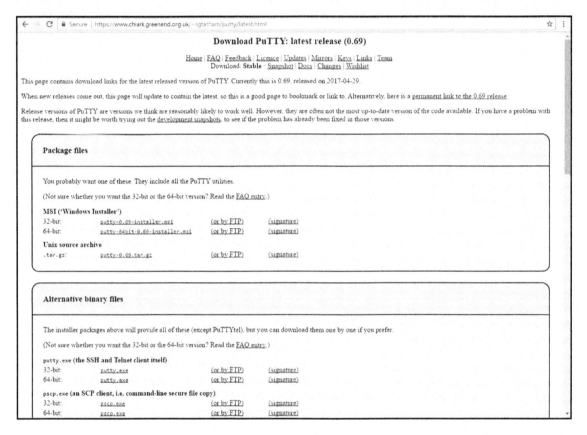

You can either install the full Windows installer or you can just install the pieces you need. The only parts you actually need are putty.exe, which is the terminal application itself and puttygen.exe. We need puttygen.exe to convert our .pem file, which contains our public/private key pair, to a .ppk file that PuTTY can use. Go and download them into your SparkCourse folder. Then, open up puttygen.exe and click on **Load**:

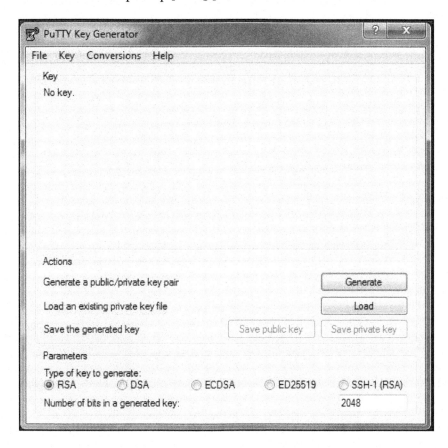

What you need to do is change the drop-down for the file filter to **All Files (*.*)**:

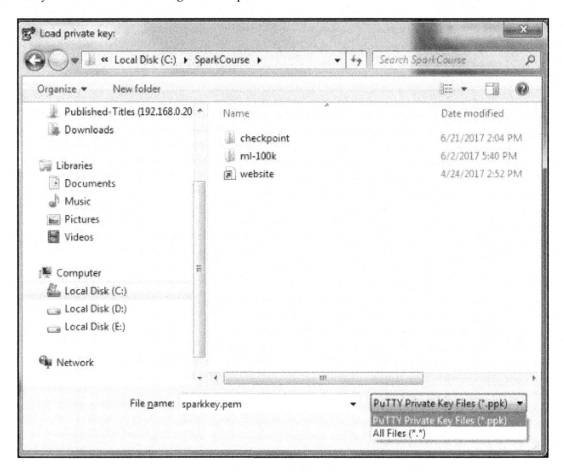

Then select your `sparkkey.pem` file:

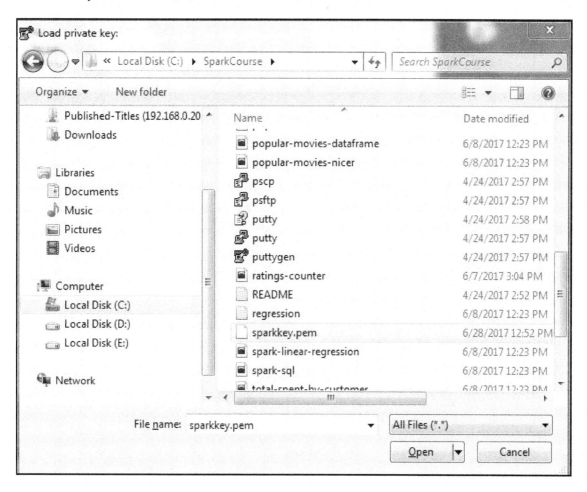

In order to save it as a PPK file that PuTTY can actually use, you now need to save it as a private key:

I'll leave the **Key passphrase** box empty because it just makes life a lot more complicated when you're actually trying to use this key file. As long as you have good physical security for your desktop, I wouldn't worry about it too much. If it does make you more comfortable to have a passphrase, put one in, but it's not as necessary as you might think. So, I'll click on **Save private key**. It'll warn me that I don't have a passphrase, but yeah, that's fine with me:

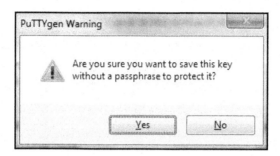

Now I'll save it as `sparkkey.ppk`:

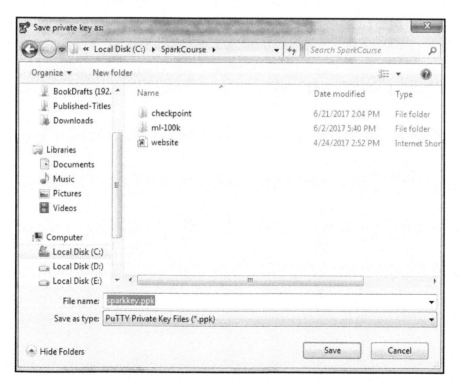

At this point, we have a `sparkkey.ppk` file that will let you log in to any cluster that you spin up using the `sparkkey` key pair later on.

Let's open up PuTTY itself to see how we use our PPK file within PuTTY. Double-click on `putty.exe` in your `SparkCourse` folder:

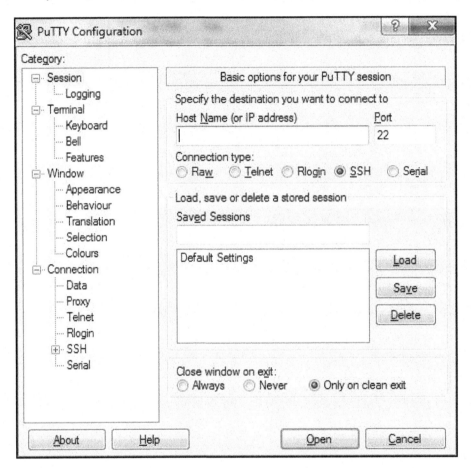

When you actually spin up your cluster, you'll get back a hostname that you can use to log in to the master node of your Spark cluster. However, the first thing you want to do is go to the **SSH** tab, open it up, and click on **Auth**:

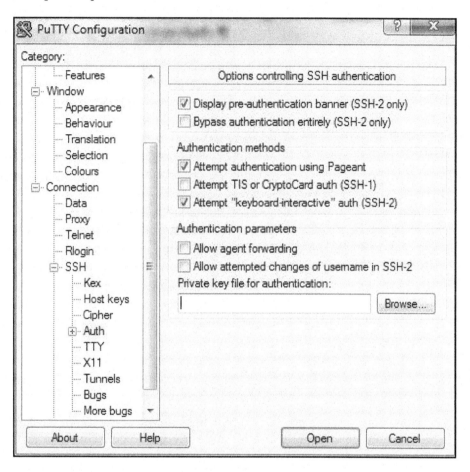

Here you will select your PPK file, so click on **Browse...** and locate that:

Once you have done that, you can just click on the **Session** tab at the top of the category list and enter in the **Host Name** field of the master node of your cluster. This allows you to log in automatically without having to sign in with username and password, which is actually more secure:

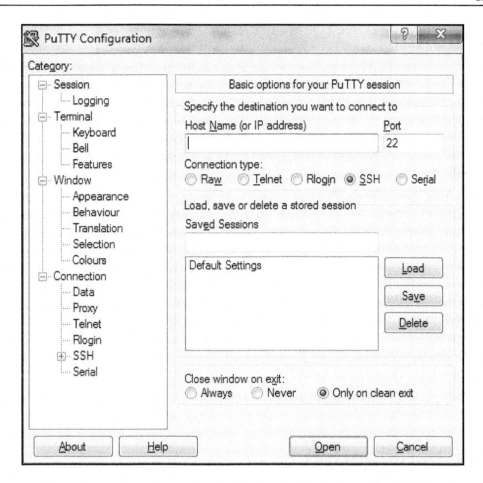

So there you have it, you have an **EMR(Elastic MapReduce)** Amazon Web Services account ready to go, you have a Terminal ready, and you are able to connect to that cluster as soon as you spin it up. We want to make sure we have all these pieces in place beforehand because time is money on that cluster once we spin it up. We're ready to spin up a cluster and connect to it. I'm not going to actually connect to it yet though, because as soon as I spin up that cluster, the clock's going to start ticking and my bill is going to start getting run up. Wait until the last second to actually do that because this really costs money and you should be very careful if you're actually going to be running these clusters yourself. I cannot caution you enough to be careful when you're experimenting with EMR and running Spark in the cloud. For that reason, you might want to consider just following along without joining in yourself here.

Partitioning

Now that we are running on a cluster, we need to modify our driver script a little bit. We'll look at the movie similarity sample again and figure out how we can scale that up to actually use a million movie ratings. To do so, you can't just run it as is and hope for the best, you wouldn't succeed if you were to do that. Instead, we have to think about things such as how is this data going to be partitioned? It's not hard, but it is something you need to address in your script. In this section we'll cover partitioning and how to use it in your Spark script.

Let's get on with actually running our `movie-similarities` script on a cluster. This time we're going to talk about throwing a million ratings at it instead of a hundred thousand ratings. Now, if we were to just modify our script to use the 1 million rating dataset from `grouplens.org`, it's not going to run on your desktop obviously. The main reason is that when we use `self-join` to generate every possible combination of movie pairs, it blows up like you wouldn't believe. You'll run out of memory and your job will fail pretty quickly if you just run it on your desktop. Even if you were to run it on a cluster on Elastic MapReduce, no matter how many computers you throw at it, it's still not going to run. When you just run it as is, your executors will start failing and they'll just hang, you won't know why and it's not very easy to track down what's going on. There are lots of things about Spark that I love, but one thing that's not so hot is that it does not automatically optimally spread out the work of your job throughout a cluster; you have to think about that yourself and deal with it manually to some extent. This is where partitioning comes in.

Using .partitionBy()

The `partitionBy()` method is on an RDD that you can use to say, "I'm going to run some large operation and I know I have enough compute resources to actually split this up into many different executors, many different runs", This tells you how many pieces we want to break this job up into. If we call `partitionBy()` on the RDD that we do a self-join operation on first, we can then split it up into smaller chunks that a given executor can actually deal with. Then our job will complete successfully. Once you do that, Spark will attempt to preserve that partitioning going forward.

I want you to take a look at this list of different RDD methods:

- `Join()`
- `cogroup()`
- `groupWith()`
- `join()`
- `leftOuterJoin()`
- `rightOuterJoin()`
- `groupByKey()`
- `reduceByKey()`
- `combineByKey()`
- `lookup()`

Some of these methods are very common. We've used `groupByKey()` and `reduceByKey()` a lot. We've used `Join()` in this `movie-similarities` example already. Anytime you call one of these operations on a very large RDD, they will benefit if you use `partitionBy()` on it beforehand. Keep that in mind. As part of your code review, before running a large job on a cluster, look for places where you're calling any of these methods and ask yourself, do I need to call `partitionBy` on it first? Odds are you do.

Choosing a partition size

So how do I choose the argument for `partitionBy()`? How many partitions is the right partition size? If you have too few partitions, it won't take full advantage of your cluster, it can't spread it out effectively. On the other hand, if you have too many you end up shuffling data around and breaking things up into chunks that are too small; there's some overhead associated with running an individual executor job, so you don't want too many executors either. You want at least as many partitions as you have cores in your cluster or as many will fit in your available memory. A hundred is usually a reasonable place to start. Let's say you have five or ten computers in your cluster-that will split it up into a reasonable amount of operations. I found that 100 actually worked well on my own example across a cluster of ten computers.

Let's go back and make some modifications to our movie-similarities scripts to make it work on the 1 million ratings dataset. We'll also make it work on a cluster by making sure we think about partitions. At this point, we know about partitioning and we have the tools we need to go back to our `movie-similarities` script and modify it to work with a much larger set of ratings.

Creating similar movies from one million ratings - part 1

Let's modify our `movie-similarities` script to actually work on the 1 million ratings dataset and make it so it can run in the cloud on Amazon Elastic MapReduce, or any Spark cluster for that matter. So, if you haven't already, go grab the `movie-similarities-1m` Python script from the download package for this book, and save it wherever you want to. It's actually not that important where you save this one because we're not going to run it on your desktop anyway, you just need to look at it and know where it is. Open it up, just so we can take a peek, and I'll walk you through the stuff that we actually changed:

```python
import sys
from pyspark import SparkConf, SparkContext
from math import sqrt

#To run on EMR successfully + output results for Star Wars:
#aws s3 cp s3://sundog-spark/MovieSimilarities1M.py ./
#aws s3 sp c3://sundog-spark/ml-1m/movies.dat ./
#spark-submit --executor-memory 1g MovieSimilarities1M.py 260

def loadMovieNames():
    movieNames = {}
    with open("movies.dat") as f:
        for line in f:
            fields = line.split("::")
            movieNames[int(fields[0])] = fields[1].decode('ascii', 'ignore')
    return movieNames

def makePairs((user, ratings)):
    (movie1, rating1) = ratings[0]
    (movie2, rating2) = ratings[1]
    return ((movie1, movie2), (rating1, rating2))
```

Changes to the script

Now, first of all, we made some changes so that it uses the 1 million ratings dataset from Grouplens instead of the 100,000 ratings dataset. If you want to grab that, go over to `grouplens.org` and click on **datasets**:

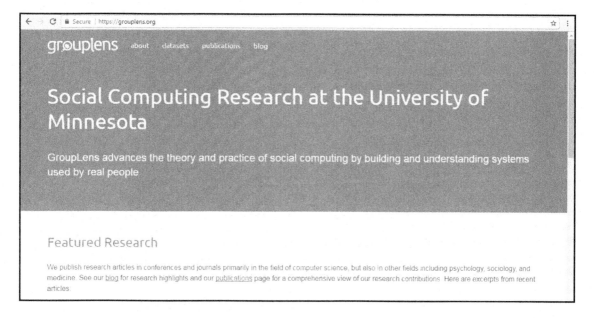

You'll find it in the **MovieLens 1M Dataset**:

MovieLens 1M Dataset

Stable benchmark dataset. 1 million ratings from 6000 users on 4000 movies. Released 2/2003.

- README.txt
- ml-1m.zip (size: 6 MB, checksum)

Permalink: http://grouplens.org/datasets/movielens/1m/

This data is a little bit more current, it's from 2003. They do have a current dataset that is updated as of this month, but you're going to need a pretty large cluster to handle the 40 million plus ratings in that dataset, so let's stick with 1 million for now, just to keep costs under control if nothing else. Go ahead and download that if you want to. When you get it, you'll see that it's structured a little bit differently, and we need to account for that in our script.

Go back to the `movie-similarities.py` script. If you look at line 12, you should see that the movie ID to movie name lookup table is now in a file called `movies.dat`. We need to make sure that this file exists in the same directory as our driver script when we're running this on the master node of our cluster:

```
def loadMovieNames():
    movieNames = {}
    with open("movies.dat") as f:
        for line in f:
            fields = line.split("::")
            movieNames[int(fields[0])] = fields[1].decode('ascii',
'ignore')
    return movieNames
```

The function that just loads up that dictionary of movie ID to movie names is going to look locally in our current directory for `movies.dat`. We know that's actually delimited by this double colon in line 14, which is kind of a new format:

```
fields = line.split("::")
```

Otherwise, it's doing the same thing as before.

There are other things that I changed. Go to line 53. You'll notice that we're loading the actual ratings data from s3:

```
data = sc.textFile("s3n://sundog-spark/ml-1m/ratings.dat")
```

This is Amazon's simple storage service. It is actually a distributed and redundant data store, so if you are going to be dealing with really big data, often it's data that's going to be living in the cloud itself on some distributed file system. If you have an HDFS data store, you can also have an HDFS URI here if you wanted to. This basically tells Spark to go out to Amazon's s3 service, with this s3n URL, and look in the sundog-spark bucket that I created. There, it knows where to find the large `ratings.dat` file that I got from the Grouplens 1M ratings dataset. Technically speaking, you should install this yourself in your own s3 bucket. You're supposed to go get it from their website and not from me, according to their license agreement, but hey, the secret's safe with me.

The other thing I changed is the format of that data file for ratings. It's also delimited by these double colon characters- (`"::"`):

```
# Map ratings to key / value pairs: user ID => movie ID, rating
ratings = data.map(lambda l: l.split("::")).map(lambda l:
    (int(l[0]), (int(l[1]), float(l[2]))))
```

There's one other thing worth pointing out. Notice in line 47, when I'm creating `SparkContext`, that my `SparkConf` object is empty:

```
conf = SparkConf()
sc = SparkContext(conf = conf)
```

I'm not putting anything in here at all for what the master is or what the name is because, instead, I'm going to pass that on the command line when I actually run the script on the master. By doing so, I can take advantage of some preconfigured stuff on **EMR (Elastic MapReduce)**, which will automatically tell Spark to run on top of Hadoop YARN, using the cluster that I created with EMR. So, if I were to actually keep my master equals local here, it would only run on the master node and that's certainly not what we want. By leaving that empty, it will fall back to the command-line arguments and the built-in configuration files for Spark that Amazon sets up for me. This is a very important point: if I did not change that, I wouldn't really be running on a cluster at all and I would not have very good results.

So that's pretty much it. The main differences here again, just to recap, are that I have moved `textFile` to be in the cloud from `s3`:

```
data = sc.textFile("s3n://sundog-spark/ml-1m/ratings.dat")
```

I have left my Spark configuration empty:

```
conf = SparkConf()
sc = SparkContext(conf = conf)
```

I have changed the format in the file names of the data file to actually account for the differences between MovieLens' 1 million rating dataset and the 100, 000 ratings dataset:

```
# Map ratings to key / value pairs: user ID => movie ID, rating
ratings = data.map(lambda l: l.split("::")).map(lambda l:
    (int(l[0]), (int(l[1]), float(l[2]))))
```

We're just about ready to start spinning things up and start playing with it. Everything else in this script is pretty much the same.

One other note is that the IDs for movies have changed between the 100,000 and 1 million movie rating dataset. *Star Wars* is no longer movie ID 50, it's movie ID 260. I left myself a little bit of a cheat sheet up in lines 5-8, outlining how to actually run this on the cluster when we get there. We'll talk about that more next:

```
#To run on EMR successfully + output results for Star Wars:
#aws s3 cp s3://sundog-spark/MovieSimilarities1M.py ./
#aws s3 sp c3://sundog-spark/ml-1m/movies.dat ./
#spark-submit --executor-memory 1g MovieSimilarities1M.py 260
```

Our code is now ready to run on a cluster on Elastic MapReduce using Spark on multiple machines. What do we actually have to do to run a script on a cluster? Let's find out.

Creating similar movies from one million ratings - part 2

Now it's time to run our similarities script on a Spark cluster in the cloud on Elastic MapReduce. This is a pretty big deal, it's kind of the culmination of the whole course here, so let's kick it off and see what happens.

Our strategy

Before we actually run our script on a Spark cluster using Amazon's Elastic MapReduce service, let's talk about some of the basic strategies that we're going to use to do that.

Specifying memory per executor

Like we talked about earlier, we're going to use the default empty `SparkConf` in the driver script. That way we'll use the defaults that Elastic MapReduce sets up for us, and that will automatically tell Spark that it should be running on top of EMR's Hadoop cluster manager. Then it will automatically know what the layout of the cluster is, who the master is, how many client machines I have, who they are, how many executors they have, and so on. Now, when we're actually running this, we're going to pass one extra argument to `spark-submit`. In the past, we always just called `spark-submit` followed by the script name and whatever parameters we were passing into it. However, there's a bunch of other options you can pass in to. Specifically, we're going to pass in `--executor-memory 1g`. This is because I know from past experience that if I try to run this with a default memory of 512 MB per executor, that's not enough for that self-join operation to succeed:

```
spark-submit --executor-memory 1g MovieSimilarities1M.py 260
```

So by passing `--executor-memory 1g`, I'm saying I want 1 GB of memory per executor. That should give me plenty to work with throughout that partition that's been broken up into 100 partitions for that self-join. Anything lower just won't work. Really, the only way to figure this out is through trial and error, unfortunately. I tried the default setting of 512 MB and my executors kept failing, I then increased it to 1 GB and everything was happy. There's no real science to it, you have to experiment with what works and try to do that experimentation as quickly as possible because time is money on these clusters.

Specifying a cluster manager

There are other options you can pass in as well, for example, `--master yarn` will tell `spark-submit` explicitly to run on a YARN cluster, but EMR actually sets that up for us by default. However, if you're running on your own cluster, you might need to pass that in by hand.

Running on a cluster

Ahead of time, I copied everything to AWS's S3 service, just so I can quickly access all of the scripts and data files that I need. I can use that to quickly copy over my script from S3 and also refer to my "big data" using S3 and URL. This means that I can just load my data directly from Amazon's S3 service. One of the good things about using Amazon Web Service's EMR cluster is that it has very fast and very good connectivity to S3, so S3 becomes a good choice for a distributed file system to use together with EMR. You can use `s3n://` URLs when specifying file paths. You can also spin up an HDFS file system as well if you want to.

The next thing we'll do will be to spin up a EMR cluster for Spark using the AWS console. The clock starts ticking on our bill at this point. As soon as those clusters become available, we'll get the external DNS name for the master node and log into it using PuTTY. We will then copy our driver program, shown here:

```
using aws s3 cp s3://bucket-name/filename ./
```

We'll then run it and watch the output. As soon as we're done, we're going to terminate that cluster so that we stop getting billed. If you do decide to follow along with me in this exercise, don't forget to terminate the cluster when we're done! Let's go and start the process.

Setting up to run the movie-similarities-1m.py script on a cluster

Alright, it's time to actually run this script on a real Spark cluster in the cloud, here we go. Remember that we're going to be racking up some real charges here, it's going to cost real money to run this on Amazon Web Services, so remember to terminate your cluster when you're done. It should only cost you a few dollars to run this once, but if you have any doubts about your ability to remember to terminate this cluster, don't do it, just see how I do it. It's going to be cheaper and a lot safer that way.

Preparing the script

Open up the `movie-similarities-1m.py` script:

```
1 import sys
2 from pyspark import SparkConf, SparkContext
3 from math import sqrt
4
5 #To run on EMR successfully + output results for Star Wars:
6 #aws s3 cp s3://sundog-spark/MovieSimilarities1M.py ./
7 #aws s3 sp c3://sundog-spark/ml-1m/movies.dat ./
8 #spark-submit --executor-memory 1g MovieSimilarities1M.py 260
9
10 def loadMovieNames():
11     movieNames = {}
12     with open("movies.dat") as f:
13         for line in f:
14             fields = line.split("::")
15             movieNames[int(fields[0])] = fields[1].decode('ascii', 'ignore')
16     return movieNames
17
18 def makePairs((user, ratings)):
19     (movie1, rating1) = ratings[0]
20     (movie2, rating2) = ratings[1]
21     return ((movie1, movie2), (rating1, rating2))
22
23 def filterDuplicates( (userID, ratings) ):
24     (movie1, rating1) = ratings[0]
25     (movie2, rating2) = ratings[1]
26     return movie1 < movie2
27
28 def computeCosineSimilarity(ratingPairs):
29     numPairs = 0
30     sum_xx = sum_yy = sum_xy = 0
31     for ratingX, ratingY in ratingPairs:
32         sum_xx += ratingX * ratingX
33         sum_yy += ratingY * ratingY
34         sum_xy += ratingX * ratingY
35         numPairs += 1
36
37     numerator = sum_xy
38     denominator = sqrt(sum_xx) * sqrt(sum_yy)
39
40     score = 0
41     if (denominator):
42         score = (numerator / (float(denominator)))
43
44     return (score, numPairs)
45
46
47 conf = SparkConf()
48 sc = SparkContext(conf = conf)
```

As you can see, to make life easier, I actually went ahead and copied the `ml-1m` 1 million rating dataset to a `sundog-spark` bucket on Amazon's S3 service, so that my Spark cluster can access it:

```
#aws s3 cp s3://sundog-spark/m1-1m/movies.dat ./
```

I've also copied the script itself to my `sundog-spark` S3 bucket as well. This way I can quickly obtain a copy of it from my master node on my cluster:

```
#aws s3 cp s3://sundog-spark/MovieSimilarities1M.py ./
```

Once I spin up that cluster, the first thing I'm going to do, because time is money and the clock starts ticking right away, is call this little script shown in line 6 to copy the `MovieSimilarities1M.py` script from S3 to that master node. Then I copy the `movies.dat` file that it's going to use to load up and create our movie ID to movie name lookup table used in the final output:

```
#aws s3 cp s3://sundog-spark/m1-1m/movies.dat ./
```

Finally, I left myself a little cheat sheet, here in line 8, of what to actually run to execute this job:

```
#spark-submit --executor-memory 1g MovieSimilarities1M.py 260
```

Creating a cluster

Let's do it. Go to the `aws.amazon.com` console and sign in:

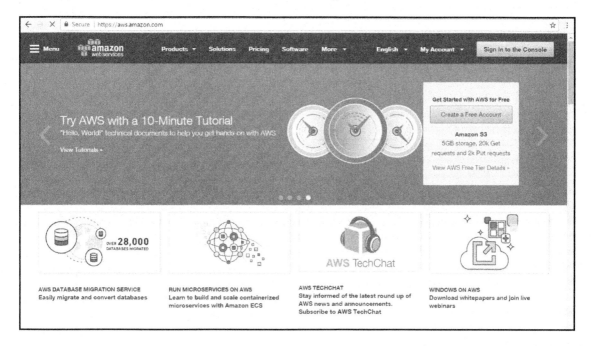

Then, click on **EMR**:

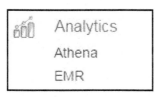

I'm going to create a new cluster, clicking on **Create cluster**:

I then get this page:

I'll type in a cluster name of *One Million Ratings*. I don't really need **Logging** because there's no easy way for me to look at it anyway, so I'll uncheck that box. Where it says **Launch mode**, I'll keep **Cluster** checked, I'm just going to go ahead and launch the cluster as opposed to using steps:

Moving down to the software configuration settings on the page, I want to use the latest EMR release. For **Applications**, I want to use Spark, so I'll check that. To save a little bit of time, I'm not going to bother installing Hive, Mahout, Pig, and stuff that I don't need, I just want Spark running on top of Hadoop's YARN cluster manager:

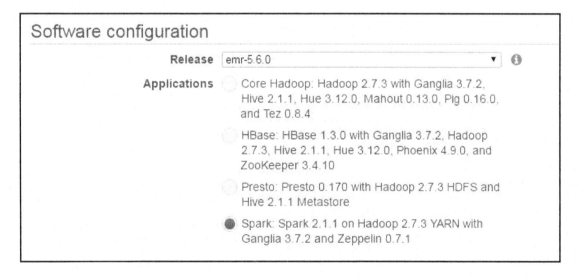

For **Hardware configuration**, I will stick with the default instance type of m3.xlarge, and the default instance number of 3. Please do feel free to go ahead and change that number to 5 or even 10 - more is definitely better here.

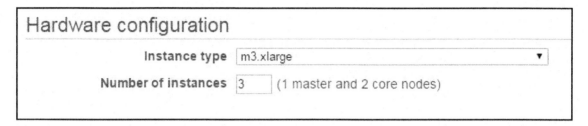

Let's move down to the **Security and access** settings. I need to choose an **EC2 key pair**. Remember, in the previous sections we actually created a key pair? I will select that now; for me, I'm using the sparkkey key pair, which will correspond to the PPK file that I'm going to use to connect to my master node using PuTTY (or whatever terminal you might have). I will leave everything else as default:

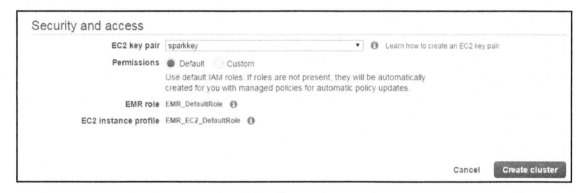

Now we can click on **Create cluster**. At this point, the bill starts adding up, so again, don't hit this button unless you're comfortable spending a few dollars here. If you're not comfortable with that, just watch me, here I go.

This is what we see when we click on **Create cluster**:

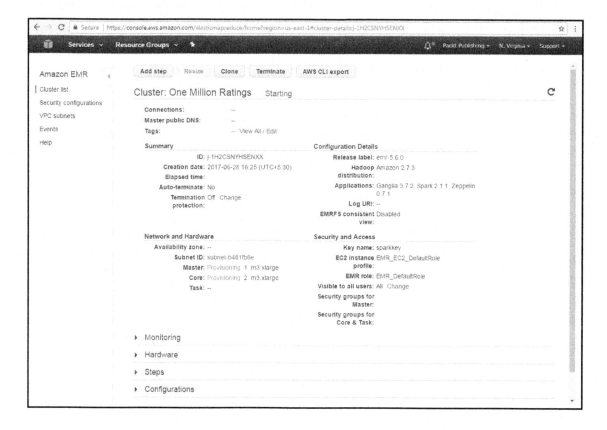

This is going to take about five minutes for these to actually get provisioned. Under the hood, Amazon's Web Services framework is going out, it's finding the available `m3.xlarge` instances in its data centers that I can have, and it's going to reserve those for me. It's going to install the operating system on them, Spark, and Hadoop. This will take a few minutes:

Network and Hardware

Availability zone: --

Subnet ID: subnet-b481fb8e

Master: Provisioning 1 m3.xlarge

Core: Provisioning 2 m3.xlarge

Task: --

Until this page stops saying provisioning and says that these systems are ready to go, we can't actually do anything quite yet.

After about 5 minutes my instances have spun up, so I now have a running master node of one `m3.xlarge` instance and have my core nodes of an `m3.xlarge` running as well:

Network and Hardware

Availability zone: us-east-1e

Subnet ID: subnet-b481fb8e

Master: Running 1 m3.xlarge

Core: Running 2 m3.xlarge

Task: --

Without further ado, let's connect to that and kick off our script.

Connecting to the master node using SSH

Up in the left-hand corner of our page, we have the public DNS name of our master node:

If you click on the **SSH** tab next to that, it will give you instructions on exactly what you need to do to connect to it. We have instructions for Windows, which I've been describing, and also for Mac and Linux. So if you are doing this from Linux or macOS, this will tell you in a little more detail what you need to do:

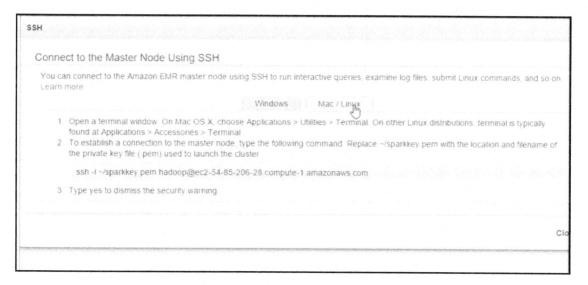

You just need that `sparkkey.pem` file that we got from the key pair from EC2 earlier and you can type in something like this to actually connect to it:

```
ssh -i ~/sparkkey.pem hadoop@ec2-54-85-206-28.compute-1.amazonws.com
```

But we are using PuTTY on Windows:

I'm going to copy this bit shown here:

```
hadoop@ec2-54-85-206-28.compute-1.amazonaws.com
```

Then I'll open PuTTY and paste that into the **Host Name** field:

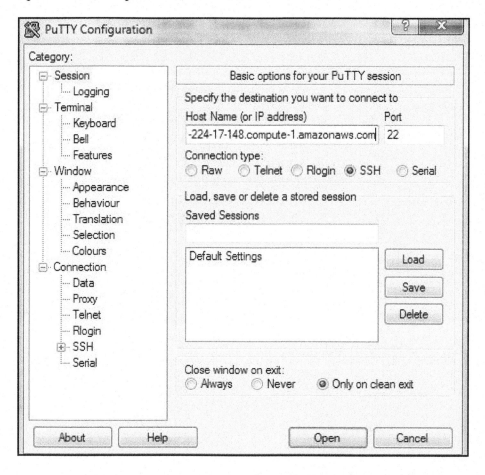

I'll go to my **SSH** section, to **Auth**, and select my PPK file that I created earlier. This should get me right in:

There we are, isn't that cute, we get some ASCII art!

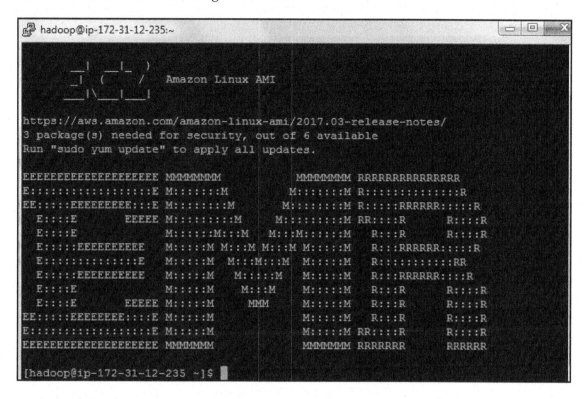

Now it's time to get busy. Let's kick this thing off.

Running the code

If you recall, I left myself a little cheat sheet in my script comments, telling me what I need to do, so let's go ahead and do all of that. The first thing I want to do is copy the script itself down. So I'm going to type in `aws s3 cp s3://sundog-spark/MovieSimilarities1M.py./`:

```
[hadoop@ip-172-31-12-235 ~]$ aws s3 cp s3://sundog-spark/MovieSimilarities1M.py ./
```

What that's going to do is go to S3 and copy my Python script and my driver script to this local directory here in my home directory:

```
download: s3://sundog-spark/MovieSimilarities1M.py to ./MovieSimilarities1M.py
[hadoop@ip-172-31-12-235 ~]$
```

I also need the lookup file for movie IDs to movie names, so let's do that next. Add `aws s3 cp s3://sundog-spark /ml-1m/movies.dat` also to the current directory:

```
[hadoop@ip-172-31-12-235 ~]$ aws s3 cp s3://sundog-spark/ml-1m/movies.dat ./
download: s3://sundog-spark/ml-1m/movies.dat to ./movies.dat
```

There we have that:

```
[hadoop@ip-172-31-12-235 ~]$
```

Finally, I'm going to kick off the job itself. Here we go, I'll type `spark-submit --executor-memory 1g` to give 1 GB of memory per executor. Then I'll type the name of the script, `MovieSimilarities1M.py`, and finally, the movie ID for *Star Wars*, which I am interested in getting similarities for-260:

```
[hadoop@ip-172-31-12-235 ~]$ spark-submit --executor-memory 1g MovieSimilarities
1M.py 260
```

Off we go.

If you're running this yourself, you'll see it's doing all sorts of stuff. We're getting a bunch of info messages that we had filtered out on our desktop configuration. However, while you're running on the cluster, you want a little bit more insight as to what's going on, in case something goes wrong. You'll see it kicking off that `sortByKey` operation with 16 output partitions and doing all sorts of good stuff. This will take a little bit of time to finish, so we'll take a look at the results in the next section when it's done. Well, there we have it, we've kicked off our job, it's running on a cluster at this point, which is pretty awesome. I'd say we're actually doing "big data" now! We'll take a look at the results in the next section.

Creating similar movies from one million ratings – part 3

About 15 minutes after I set off our `movie-similarities-1m` script on a cluster using EMR, I have some actual results to look at. Let's review what happened.

Assessing the results

Here are the results:

```
Top 10 similar movies for Star Wars: Episode IV - A New Hope (1977)
Star Wars: Episode V - The Empire Strikes Back (1980)    score: 0.989791710657    strength: 2355
Sanjuro (1962)  score: 0.987715715754    strength: 60
Raiders of the Lost Ark (1981)  score: 0.985554827857    strength: 1972
Star Wars: Episode VI - Return of the Jedi (1983)    score: 0.984124835993    strength: 2113
Run Silent, Run Deep (1958)    score: 0.979146338933    strength: 145
Laura (1944)    score: 0.978729003724    strength: 187
Close Shave, A (1995)    score: 0.978216762084    strength: 436
Wrong Trousers, The (1993)    score: 0.978051224484    strength: 596
Captain Horatio Hornblower (1951)    score: 0.977892172004    strength: 81
Indiana Jones and the Last Crusade (1989)    score: 0.977444002865    strength: 1397
```

The top similar movie to *Star Wars* Episode Four, was *Star Wars* Episode Five, not too surprising. But the next entry is a little bit surprising, some little movie called *Sanjuro* had a very high similarity score. Let's look at what's going on there. Its actual strength, the number of people that rated that together with *Star Wars*, was only 60, so I think it's safe to say that is kind of a spurious result. Now that we're using a million ratings, we probably need to increase that minimum threshold on the number of co-raters in order to actually display a result. By doing so, we could probably pretty easily filter out movies like that and instead get *Raiders of the Lost Ark* as our second result instead of as our third. I think the position of *Raiders of the Lost Ark* is interesting because it's actually scoring better than *Return Of The Jedi*. I'm no film critic, but maybe you too also enjoyed Raiders of the *Lost Ark more than Return of the Jedi*, I know I did. That's not that crazy a result. We then get *Run Silent, Run Deep* from 1958, which is another kind of a spurious result, with only 145 co-raters. This sounds like a lot of people, but in the context of a million ratings, it isn't so much.

The moral of the story is you'll often need to go back, adjust your algorithms, and clean your data a little bit differently when you're running at a larger scale in order to get the results you want. Data mining and using big data is not magic, you do not automatically get better results just because you have more data, in fact, often the opposite is true. So let that be a lesson to you. But hey, we successfully ran this thing so that's cool. Let's shut down this cluster before we forget.

Terminating the cluster

Now that I have a result, the most important thing is to remember to terminate that cluster so that I don't keep getting billed for it. Let's go to `console.aws.amazon.com`. I'll click on **EMR** and find my cluster. It is shown with the green circle next to it, which means that it is currently running, racking up a bill for me:

Let's click on that cluster and then click on **Terminate**:

Now it'll ask me if I'm sure I want to lose everything. I'm totally okay with that, just stop billing me for it. So I'll click on **Terminate**:

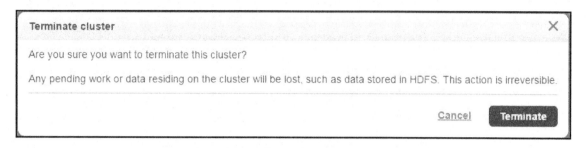

I want to make sure that actually terminates, that the status goes from running to terminated. When it does, I will stop getting billed and that's all there is to it.

We have successfully run a 1 million ratings analysis on a cluster on Elastic MapReduce using Spark on top of Hadoop, and we shut down the cluster now that we're done with it-pretty cool. Remember to terminate your cluster when you're done. I'm just going to keep saying that over and over again because I don't want you to get a big bill. If you're actually running this yourself, terminate any clusters in the Amazon Web Services console using the **EMR** tab okay? But hey, we got some results, that's awesome. You are now officially processing big data in the cloud, which is what this course is all about, so congratulations! Let's talk about troubleshooting jobs next and what you need to do when things go wrong.

Troubleshooting Spark on a cluster

So let's start talking about what we do when things go wrong with our Spark job. It has a web-based console that we can look at in some circumstances, so let's start by talking about that.

Troubleshooting Spark jobs on a cluster is a bit of a dark art. If it's not immediately obvious what is going on from the output of the Spark driver script, a lot of times what you end up doing is throwing more machines at it and throwing more memory at it, like we looked at with the executor memory option. But if you're running on your own cluster or one that you have within your own network, Spark does offer a console UI that runs by default on port 4040. It does give you a little bit more of a graphical, in-depth look as to what's going on and a way to access the logs and see which executor is doing what. This can be helpful in understanding what's happening. Unfortunately, in Elastic MapReduce, it's pretty much next to impossible to connect to Spark's UI console from outside Amazon's network.

However, but if you have your own cluster running on your own network, it might be a good option for you, so you can see what it looks like, in case you end up using a Spark cluster that's run by your employer or something where you do have access to the console. Let's take a look at Spark's UI console just running on our local machine. We'll kick off a larger similarities build script and take a peek at it to see what it looks like.

If you ever need the Spark UI console and you have local network access to your master node on your cluster, then you should be able to access it on port 4040. I'm going to kick off a script in Command Prompt that takes at least a minute. I run our original movie similarities script on my desktop:

```
(User) c:\SparkCourse>spark-submit movie-similarities.py 50
```

As soon as that starts running, I can open up a browser and navigate to localhost:4040 to open up port 4040 on my computer. You can see here that we have this display of any active jobs currently running and we can click on the displayed job to drill in and see some cool stuff:

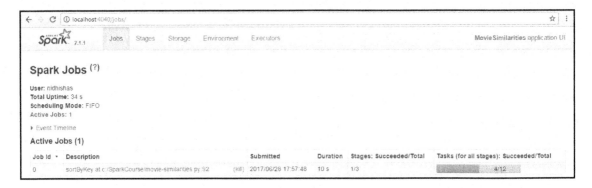

We have an actual visualization of the directed acyclic graph that Spark used:

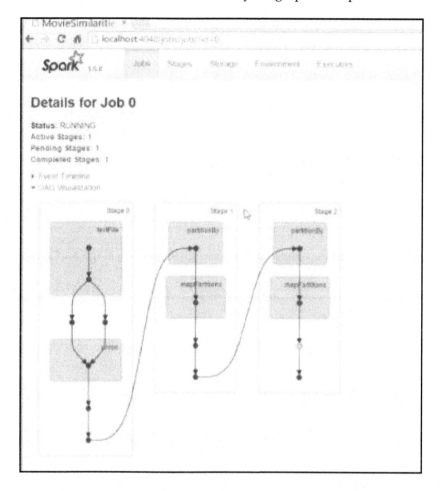

We have a timeline here that we can use for troubleshooting where all the time is being spent on our job, for example:

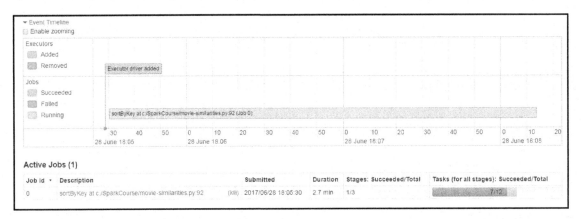

We can click on one of these, say the green **Active groupByKey** stage and get more details on it:

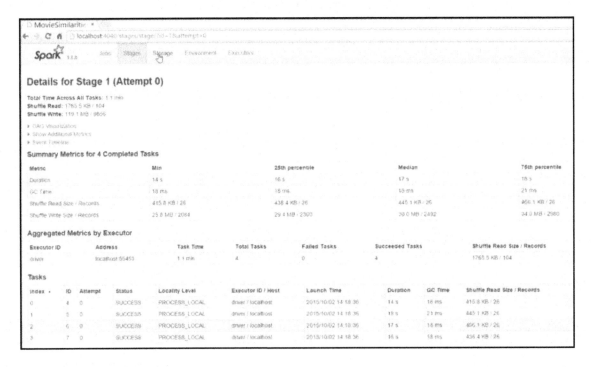

You can just drill down there and try to figure out what's taking all the time, what you might need to optimize, and what might need to be partitioned better.

Another useful thing is the **Environment** tab, which tells you all the various passing dependencies and software versions that are installed:

If you're running on a cluster that you don't necessarily have direct control over, that can be useful information.

If we look at our **Executors** tab, we can see individual executors:

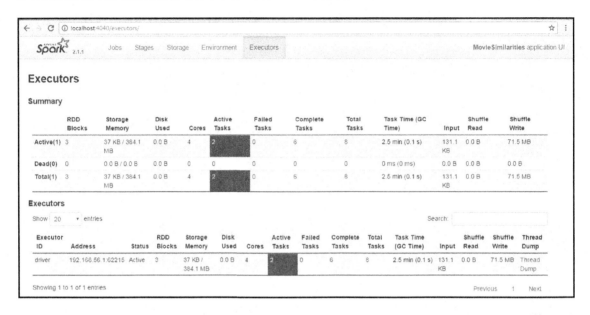

You can drill into **Thread dumps** and actually see what's going on there in as much depth as you want to:

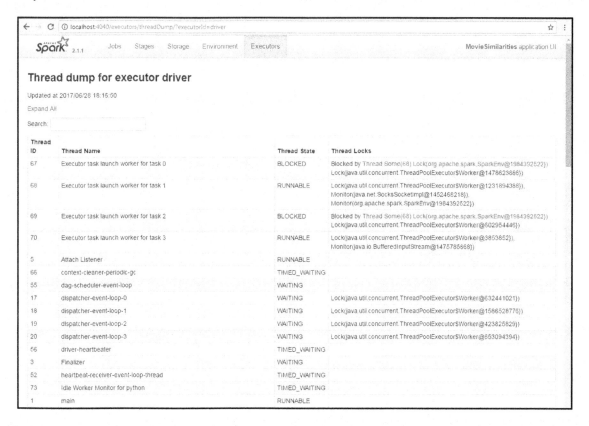

The **Stages** tab also shows you details of each individual stage running:

If you need to get more insight into where your Spark job is at, where it might be stuck at, and things you might need to optimize, this gives you all the information you might need. It's actually pretty slick. As I mentioned earlier, the Spark console is hard to get to on EMR. That might change in the future, and I hope it does. If you're running on some other cluster that you have more direct access to or even within your own network, it's a good way to figure out what's going on and to get a good sense of how long different steps are taking. You can also just watch the output of your driver script to get a good sense of what's going on, but obviously, the UI gives you a better idea of what's happening under the hood. Let's talk about some more troubleshooting tips next.

More troubleshooting and managing dependencies

In this section, I want to talk about a few more troubleshooting tips with Spark. There are weird things that will happen and have happened to me in the past when working with Spark. It's not always obvious what to do about them, so let me impart some of my experience to you here. Then we'll talk about managing code dependencies within Spark jobs as well.

Troubleshooting

So let's talk about troubleshooting a little bit more. I can tell you, I did need to do some troubleshooting to get that million ratings job running successfully on my Spark cluster. We'll start by talking about logs. Where are the logs? We saw some stuff scroll by from the driver script, and in practice, if you're running on EMR, that's pretty much all you'll have to go on. Now, as I showed you, if you're in standalone mode and you have access directly, on the network to your master node, all the log information is displayed in this beautiful graphical form in the web UI. However, when you're running on top of YARN, those logs end up getting distributed and you need to collect them after the fact using this command: `yarn logs -applicationID <app ID>`. You use that to actually bring them all back together so you can see them. Your job is distributed and therefore the logs are distributed, that makes them a little bit difficult to consolidate and see what's going on. In saying that, a lot of the time you can kind of intuit what's happening.

What happened to me when I was trying to get this movie similarities with one million ratings script running was that, when I first started running it, I kept getting errors in the driver script that said that executors were failing to issue heartbeats. It would kick off an executor to do some job and that executor would just go away and never respond again-it just hung. When that happens, it's probably a sign that you're asking too much of each executor. One thing you can do is throw more machines at it. Indeed, I found that by going up to 10 machines in my cluster it ran a lot more reliably than with four or five. It might also mean that each executor needs more memory, so they still hung unless I gave them 1 GB per executor, like we did earlier. With the default value of 512 MB, it just wasn't enough even with a hundred partitions. This brings me to the last point: you can always increase the number of partitions in order to demand less work from each individual executor job. You do this using smaller partition sizes to split up your job into smaller bits. Whenever you have executors that just get hung and start losing their heartbeat, Spark's going to start to try to destroy those executors and create new ones to try again, but after about four tries, it will just give up and your entire job will fail.

So, even though Spark in Hadoop and YARN bill themselves as being extremely fault-tolerant, at the end of the day, if you're asking too much of one of your executors and it just plain can't do it, your job will still fail. Don't rely on fault-tolerance from Hadoop to ensure that your script will run successfully because there is no such guarantee. Once you've configured things such that you are asking a reasonable amount of work from each executor, then yeah, fault-tolerance does what it should be doing. If you have a genuine failure of one of your nodes or some weird network area, then it can recover from that. But nothing Hadoop does can recover from poorly structured code, having a wrong number of partitions, not having enough memory, or asking too much of each executor. These are problems you need to identify and fix before you put your job into production, okay?

Managing dependencies

Another thing I want to talk about is managing dependencies. Something to remember is, even if something runs perfectly on your desktop, it doesn't mean it will run on your cluster. This is because you might not have the same Java environment, the same Scala environment, or the same Python environment. Another point to make is that the same data won't be there. If your scripts are referring to absolute file paths or file paths on your local desktop system, you're going to want to make sure you fix those before you run them on the cluster. What you could do is refer to a path that's on some distributed file system that each node has access to, or use things such as broadcast variables to actually share data outside of your RDDs and broadcast out to all the nodes. However, your master node needs to get to that data somehow originally, before it can broadcast it to all the core nodes.

Try not to depend on obscure Python packages. If you do have a driver script that needs some weird Python package as a dependency and it's not preloaded on your Spark cluster, you can always set up a step in Elastic MapReduce to run `pip` and install whatever you need as it's in the process of spinning up each node. There's also a `--py-files` argument you can pass to `spark-submit` to add individual libraries and pass them off to the executor nodes, but again, that's only going to work if you already have the packages you need on the master node. Its a bit of a chicken and egg situation: `pip` is probably the only realistic way to deal with this problem, otherwise, you still have to get what you need to the master node somehow. However, just try to avoid using obscure packages if you can. Time is money in your cluster and the less time you spend fiddling with dependency issues the better. The best solution is: if you don't need some weird package that doesn't come pre-installed on your cluster, don't use it. If you do need some weird cluster, you can use a step in the EMR process to get that installed as part of the bootstrap process for setting up your individual nodes. This is my brain dump on running Spark in a cluster.

Summary

This concludes the part of the course about Spark core, covering the things you can do with Spark itself. We did pretty much everything there is to do, and we actually ran a million ratings, and analyzed on a real cluster in the cloud using Spark. So congratulations, if you've got this far! You are now pretty knowledgeable about Spark. In the next chapter, we'll talk about some of the technologies built on top of Spark that are still part of this greater Spark package.

5
SparkSQL, DataFrames, and DataSets

In this chapter, we'll spend some time talking about SparkSQL. This is becoming an increasingly important part of Spark; it basically lets you deal with structured data formats. This means that instead of the RDDs that contain arbitrary information in every row, we're going to give the rows some structure. This will let us do a lot of different things, such as treat our RDDs as little databases. So, we're going to call them DataFrames and DataSets from now on, and you can actually perform SQL queries and SQL-like operations on them, which can be pretty powerful.

Introducing SparkSQL

What is structured data? Basically, it means that when we extend the concept of an RDD to a DataFrame object, we provide the data in the RDD with some structure.

One way to think of it is that it's fundamentally an RDD of row objects. By doing this, we can construct SQL queries. We can have distinct columns in these rows, and we can actually form SQL queries and issue commands in a SQL-like style, which we'll see shortly. Because we have an actual schema associated with the DataFrame, it means that Spark can actually do even more optimization than what it normally would. So, it can do query optimization, just like you would on a SQL database, when it tries to figure out the optimal plan for executing your Spark script. Another nice thing is that you can directly read and write to JSON files or JDBC-compiled and compliant databases. This means that if you do have your source data that's already in a structured format, for example, inside a relational database or inside JSON files, you can import it directly into a DataFrame and treat it as if it were a SQL database. So, powerful stuff, isn't it?

Using SparkSQL in Python

In Python, it's pretty straightforward to use structured data. There are actually a couple of different interfaces that I'm going to look at in more detail in the examples to come. In short, you can do any of the following:

- Import things directly from a JSON file
- Import things directly from a Hive database
- Connect directly to a JDBC database
- Convert RDDs into DataFrames if you know their schema under the hood

Here's a quick example to showcase some of those imports:

```
from pyspark.sql import SparkSession, Row
hiveContext = HiveContext(sc)
inputData = spark.read.json(dataFile)
```

Once you have a DataFrame, you can do things such as create or replace `TempView` to create a table in memory that you can issue SQL queries on, for example:

```
inputData.createOrReplaceTempView("myStructuredStuff")
```

Pretty cool, isn't it? Then you can use the `SELECT foo FROM bar ORDER BY foobar` SQL query

```
myResultDataFrame = hiveContext.sql('"""'SELECT foo FROM bar ORDER BY
foobar'"""')
```

You can do whatever you want to, and you don't even have to use SQL queries – there are ways to do this programmatically as well.

More things you can do with DataFrames

As you can see, DataFrame is a very powerful syntax. Let's look at a few more examples. You can call `show` if you're debugging to show the top 20 rows in your DataFrame:

```
myResultDataFrame.show()
```

You can select a given row and create a new DataFrame out of it:

```
myResultDataFrame.select("someFieldName")
```

Another neat thing is that you can construct little expressions inside these queries. For example, you could do the following:

```
myResultDataFrame.filter(myResultDataFrame("someFieldName" > 200))
```

From the DataFrame, this would filter out anything where the value of a given row's `someFieldName` column is greater than 200. You can use very intuitive syntactic expressions to actually express complicated logic inside your queries.

You can also do `groupBy` on a DataFrame, a `mean` or `count` operation, or whatever you want. So things that were more challenging earlier in the book, such as counting the number of movie ratings or a number of ratings for a given movie ID, have suddenly become a lot simpler. We don't have to go through all the contortions we've discussed to map things to key/value pairs, where the value is 1, and then count up and add all those 1 values together. You can just do `groupBy` and count, and you're done with one line of code:

```
myResultDataFrame.groupBy(myResultDataFrame("someFieldName")) mean()
```

Again, this is a high-level API that actually gives you a lot more power, and it can often result in much simpler code. So, in general, if you can express your problem in terms of DataFrames, you should.

Differences between DataFrames and DataSets

Until Spark 2.0, people talked about DataFrames a lot, and the term made its way into the lexicon of Spark. You'd hear people talking about DataFrame APIs. However, in Spark 2.0, a DataFrame is a DataSet of Row objects. So now, in Spark 2.0, they talk about DataSets, and this can get a little bit confusing. A DataSet is just a DataFrame of structured data, so it can contain more than one Row object; it can contain a specific type of class. This is more important if you're coding in Scala or Java. Since Python is untyped to begin with, you're not really going to sense the difference when you're coding Spark code in Python. You just need to be aware of the terminology. Therefore, when people talk about DataSets, they're really talking about a DataFrame full of structured data. Of course, more accurately, a DataFrame is a DataSet of Row objects. We're going to use Python here, so you don't need to worry about it too much. Within Python, you can use those terms interchangeably, but given the choice, use a DataSet; that's the way to go in future.

Shell access in SparkSQL

Another cool thing about SparkSQL is that with it, you can actually expose a shell that you can connect to. So if you cache a table, you can actually connect to it by starting a server and issuing SQL queries to it, just like you would with any other database. Here are the key features of the process:

- SparkSQL exposes a JDBC/ODBC server (if you build Spark with Hive support)
- You start SparkSQL with `sbin/start-thriftserver.sh`
- It listens on port `10000` by default
- You connect to it using `bin/beeline -u jdbc:hive2://localhost:10000`
- Voila, you have a SQL shell for SparkSQL
- You can create new tables or query existing ones that were cached using `hiveCtx.cacheTable("tableName")`

Think about how powerful this is: You can have a Spark cluster running that would encompass a massive database spread out across an entire cluster of computers, and you can query that cluster as if it were a relational database, using a SQL prompt. One example of this power is that databricks (`www.databricks.com`) has something called the Databricks Community Edition, which is a product that lets you play around with Spark inside a Python notebook. You can issue SQL queries interactively using this system as well. So it's kind of a neat feature.

User-defined functions (UDFs)

One last thing to talk about SparkSQL is that you can also have user-defined functions, so you can create your own functions. For example, in the following piece of code, we'll define a square function that takes x and returns x times x:

```
from pyspark sql.types import IntegerType
hiveCtx.registerFunction("square", lambda x: x*x, IntegerType())
df = hiveCtx.sql("SELECT square('someNumericField') FROM tableName)
```

Once you define this type of function and register it, you can use it within your SQL queries. So you can extend the SQL syntax yourselves to do specialized operations, which will get executed across your cluster automatically.

Let's look at a few real examples of using SparkSQL. We're going to do three things:

- First, we'll look at using SQL commands directly
- Next, we'll look at using more SQL-style functions in a problem
- Finally, we'll go back to an RDD-based solution, which we covered earlier in the book, and actually implement it with DataSets instead

Again, DataSets are the way of the future in Spark 2.0. You'll see it being used more widely as a common interface between the different components of Spark. Therefore, MLlib now has a DataSet-based API, Spark Streaming has a DataSet-based API, and so on. DataSets are a very important concept to understand, especially as Spark develops in the future. Let's go ahead and look at some examples.

Executing SQL commands and SQL-style functions on a DataFrame

Alright, open up the `sparksql.py` file that's included in the download files for this book. Let's take a look at it as a real-world example of using SparkSQL in Spark 2.0. You should see the following code in your editor:

```
1  from pyspark.sql import SparkSession
2  from pyspark.sql import Row
3
4  import collections
5
6  # Create a SparkSession (Note, the config section is only for Windows!)
7  spark = SparkSession.builder.config("spark.sql.warehouse.dir", "file:///C:/temp").appName("SparkSQL").getOrCreate()
8
9  def mapper(line):
10     fields = line.split(',')
11     return Row(ID=int(fields[0]), name=str(fields[1].encode("utf-8")), age=int(fields[2]), numFriends=int(fields[3]))
12
13 lines = spark.sparkContext.textFile("fakefriends.csv")
14 people = lines.map(mapper)
15
16 # Infer the schema, and register the DataFrame as a table.
17 schemaPeople = spark.createDataFrame(people).cache()
18 schemaPeople.createOrReplaceTempView("people")
19
20 # SQL can be run over DataFrames that have been registered as a table.
21 teenagers = spark.sql("SELECT * FROM people WHERE age >= 13 AND age <= 19")
22
23 # The results of SQL queries are RDDs and support all the normal RDD operations.
24 for teen in teenagers.collect():
25   print(teen)
26
27 # We can also use functions instead of SQL queries:
28 schemaPeople.groupBy("age").count().orderBy("age").show()
29
30 spark.stop()
31
```

Notice that we're importing a few things here. We're importing the `SparkSession` object and the `Row` object. The `SparkSession` object is basically Spark 2.0's way of creating a context to work with SparkSQL. We'll also import collections here:

```
from pyspark.sql import SparkSession
from pyspark.sql import Row

import collections
```

Earlier, we used to create `sparkContext` objects, but now, we'll create a `SparkSession` object:

```
# Create a SparkSession (Note, the config section is only for Windows!)
spark = SparkSession.builder.config("spark.sql.warehouse.dir",
"file:///C:/temp").appName("SparkSQL").getOrCreate()
```

So what we're doing here is creating something called `spark` that's going to be a `SparkSession` object. We'll use a `builder` method on it, then we will just combine these different parameters to actually get a session that we can work with. This will give us not only `sparkContext`, but also a SQL context that we can use to issue SQL queries on. Here goes the first part:

```
config("spark.sql.warehouse.dir", file:///C:temp)
```

This part is only needed on Windows. It's kind of a workaround, well frankly, a bug in Spark 2.0. If you're not on Windows, go ahead and delete this part. If you are on Windows, leave that part as is and make sure you have a `temp` folder in your `C:` drive; otherwise, point it to someplace else.

Alright, we're going to give `appName` a name-SparkSQL-and then call `getOrCreate` to create it. This gives back a `SparkSession` object that we can start using.

Now what we're going to do is take our fake social network data and use SQL queries to analyze it instead of doing RDD operations. Unfortunately though, this data is not structured to begin with. It's just a CSV file, a bunch of text as far as we're concerned. So, before we can import the data into a structured DataFrame object, we need to provide some structure to it. Just like we would normally, open up the text file and give it to a mapper to convert it into a `Row` object:

```
def mapper(line):
    fields = line.split(',')
    return Row(ID=int(fields[0]), name=str(fields[1].encode("utf-8")),
age=int(fields[2]), numFriends=int(fields[3]))

lines = spark.sparkContext.textFile("fakefriends.csv")
```

```
people = lines.map(mapper)
```

This is basically converting an RDD that's splits comma-separated values into a DataFrame. Remember that a DataFrame in Python is really just an RDD of Row objects. Let's go into this in a little bit of more detail; let's give it a little more attention.

First of all, we call sparkContext on the SparkSession object we created:

```
lines = spark.sparkContext.textFile("fakefriends.csv")
```

This gives us the same kind of sparkContext we saw previously in this book. From there, we can just call textFile with fakefriends.csv.

Now that we have sparkContext, we can pass it to our mapper function:

```
def mapper(line):
    fields = line.split(',')
    return Row(ID=int(fields[0]), name=str(fields[1].encode("utf-
    8")), age=int(fields[2]), numFriends=int(fields[3]))
```

This just splits up each line by commas and then creates Row objects, and as you can see, we're giving some structure to these objects. We're going to have an ID column that would consist of the customer ID, a name column for a string name, an age column that would be integer-based, and a numFriends column that would be integer-based as well. So this mapper basically provides the structure and specifically typed information back to our RDD. Under the hood, Spark can use this information-how each row is structured and what these columns are-to more compactly represent the DataFrame and deal with it in a more optimal manner.

So, at this point, you can think of people as almost a DataFrame. We just need to call spark.createDataFrame to officially make it a DataFrame and take the RDD of row objects and treat it as a DataFrame:

```
# Infer the schema, and register the DataFrame as a table.
schemaPeople = spark.createDataFrame(people).cache()
```

You'll also see that at the end of the line, we'll cache spark.createDataFrame because we're going to do more than one thing to it. Let's start by issuing actual SQL queries to it. So we first call createOrReplaceTempView:

```
schemaPeople.createOrReplaceTempView("people")
```

What this line does is to create a sort of a temporary SQL table in memory, called people, that we can issue queries on. Because schemaPeople is now a DataFrame, it'll look at those rows and the names of those rows and subsequently create columns.

Let's look at how to define this row:

```
return Row(ID=int(fields[0]), name=str(fields[1].encode("utf-8")),
age=int(fields[2]), numFriends=int(fields[3]))
```

These parameters are our column names, and we can issue them in actual queries. So we can say:

```
# SQL can be run over DataFrames that have been registered as a table.
teenagers = spark.sql("SELECT * FROM people WHERE age >= 13 AND age <= 19")
```

Remember that spark is the name of SparkSession. Next, we write out our SQL query, just like it were a SQL database. Also, because we defined our Row object with a parameter of age, it knows that the age corresponds to the third column of the DataFrame. That's it! Everything works. It's some kind of magic, but it's pretty cool.

So there you have a high-level API. Now we can issue arbitrary SQL queries to a DataFrame. All we had to do was structure our data and then put it into a DataFrame using Row objects. At this point, I could just call teenagers.show to print out the top 20 results, or I can treat it as an RDD, like so:

```
# The results of SQL queries are RDDs and support all the normal RDD
operations.
for teen in teenagers.collect():
  print(teen)
```

I can collect the results and print them out, and it'll print out the individual Row objects of that DataFrame.

Using SQL-style functions instead of queries

You don't have to use SQL queries anymore; it's arguably a little bit more efficient to use SQL-style functions instead. Let's discuss a way to do this. Remember in the previous chapters we had to jump through some hoops to reduce things together and actually do things, such as count the number of people by identifying how many people of each age exist, for example? We can do all of this with just one line of code using DataFrames:

```
# We can also use functions instead of SQL queries:
schemaPeople.groupBy("age").count().orderBy("age").show()
```

Let's take a look at what we're doing here. We're using the cached `schemaPeople` DataFrame and calling `groupBy`, using the `age` column, and then doing a count. This is exactly like issuing a SQL query that's grouped by age and counting and then ordering the results by age and showing them. So what this particular line of code does is it groups together all the people of a given age and counts them up-at this point, we have a DataFrame of ages-and how many people of that age occur in the DataFrame. We can order the result by age and show the top 20 results.

So, in one line of code, we've done what would otherwise have been a more complicated and convoluted implementation using straight-up RDDs. You know we don't have to actually create key/value RDDs, where the value is 1, and then reduce them together to count them up; we can just say `groupBy` and `count` to do the same thing in one line.

Let's run this code and see whether it actually does what we think it will do. Open up your Command Prompt and go to wherever you are storing your course materials and type:

```
spark-submit spark-sql.py
```

You could do this just as well in the interactive Python prompt as well, if you want to. Check it out:

```
Row(ID=21, age=19, name=u'Miles', numFriends=268)
Row(ID=52, age=19, name=u'Beverly', numFriends=269)
Row(ID=54, age=19, name=u'Brunt', numFriends=5)
Row(ID=106, age=18, name=u'Beverly', numFriends=499)
Row(ID=115, age=18, name=u'Dukat', numFriends=397)
Row(ID=133, age=19, name=u'Quark', numFriends=265)
Row(ID=136, age=19, name=u'Will', numFriends=335)
Row(ID=225, age=19, name=u'Elim', numFriends=106)
Row(ID=304, age=19, name=u'Will', numFriends=404)
Row(ID=341, age=18, name=u'Data', numFriends=326)
Row(ID=366, age=19, name=u'Keiko', numFriends=119)
Row(ID=373, age=19, name=u'Quark', numFriends=272)
Row(ID=377, age=18, name=u'Beverly', numFriends=418)
Row(ID=404, age=18, name=u'Kasidy', numFriends=24)
Row(ID=409, age=19, name=u'Nog', numFriends=267)
Row(ID=439, age=18, name=u'Data', numFriends=417)
Row(ID=444, age=18, name=u'Keiko', numFriends=472)
Row(ID=492, age=19, name=u'Dukat', numFriends=36)
Row(ID=494, age=18, name=u'Kasidy', numFriends=194)
```

The first thing we did was we printed out the actual contents of the DataFrame we had; after that, we used SELECT * FROM people WHERE age >= 13 AND age <= 19. This should give us all the teenagers in our DataFrame and sure enough it does. What we're getting back here are the actual Row objects of that DataFrame, with the individually named columns inside each object. Let me give you a little bit of a peek into the inner structure of this DataFrame. I could just call show and it would show the result in a more compact manner; alternatively, I could use a SELECT command on it to extract specific rows that I care about.

The next thing we did was we used this syntax:

```
schemaPeople.groupBy("age").count().orderBy("age").show()
```

This counts up how many people of each age exist and sorts that by age. Sure enough, it has worked as well:

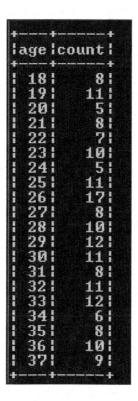

In this output, you can see that in our DataSet, we had eight 18 year olds, eleven 19 year olds, and so on and so forth. The `show` command will just print out the top 20, but you could collect the whole thing and print it out if you want to as well.

So there you have it, SparkSQL in action. Like I said before, this is the direction that Spark is going toward. As you can see, it's a very powerful and high-level API, and it also allows Spark to do more optimization under the hood. Although not everything can be thought of in terms of SQL queries, a lot of times it can; if you can, then you should use DataFrames instead of straight-up RDDs. It may seem a little bit counterintuitive that this high-level API can be faster and more efficient, but it does allow Spark more opportunities to optimize things under the hood. So, once again, DataFrames are very important to understand.

Using DataFrames instead of RDDs

Just to drive home how you can actually use DataFrames instead of RDDs, let's go through an example of actually going to one of our earlier exercises that we did with RDDs and do it with DataFrames instead. This will illustrate how using DataFrames can make things simpler. We go back to the example where we figured out the most popular movies based on the MovieLens DataSet ratings information. If you want to open the file, you'll find it in the download package as `popular-movies-dataframe.py`, or you can just follow along typing it in as you go. This is what your file should look like if you open it in your IDE:

```python
1 from pyspark.sql import SparkSession
2 from pyspark.sql import Row
3 from pyspark.sql import functions
4
5 def loadMovieNames():
6     movieNames = {}
7     with open("ml-100k/u.ITEM") as f:
8         for line in f:
9             fields = line.split('|')
10            movieNames[int(fields[0])] = fields[1]
11    return movieNames
12
13 # Create a SparkSession (the config bit is only for Windows!)
14 spark = SparkSession.builder.config("spark.sql.warehouse.dir", "file:///C:/temp").appName("PopularMovies").getOrCreate()
15
16 # Load up our movie ID -> name dictionary
17 nameDict = loadMovieNames()
18
19 # Get the raw data
20 lines = spark.sparkContext.textFile("file:///SparkCourse/ml-100k/u.data")
21 # Convert it to a RDD of Row objects
22 movies = lines.map(lambda x: Row(movieID =int(x.split()[1])))
```

Let's go through this in detail. First comes our import statements:

```python
from pyspark.sql import SparkSession
from pyspark.sql import Row
from pyspark.sql import functions
```

We start by importing `SparkSession`, which again is our new API in Spark 2.0 for doing DataFrame and DataSet operations. We will import the `Row` class and `functions`, so we can do SQL functions on them:

Next, we have our `loadMovieNames` function:

```python
def loadMovieNames():
    movieNames = {}
    with open("ml-100k/u.ITEM") as f:
        for line in f:
            fields = line.split('|')
            movieNames[int(fields[0])] = fields[1]
    return movieNames
```

This just creates a map of movie IDs to `movieNames`, and that's unchanged from the earlier example. We're going to use `loadMovieNames` to look up the movie names as we print out results at the end.

So let's get into the meat of the script. We'll create a `SparkSession` object, just like we did earlier:

```
# Create a SparkSession (the config bit is only for Windows!)
spark = SparkSession.builder.config("spark.sql.warehouse.dir",
"file:///C:/temp").appName("PopularMovies").getOrCreate()
```

 Remember that if you're on a non-Windows system, you need to delete the config clause in the middle of the line. This clause is only needed on Windows, and it's only to work around a Windows bug in Spark 2.0. Refer to the earlier part of this chapter if you need more details. So, if you are on Windows, leave the clause as is and make sure you have a `C:/temp` folder. If you're not on Windows, delete that part.

We give our app a name, called `PopularMovies`, and then have a `SparkSession` object that we can work with.

First, we load up our dictionary of movie IDs to `movieNames`:

```
# Load up our movie ID -> name dictionary
nameDict = loadMovieNames()
```

We'll use this later in the script for printing out human-readable results. First, though, let's start by getting the `sparkContext` object that's part of `SparkSession` and calling `textFile` to import our unstructured data:

```
# Get the raw data
lines = spark.sparkContext.textFile("file:///SparkCourse/ml-100k/u.data")
```

So, `u.data` again is just a text file as far as Spark is concerned. Now, if it were in a structured format, such as JSON, we would have done something like `spark.read.json` instead. This would have converted it directly into a DataFrame, which would be pretty cool. In this case, though, we have to first provide our own structure to it. Fortunately, it's pretty simple:

```
# Convert it to a RDD of Row objects
movies = lines.map(lambda x: Row(movieID =int(x.split()[1])))
```

To do this, we'll call map by taking each line of the input and creating a Row object consisting of a single column named movieID. Since all we're doing is counting how many times each movie ID occurs, the only column that we really care about is the movieID column. So let's go ahead and split the row, extract column number 2, and call it movieID.

What we now have is an RDD called movies that consists of Row objects, where each row consists of a single column named movieID. We can convert it into a DataFrame:

```
# Convert that to a DataFrame
movieDataset = spark.createDataFrame(movies)
```

This will allow Spark to treat it as a miniature database really, and this will give it all the opportunities of optimizing queries. Alright, at this point, we have a DataFrame called movieDataset. Remember, a DataFrame is just a DataSet of Row objects as far as Spark terminology is concerned.

Now we can do something like this:

```
# Some SQL-style magic to sort all movies by popularity in one line!
topMovieIDs = movieDataset.groupBy("movieID").count().orderBy("count",
ascending=False).cache()
```

As in our previous example, we'll do movieDataset.groupBy("movieID"). Again, from the Row object we constructed, we know that movieID is the name of the column. Carrying on with the line, we count it up by movieID and order it by count in descending order. So, we can pass this extra parameter to orderBy that says I want you to go in descending order, and therefore, get the most popular movies on the top. Next, I'm going to cache the resulting DataSet to do more than one thing to it.

At this point, I can show the top 20 results with the show command:

```
topMovieIDs.show()
```

The show command is a very handy command for debugging. Here's an example of what you should see:

```
#|movieID|count|
#+-------+-----+
#|     50|  584|
#|    258|  509|
#|    100|  508|
```

This is a sample result that I've typed in as a comment for illustration. It's just a new DataSet that consists of my original `movieID` column and a new `count` column that was added by our `count` command.

Finally, to get the results I want, I can call `take(10)` to just get the top 10 results out of the DataSet:

```
# Grab the top 10
top10 = topMovieIDs.take(10)
```

I can then print them all using `nameDict`, which I had earlier, to actually map the names to human-readable movie names:

```
# Print the results
print("\n")
for result in top10:
    # Each row has movieID, count as above.
    print("%s: %d" % (nameDict[result[0]], result[1]))
```

When you're done, remember to stop the session:

```
# Stop the session
spark.stop()
```

From a coding standpoint, `SparkSession` is just like opening a connection to a database. You want to make sure you close that connection when you're done.

Let's go ahead and run this code. We're going to open up the Command Prompt to put our course materials. Again, if you want to do this through a Canopy Command Prompt, that's fine too; it doesn't really matter. I'm just showing you more than one way of doing it. Enter the following command:

```
spark-submit popular-movies-dataframe.py
```

Let's go ahead and run this. It's a large DataSet: 100,000 ratings, remember? So it's going to move forward on this and do a little bit of more work than we normally do. You'll see Spark's progress as it breaks it up into multiple stages. When it's finished, you should see something like the following:

```
+-------+-----+
|movieID|count|
+-------+-----+
|     50|  584|
|    258|  509|
|    100|  508|
|    181|  507|
|    294|  485|
|    286|  481|
|    288|  478|
|      1|  452|
|    300|  431|
|    121|  429|
|    174|  420|
|    127|  413|
|     56|  394|
|      7|  392|
|     98|  390|
|    237|  384|
|    117|  378|
|    172|  368|
|    222|  365|
|    313|  350|
+-------+-----+
only showing top 20 rows


Star Wars (1977): 584
Contact (1997): 509
Fargo (1996): 508
Return of the Jedi (1983): 507
Liar Liar (1997): 485
English Patient, The (1996): 481
Scream (1996): 478
Toy Story (1995): 452
Air Force One (1997): 431
Independence Day (ID4) (1996): 429
```

So, remember, we started off by printing the table of intermediate results where we looked at the contents of the `topMovieID` DataSet. You can see that we ended up with our `movieID` column and our `count` column that were added by the `count` command. This is why we see the list of movie IDs and their total counts. We also showed the top 20 results for debugging purposes. To get our final results, we took the top 10 and mapped them to their human-readable names using our dictionary, and the results are the same as before. You can see *Star Wars* is the most rated movie, just as we expected, followed by *Contact*, *Fargo, Return of the Jedi, Liar Liar*, and *The English Patient*. This DataSet is showing age from the 1990's, but it is accurate data, so there you have it.

Summary

It is interesting how you can actually use these high-level APIs using SparkSQL to save on coding. For example, just look at this one line of code:

```
topMovieIDs = movieDataset.groupBy("movieID").count().orderBy("count",
ascending=False).cache()
```

Remember that to do the same thing earlier, we had to kind of jump through some hoops and create key/value RDDs, reduce the RDD, and do all sorts of things that weren't very intuitive. Using SparkSQL and DataSets, however, you can do these exercises in a much more intuitive manner. At the same time, you allow Spark the opportunity to represent its data more compactly and optimize those queries in a more efficient manner.

Again, DataFrames are the way of the future with Spark. If you do have the choice between using an RDD and a DataFrame to do the same problem, opt for a DataFrame. It is not only more efficient, but it will also give you more interoperability with more components within Spark going forward. So there you have it: Spark SQL DataFrames and DataSets in a nutshell and in action. Remember, this lesson is very important going forward. Let's move on and take a look at some of the other technologies and libraries available with Spark.

6
Other Spark Technologies and Libraries

Introducing MLlib

If you're doing any real data or science data mining or machine learning stuff with Spark, you're going to find the MLlib library very helpful. **MLlib (machine learning library)** is built on top of Spark as part of the Spark package. It contains some useful libraries for machine learning and data mining and some functions that you might find helpful. Let's review what some of those are and take a look at them. When we're done, we'll actually use MLlib to generate movie recommendations for users using the MovieLens dataset again.

MLlib capabilities

The following is a list of different features of MLlib. They have support in the library to help you with these various techniques:

- Feature extraction
  - Term Frequency / Inverse Document frequency useful for search
- Basic statistics
  - Chi-squared test, Pearson or Spearman correlation, min, max, mean, and variance

- Linear regression and logistic regression
- Support Vector Machines
- Naïve Bayes classifier
- Decision trees
- K-Means clustering
- Principal component analysis and singular value decomposition
- Recommendation using Alternating Least Squares

I don't really have time to go into what machine learning is and what all these different techniques use in a lot of depth, but this should mean something to you if you're coming from a data science, statistics, or data mining background.

- Feature extraction

  A very common approach to handling search, especially, for web pages, is Term Frequency / Inverse Document Frequency. MLlib has some built-in ways to compute that given RDD. So, if you're dealing with a massive corpus of web pages, say you're a big web search company, for example, you might find a way of distributing that through a Spark cluster to be very useful. MLlib that can help with that.

- Basic statistics

  MLlib also gives you some very basic statistics functions. If you just want to very quickly find out the minimum or maximum value in an RDD or the mean or the variance of an RDD, it provides functions to do that really quickly. It also gives you ways to compare two RDDs together, using Pearson or Spearman correlation functions, and it gives you a function for the Chi-squared test. Even if you just take Statistics 101 or read Statistics For Dummies, you should learn what all those various terms mean, if you don't know already.

- Linear regression and logistic regression

  MLlib also has functions for linear regression and logistic regression. If you have an RDD full of data points that are a time series of some sort, you can predict future performance based on past performance just by basically fitting a line or curve to the set of data and extrapolating it to where it goes.

- Naive Bayes classifier

  A common example of using a Naïve Bayes classifier is for a spam filter. You can actually train a Bayes classifier as to what is spam and what is real email by giving it a set of known spam and known email. You can use that to try to classify future emails as spam or not spam. This is an example of supervised learning.

- Decision trees

  You can use MLlib to construct decision trees from a group of data, and automatically compute what tree of various conditions you need to follow in order to get to a certain point in your data. There's some cool stuff you can do there.

- K-Means clustering

  This is a way to automatically discover interesting groups that exist in your data.

- Principal component analysis and singular value decomposition

  This is a very big, complicated topic but it's a very powerful one. I've actually used this in the past for movie recommendations. Although it's a very expensive thing to do, splitting it out on a Spark cluster makes it a little bit more accessible, which excites me because the results I've seen from that have been creepy good. With singular value decomposition-based approaches, you have to wonder if it's some insight into how the human brain works because what can come out of this stuff really borders on artificial intelligence. I'm excited to see what people do with that part of MLlib in the future.

- Recommendations using Alternating Least Squares

    Finally, MLlib gives us a built-in recommendations algorithm using Alternating Least Squares. This is important because that's actually the approach that the Netflix prize took. A long time ago, Netflix actually offered a large cash prize to any researcher that could improve upon their movie recommendation algorithm. The winner was actually an approach that used this technique called Alternating Least Squares. MLlib has a way of creating, with just a few lines of code, recommendations of not just movies but anything else. These recommendations can be based on either explicit ratings like we've been seeing in the MovieLens dataset, or implicit ratings, which might just be the act of somebody viewing something or purchasing something. Given that we looked at movie recommendations before in this book, let's do it again in this section.

Special MLlib data types

One thing you need to understand with MLlib is that it does have a few special data types. For example, it has a `Vector` type that can be either dense or sparse. Sparse vectors can be useful if you have a matrix in machine learning, where most of the cells are empty. It's a more compact way of representing vectors or arrays of data where a lot of the values have nothing in them. This actually happens pretty often when you're doing things such as recommendations. It also has `LabeledPoint`, allowing you to attach some sort of meaning to a data point. Finally, in the context of recommendations, it has a `Rating` type that we'll look at later in this section.

For more information on machine learning

If you want to learn more about this stuff, as I mentioned earlier, there are various basic statistics books you can use and I'll suggest more resources you can go into at the end of this book. A quick recommendation, for now, I like the book *Advanced Analytics with Spark, O'Reilly*. Not only does this show you how to use this stuff in more depth, stuff that is really worthy of a course of its own, but it also assumes that you're not a machine learning expert already. It actually takes the time to very concisely and accurately convey some of these concepts for you. So, if you want to learn more about MLlib, I'd recommend starting there and hey, I might actually write a book on it myself at some point too. Alright, let's make some movie recommendations.

Making movie recommendations

Believe it or not, the following code is all you need to replicate what was done with the Netflix prize and actually create what should be really good movie recommendations. However, as we'll see, your mileage may vary.:

```
data = sc.textFile("file:///SparkCourse/ml-100k/u.data")

    ratings = data.map(lambda l: l.split()).map(lambda l: Rating(int(l[0]),
    int(l[1]), float(l[2]))).cache()

rank = 10
numIterations = 20
model = ALS.train(ratings, rank, numIterations)

recommendations = model.recommendProducts(userID, 10)
```

Let's walk through it. All it's doing is opening up a text file from your hard drive, the same old `u.data` file you're used to all the time:

```
data = sc.textFile("file:///SparkCourse/ml-100k/u.data")
```

Next, it's going to map it out just like we did before. It's going to split it out based on whitespaces and then map that to a rating structure:

```
ratings = data.map(lambda l: l.split()).map(lambda l: Rating(int(l[0]),
int(l[1]), float(l[2]))).cache()
```

As we discussed, MLlib has some special types and rating is one of them. Rating is basically saying you rated something some value, so we're going to pull out the user, the movie, and the rating itself. Then, we'll cache that because we're going to use that `ratings` RDD more than once. So remember, if you want to use more than one action on ratings, under the hood, our ALS MLlib function is going to call that `ratings` RDD multiple times. So we need to make sure that we cache or persist that RDD for it to work efficiently:

```
rank = 10
numIterations = 20
model = ALS.train(ratings, rank, numIterations)
```

From here, it's just a one line of code thing **ALS (Alternating Least Squares)** is part of the MLlib library:

```
model = ALS.train(ratings, rank, numIterations)
```

We tell it to train itself based on our ratings data. There are several magic numbers that you need to pass into it that are extremely important and affect the results greatly. Unfortunately, there's no real guidance given as what you should set those to, so you kind of have to experiment, iterate, and try different values until you get results that you like. In our example, we'll use a rank of 10 and a number of iterations of 20. I find that the more iterations you have, the better it does. Although, the more iterations you have, the more work it needs to perform and the less likely it is to succeed on a single node. Finally, we will just use the resulting model to actually recommend products, movies in this case, for a given user ID. We're saying we want 10 recommendations for whatever user ID we want:

```
recommendations = model.recommendProducts(userID, 10)
```

That's all there is to it. That's only 8 lines of code to make movie recommendations!

That's MLlib in a nutshell. Since we've been dealing a lot with movie recommendations here in this book, I can't resist showing you what the Alternating Least Squares part of MLlib can actually do. Let's kick off an ALS movie similarities job using the MovieLens data and see what happens.

Using MLlib to produce movie recommendations

Let's take a look at some code to actually run Alternating Least Squares recommendations on the MovieLens dataset. You'll see just how simple it is to do and we'll take a look at the results.

You can download the script from the download package for this book. Look for movie-recommendations-als.py, download that into your SparkCourse folder, and then we can play with it. This is going to require us to input a user ID that I want recommendations for. So, how do we know if recommendations are good? Since we don't personally know any of the people that are in this dataset from MovieLens, we need to create a fictitious user; we can kind of hack their data to stick it in there. So, in the ml-100k folder, I've edited the u.data file. What I've done here is I've added three lines to the top for user ID 0, because I happen to know that user ID 0 does not exist in this dataset:

0	50	5	881250949
0	172	5	881250949
0	133	1	881250949

I looked up a few movies that I'm familiar with, so I can get a little more of a gut feel as to how good these recommendations might be. So, movie ID 50 is actually *Star Wars* and I've given that a five star rating. ID 172 is *The Empire Strikes Back*, and I've given that a five star rating as well, and 133 is *Gone With The Wind*, for which I gave a one star rating. Actually, I didn't hate it that much but the point here is I'm trying to create a persona of a science fiction nerd who really likes *Star Wars* and really doesn't like old movies from the 1930s that are about melodramatic people, to put it politely. So, let's see what kind of recommendations we get. I'd expect to see other similar science fiction-related, blockbuster action films and not movies such as Gone With The Wind.

Examining the movie-recommendations-als.py script

We already looked at the code, but we'll open it up and take a look at it in Python just for completeness. So, open up the `movie-recommendations-als.py` file. A lot of this code is the same. We have the same boilerplate stuff. One thing to point out is that we do need to explicitly import the ALS and ratings classes from `pyspark.mllib.recommendation` in order to use them:

```
import sys
from pyspark import SparkConf, SparkContext
from pyspark.mllib.recommendation import ALS, Rating
```

Down in line 13, you can see we're going to run this across our entire set of cores that we have:

```
conf =
SparkConf().setMaster("local[*]").setAppName("MovieRecommendationsALS")
```

Otherwise, everything is like we had it before in the previous section. In line 27, we train it based on the 100k MovieLens ratings:

```
model = ALS.train(ratings, rank, numIterations)
```

Then, down in line 37, we simply ask you to use that same model to generate rmmendations for a given user ID that we have put as a parameter:

```
recommendations = model.recommendProducts(userID, 10)
```

This will give us the top ten recommendations for user ID 0, assuming that's what I pass in. So let's kick it off and see what happens.

Analyzing the ALS recommendations results

Open up **Command Prompt** and type `spark-submit movie-recommendations-als.py` with user 0:

```
(User) c:\SparkCourse>spark-submit movie-recommendations-als.py 0
```

That user 0 is my Star Wars fan that doesn't like Gone With The Wind.

Off it goes, using all the cores that I have. It should finish quite quickly. For such a fancy algorithm, that came back creepily fast, almost suspiciously so:

```
Ratings for user ID 0:
Star Wars (1977): 5.0
Empire Strikes Back, The (1980): 5.0
Gone with the Wind (1939): 1.0

Top 10 recommendations:
Love in the Afternoon (1957) score 6.42090083536
Roommates (1995) score 6.39431215726
Burnt Offerings (1976) score 6.38702183096
Lost in Space (1998) score 6.38680899253
Endless Summer 2, The (1994) score 6.30275992511
Primary Colors (1998) score 6.03035775839
Drunks (1995) score 5.92894606542
Cronos (1992) score 5.71380632161
unknown score 5.676838214
Double Team (1997) score 5.65588319517

(User) c:\SparkCourse>
```

So, for my fictitious user who loves *Star Wars* and *The Empire Strikes Back*, but hated *Gone With The Wind*, the number one recommendations it produced was something called *Love in the Afternoon* and *Roommates*. What? What is this stuff? That's crazy. *Lost in Space*, okay, I can go with that, but the rest of this just doesn't make sense. What's worse is if I run it again, I'll actually get different results! Now, it could be that the algorithm is taking some shortcuts and randomly sampling things to save time, but even so, that's not good news.

Let's see what we get if we run it again. We get a totally different set of results:

```
Ratings for user ID 0:
[Stage 280:>                                                    (0 + 2) / 2]
[Stage 280:============================>                        (1 + 1) / 2]

Star Wars (1977): 5.0
Empire Strikes Back, The (1980): 5.0
Gone with the Wind (1939): 1.0

Top 10 recommendations:
Roommates (1995) score 7.87966702947
I'll Do Anything (1994) score 7.57841013131
Shall We Dance? (1937) score 7.23874848332
Don't Be a Menace to South Central while Drinking Your Juice in the Hood (1996)
score 6.72436905195
Low Down Dirty Shame, A (1994) score 6.13396930989
Army of Darkness (1993) score 5.98367809308
Underneath, The (1995) score 5.9643946162
Lord of Illusions (1995) score 5.95305643224
Hard Eight (1996) score 5.93277528025
In the Line of Duty 2 (1987) score 5.88337368104

(Canopy 64bit) C:\SparkCourse>
```

There's something in there that I might agree with- *Army of Darkness*, yeah, people who like *Star Wars* might be into that. But this other stuff? Not so much. Let's run it one more time; I mean, we've got to get something good out of here at some point:

```
Top 10 recommendations:
War, The (1994) score 6.65716239806
Low Down Dirty Shame, A (1994) score 6.44548993994
Lost in Space (1998) score 6.27515939994
Love in the Afternoon (1957) score 5.60112839882
Schizopolis (1996) score 5.56638126463
Meet John Doe (1941) score 5.11439598351
Star Wars (1977) score 5.04373210278
Addiction, The (1995) score 4.96306972202
Empire Strikes Back, The (1980) score 4.92202227603
Fast, Cheap & Out of Control (1997) score 4.91837364129
```

Well, hey, at least *The Empire Strikes Back* showed up, but wait, that was actually one of the movies I started with, so why is that even in the results? I don't know. Well, let's talk about what might be going on here.

Why did we get bad results?

These results are pretty sketchy, so let's talk about what might be going on there. The first thing to mention is there are a couple of parameters to that ALS method there for Alternating Least Squares and the results are very sensitive to the parameters you choose. It actually takes a lot of work to find the optimal parameters to get good recommendations out a given dataset. Now, there are some techniques you can use in machine learning to try to arrive at the right parameters. There's a technique called "train/test," where you withhold a portion of the data as sort of a training dataset and another portion as a testing dataset, and you evaluate your ability to predict user ratings using your algorithm going forward. There are measures of recommendation accuracy that use that technique. What you could do is actually create a nested loop to try every possible combination of those parameters you can think of, and measure which one gives you the best results. But even that's kind of a dodgy thing to do because you could end up overfitting to the dataset that you have. One algorithm might work very well, one set of parameters might work very well for this particular 100k MovieLens dataset from 1998, but that doesn't mean the same parameters will work well on a dataset from a different UI, where different people were using it, or from a different time, or a different location.

There's also this sort of bigger question of, what is a good recommendation anyway? Does the ability to predict movies that I have already seen and rated make a good recommendation? Should I be recommending things that I haven't heard of before? It's kind of debatable. Honestly, those results are so sketchy, I'm not even convinced it's working properly internally. Putting your faith into a black box like this is kind of a dodgy thing to do. We're kind of trusting that a very complicated ALS algorithm under the hood works perfectly, and that may not be the case. We'd actually get better results using our movie-similarities results from earlier to recommend similar movies to movies that you already said that you liked. So, complicated isn't always better and a black box isn't always better. Never put your blind trust into something like this when you're analyzing big data. Question things and remember that small problems in your algorithms can explode into big ones with large datasets. Often the real issue is the quality of your input data; that also needs to be looked at too. All that said, MLlib's still really cool. Some of its other components are very useful and much more simple.

There we have it, our results from Alternating Least Squares were a little bit underwhelming. All the more reason to go and do it yourself the way you want to. If you go back, I think the results we were getting out of our `movie-similarities` script just using a simple cosine metric were actually better. If you were to use that in an item-based collaborative filtering context to actually recommend new movies to people based on those similar movies, I think those results would actually be preferable. However, this is the algorithm that won the Netflix prize, so there's got to be something to it. Maybe we just didn't choose the right parameters, who knows? Maybe the data isn't really amenable to it. But this is what you get when you have a black box algorithm like that, you don't have a whole lot of insider control as to what's actually going on within there. However, MLlib is in there, free to use, and some of its more basic functions will be a lot more straightforward and easy to understand. You definitely shouldn't shy away from MLlib because of this; it has a lot to offer and a lot of useful functionality in there that you may find useful to have in your toolbox going forward. Let's talk about some more Spark technologies next.

Using DataFrames with MLlib

So, back when we mentioned Spark SQL, remember I said DataFrames are kind of the way of the future with Spark and it's going to be tying together different components of Spark? Well, that applies to MLlib as well. There's a new DataFrame-based API in Spark 2.0 for MLlib, which is the preferred API going forward. The one that we just mentioned is still there if you want to keep using RDDs, but if you want to use DataFrames instead, you can do that too, and that opens up some interesting possibilities. Using DataFrames means you can import structured data from a database or JSON file or even a streaming source, and actually execute machine learning algorithms on that as it comes in. It's a way to actually do machine learning on a cluster using structured data from a database.

We'll look at an example of doing that with linear regression, and just to refresh you, if you're not familiar with linear regression, all that is fitting a line to a bunch of data. So imagine, for example, that we have a bunch of data of people's heights and weights. We imagine there's some linear relationship between these two things, so taller people tend to weigh more, right? Makes sense. If we have a bunch of known data points of people's heights and weights, we can actually use that to construct a linear regression model, where we actually create an equation of a line with the given slope that actually is the best fit and minimizes the error between the actual observed heights and weights and what we're predicting with our line. Once we have that line, we can use it to predict new heights for people, given their weight or vice versa. So that's the idea behind linear regression. Let's see how it works with MLlib using DataFrames.

Examining the spark-linear-regression.py script

Open up `spark-linear-regression.py` file and have a look at the code. First we'll import, from the ML library, a regression, a `LinearRegression` class:

```
from pyspark.ml.regression import LinearRegression
```

Note that we're using `ml` instead of MLlib here. `ml` is basically where the new data frame APIs live, and going forward, that's going to be where Spark wants you to start using these. We're also going to import `SparkSession` and `Vectors`, which we're going to need in order to represent our feature data within our algorithm:

```
from pyspark.sql import SparkSession
from pyspark.ml.linalg import Vectors
```

Let's go ahead and look at the script itself, down in line 11. We'll start by creating a `SparkSession` object just like we did back in the Spark SQL lectures. Remember that this `.config` clause in this line should be removed if you're not on Windows. This is a Windows specific hack to work around a bug in Spark 2.0 on Windows. Make sure you have a `C:/temp` folder if you want to run this on Windows. We'll just call this `appName("LinearRegression")` and get our `SparkSession` that we can work with:

```
# Create a SparkSession (Note, the config section is only for Windows!)
spark = SparkSession.builder.config("spark.sql.warehouse.dir",
"file:///C:/temp").appName("LinearRegression").getOrCreate()
```

We're going to start with unstructured data, so I've provided a `regression.txt` file within the download package for this book that you should be working with. Along with the `spark-linear-regression.py` script file, you should also have saved the `regression.txt` data file into your course materials. This could represent anything, it's just normalized data. We've actually mapped this to a normal distribution, the idea being that you would scale it back up when you're done to its actual value:

```
# Load up our data and convert it to the format MLLib expects.
inputLines = spark.sparkContext.textFile("regression.txt")
data = inputLines.map(lambda x: x.split(",")).map(lambda x:
(float(x[0]), Vectors.dense(float(x[1]))))
```

You can imagine it represents anything, let's stick with heights and weights in this example. So, it's basically two columns of information that are separated by columns. In machine learning terminology, we talk about labels and features. Typically, a label is the thing you're trying to predict and a feature is a set of attributes of objects that you can use to make that prediction. So, let's imagine we are trying to predict heights based on your weight, in that case, the label would be the height and the feature would be the weight. To express things in that terminology, the format that MLlib is going to expect, we'll map that input data and split it with commas:

```
data = inputLines.map(lambda x: x.split(","))
```

Next, we'll map it into this format shown here, where we have our label, let's call it the height:

```
data = inputLines.map(lambda x: x.split(",")).map(lambda x: (float(x[0]),
```

Then we'll construct a dense vector of our feature data:

```
data = inputLines.map(lambda x: x.split(",")).map(lambda x: (float(x[0]),
Vectors.dense(float(x[1]))))
```

Whatever our features are, it has to go into a dense vector, that's what MLlib expects. In this case, we only have one thing in that vector, which is the weight.

At this point, we can actually then convert that to something MLlib can understand. Let's convert that to a DataFrame:

```
# Convert this RDD to a DataFrame
colNames = ["label", "features"]
df = data.toDF(colNames)
```

We need to give these columns some names, right, so we're going to say explicitly, the first column we showed in line 15-(float (x[0])-is going to be called label. The second column-Vectors.dense(float(x[1]))))-will be called features. Now we have a DataFrame that ML can work with.

We have a DataFrame of feature and label data, our heights and weights. It's time to construct a model from that. I'll give you a little bonus lesson here on machine learning in general. The way you can evaluate the effectiveness of a model of machine learning is using a technique called train/test. The idea is that you split your input data into two sets randomly, you take a set of that data and use it for actually constructing your model and training your model, and then you hold aside a set of other data that you use to test that model. The idea is that if you take a bunch of data that your model has never seen before, you can evaluate how well that model can predict the labels in that test dataset:

```
# Let's split our data into training data and testing data
trainTest = df.randomSplit([0.5, 0.5])
trainingDF = trainTest[0]
testDF = trainTest[1]
```

What we're doing here in these lines of code is, first, we're splitting up our DataFrame into two sets, randomly, 50-50:

```
trainTest = df.randomSplit([0.5, 0.5])
```

We then take the first dataset that comes back and call it our training DataFrame:

```
trainingDF = trainTest[0]
```

Then we're going to call the second one our test DataFrame:

```
testDF = trainTest[1]
```

Next, we'll create a linear regression model with some certain parameters that we've chosen:

```
# Now create our linear regression model
lir = LinearRegression(maxIter=10, regParam=0.3, elasticNetParam=0.8)
```

Then we'll fit that model to our training data, we call fit on that fifty percent of data that we held aside for training the model:

```
# Train the model using our training data
model = lir.fit(trainingDF)
```

Since that is in exactly the right format that the linear regression model expects-a DataFrame of labels and dense vectors of features-you can use that to create a linear model that fits that data.

Now we can take our test data and use our model to make predictions. We now have a new DataFrame that contains not only our labels and features but also a new prediction column. We'll cache that so we can do multiple things to it:

```
# Now see if we can predict values in our test data.
# Generate predictions using our linear regression model for all features
in our
# test dataframe:
fullPredictions = model.transform(testDF).cache()
```

Next, we'll select the prediction column out of that resulting DataFrame, and map that to just plain old values:

```
# Extract the predictions and the "known" correct labels.
predictions = fullPredictions.select("prediction").rdd.map(lambda x: x[0])
```

We'll also extract the labels:

```
# Extract the predictions and the "known" correct labels.
predictions = fullPredictions.select("prediction").rdd.map(lambda x: x[0])
labels = fullPredictions.select("label").rdd.map(lambda x: x[0])
```

We've basically taken what the model has predicted, the known labels and known correct values out of that DataFrame. We can now zip them back together and print them out side by side to compare the two. There are more principled ways of doing this, you can actually compute things such as R-squared, for example, but I don't want to get into too much machine-learning lingo here. Let's just print out the predicted and actual values side by side here as an exercise.

Getting results

Open up your shell, wherever it may be, and type in `spark-submit spark-linear-regression.py` to kick that off:

```
(User) c:\SparkCourse>spark-submit spark-linear-regression.py
```

Here are our results:

```
<0.8061518555150741, 1.19>
<0.956678266497083, 1.25>
<0.863495250174886>, 1.27>
<0.9423424178321297, 1.34>
<1.049861282819279, 1.36>
<0.9136707205022232, 1.44>
<1.0785329801491854, 1.45>
<1.0928688288141386, 1.52>
<1.1358763748089984, 1.53>
<1.1502122234739516, 1.54>
<1.1502122234739516, 1.55>
<1.1358763748089984, 1.59>
<1.0928688288141386, 1.74>
<1.3939216507781564, 1.78>
<1.2648990127935775, 1.82>
<1.3007386344559606, 1.85>
<1.2290593911311944, 1.93>
<1.5086084400977824, 1.95>
<1.479936742767876, 1.98>
<1.329410331785867, 2.0>
<1.594623532087502, 2.08>

(User) c:\SparkCourse>
```

You can see that our model is pretty good, there's a pretty good correlation between our actual observed values and the predictions, they tend to go in the right direction and they're not too far apart. There you have it, we basically constructed a linear model using MLlib, using DataFrames. The point here isn't really so much to show you how linear regression works, it's to show you how to use DataFrames with MLlib.

Let's review what we did quickly. We constructed this DataFrame of labels and features:

```
colNames = ["label", "features"]
df = data.toDF(colNames)
```

We fed that into a linear regression model, and then we could use that model to make predictions:

```
model = lir.fit(trainingDF)
```

That's all there is to it. It's actually a fairly simple API when you get down to it. So, there you have it, we've done an example of using DataFrames with MLlib. This, as I mentioned, is the way of the future in Spark 2.0 and beyond.

Spark Streaming and GraphX

The last two things I want to cover in this chapter are Spark Streaming and GraphX, which are two technologies built on top of Spark. Spark Streaming handles continually incoming real-time data, say from a series of web logs from web servers that are running all the time. GraphX offers some tools for network analysis, kind of like the social network analysis that we were doing back when we were looking at superheroes and their relationships to each other. I'm going to cover Spark Streaming and GraphX at kind of a hand-wavey high level, because they're currently incomplete. Neither one really has good support for Python yet, right now they only work in Scala and they're in the process of being ported to Java and Python. However, by the time you read this book they might very well be available. So, all we can do is talk about them at this point, but I think you'll get the idea. So, follow along and let's see what's there.

What is Spark Streaming?

Spark Streaming is useful for very specific tasks. If you have a continual stream of data that needs constant analysis, then Spark Streaming is for you. A common example of using it is if you have a fleet of web servers running and you need to process log data coming into it continuously. Who knows what you want to do, maybe you want to keep track of the most frequent occurrences, or keep an eye out for a certain kind of error; Spark Streaming can do that. The way it works is that, at some given interval that you define, it will aggregate the data that's coming in and analyze it however you say. So you can reduce things or map things for example, at some given time frame after a certain batch of data has been taken in from your stream. You can feed data to it, you know, just plain old text information over some port that you open up, that's the most straightforward way to use Spark Streaming. However, it can also connect to things such as HDFS, Amazon's Kinesis service, Kafka, Flume, and others, the list is growing all the time.

Another thing that Spark Streaming offers is something called "checkpointing." For fault-tolerance, it would kind of suck if your entire job that's been running forever suddenly lost everything that it was doing because one machine failed. Checkpointing will store the state of your Spark Streaming job to disk periodically, so if you do have some sort of hardware failure, you can seamlessly pick up where it left off-at least in theory. As I mentioned, Python support for Sparks Streaming is currently incomplete, although it is underway and partial, so by the time you read this, there's a good chance it will be done and available for you in Python as well. For now, we're stuck with Scala for it. We'll look at a little example here in Scala, knowing that Scala code in Spark looks a lot like Python code. This shouldn't be too far fetched from what you would see in Python.

Spark Streaming sets up what we call a "Dstream" object, which breaks up your incoming stream into a bunch of distinct RDDs. So, as individual time frames elapse, you'll receive a new RDD to process with your stream. Here's a simple example:

```
val stream = new StreamingContext(conf, Seconds(1))
val lines = stream.socketTextStream("localhost",8888)
val errors = lines.filter(_.contains("error"))
errors.paint()
```

In the first line, this just sets up a Streaming context based on some configuration that will actually boil things down every one second:

```
val stream = new StreamingContext(conf, Seconds(1))
```

Then it will connect that to port 8888 on our localhost:

```
val lines = stream.socketTextStream("localhost",8888)
```

Then we say `lines.filter`, lines being what's coming out of our text stream every one second, to filter out things that contain an error, put that into our `errors` RDD and print out the results:

```
val errors = lines.filter(_.contains("error"))
errors.paint()
```

This is a very simple example of Spark Streaming that just listens for lines of text that contain the word `error` and prints them out when they occur. That's not all the code you need to write, you actually need to kick this off in your driver kit, you need to call `stream.start` and `stream.awaitTermination` to start your Spark Streaming job:

```
stream.start()
stream.awaitTermination()
```

Once you do that, it'll start listening to port 8888 and print out anything it receives that contains the word error. Potentially, you can do that in a distributed manner.

There are some things to remember with Spark Streaming. Remember, your RDDs only contain one little chunk of incoming data, so if you need to aggregate data over time, there are a couple of ways that it lets you do that. One is using what's called "windowed operations." This lets you combine results over some window of time, some sliding time window. Let's say for example, you had sales data coming in through your stream and you want to print out the top sellers over the past 24 hours. You could create a sliding window of 24 hours and tell Spark to keep reducing by that 24-hour window. Operations such as window(), reduceByWindow(), and reduceByKeyAndWindow() make it very easy to do something like that:

```
reduceByWindow(), reduceByKeyAndWindow()
```

Finding top sellers or most frequently viewed web pages on your website over a period of time are some examples of applications you could very easily do using Spark Streaming. I wish I could go back in time and redo some of the stuff I did at Amazon and IMDb because that would have made life so much easier.

There's also updateStateByKey(). If you need to maintain something like a running count or some sort of state that persists across the entire run of your job, you can do that using updateStateByKey. It will maintain that state across many batches as they come in as time goes on. This is another tool in your toolbox for doing things over longer periods of time than your actual batch size in Spark Streaming. Shifting gears, let's talk about GraphX.

GraphX

GraphX is another library built on top of the Spark core. It's not that kind of graph where you have lines, pies, charts, bars, and stuff like that. It's "graph" in the sense of graph theory. For example, our social network of superheroes is an example of that kind of a graph. Currently, it is Scala only, although Java support is almost done. As soon as Java support is done, Python support will pretty much follow on top of that, so they're actually very close to getting that done at this time, and by the time you read this book, there's a good chance Python and Java support will exist for GraphX. However, it's currently only useful for some very specific things. Obviously, it's going to evolve over time, but GraphX in its current form wouldn't have actually helped us very much with our `degrees-of-separation` example that we did. It can do things such as measure the properties of a social graph or any graph of information for that matter. If you need to measure things such as connectedness or degree distribution, average path lengths, triangle counts, these are all high-level measures of the properties of a given graph and GraphX can help you compute these very quickly in a distributed manner. GraphX also has tools for quickly joining graphs together and transforming graphs quickly. If you need to do operations like that, GraphX is worth a look. Go see if you need to learn Scala, or if they actually have Python or Java support already.

Under the hood, GraphX introduces two new types of objects, the `VertexRDD` and `EdgeRDD`. For example, in our social network of superheroes, a superhero would be a vertex and a connection between two superheroes would be an edge. Apart from that, GraphX code looks like any other Spark code, it's not that hard to pick up really. There are very specific tasks and very specific fields for which you will find GraphX useful. I just want you to know that it's out there, and if you do have a problem in that realm, check it out.

Summary

That's Spark Streaming and GraphX, and with that, we've covered pretty much everything there is about Spark, at least as of this date. Congratulations! You are now very knowledgeable about Spark. If you've actually followed along and gone through the examples and done the exercises, I think you can call yourself a Spark developer, so well done Let's talk about where to go from here next and what the next steps are for continued learning.

7
Where to Go From Here? – Learning More About Spark and Data Science

If you made it this far, congratulations! Thanks for sticking through this whole book with me. If you feel like it was a useful experience and you've learned a few things, please write a review on this book. That will help me improve the book in future editions. Let me know what I'm doing right and what I'm doing wrong, and it will help other prospective students understand if they should give this course a try. I'd really appreciate your feedback.

So where do you go from here? What's next? Well, there's obviously a lot more to learn. We've covered a lot of the basics of Spark, but of course there is more to the field of data science and big data as a whole. If you want more information on this topic, *Packt* offer an extensive collection of Spark books and courses. There are also some other books that I can recommend about Spark. I don't make any money from these, so don't worry, I'm not trying to sell you anything. I have personally enjoyed *Learning Spark, O'Reilly*, that I found to be a useful reference while learning. It has a lot of good little snippets and code examples in there that you may find useful. If you're going to be using Spark for some real machine learning and data mining work, I also recommend *Advanced Analytics with Spark, O'Reilly Press*. It takes more of a data mining look at things, going into things such as MLlib in a lot more depth, for example. What I really like about this book is that it doesn't assume that you're a machine learning or a data mining expert; it takes the time to actually review things such as K-means clustering and Pearson correlation metrics. It doesn't assume that you're already an expert in this stuff, and it's written in a very conversational tone. Data mining and machine learning doesn't have to be hard. The concepts themselves are actually pretty straightforward once you grasp them; you've just got to get through the terminology and all the fancy language.

There's also a book called *Data Algorithms, O'Reilly,* which is a very thick book. It's not really Spark specific: it's actually written for Hadoop and MapReduce and also Spark, as sort of a third option. So you have a bunch of recipes for the different types of problems you might encounter in the machine learning world and some sample solutions to those problems using MapReduce and Spark side-by-side. It does spend a lot of time on the MapReduce side and Spark is always last. I'm not really sure it was written with Spark in mind in the beginning. The tone, in contrast with *Advanced Analytics with Spark,* is a little bit more academic. You might find it a little bit less accessible if you're new to the field. Nevertheless, there are some useful recipes in there, so my recommendation would be to go check out the Table of Contents on your favorite bookseller website, and just keep that handy. If you do need to figure out how to perform some specific algorithm in Spark, look to see if it's in that book and if so, it might be worth checking out.

Beyond the world of Spark itself, there's obviously a lot more to the world of data mining and data science in general. Just knowing Spark does not make you a data scientist who will make lots and lots of money, there are other tools and techniques out there. For example, MapReduce is still the Granddaddy of the tools in this area, so learning more about MapReduce is a good option and there are courses on Udemy for that. Just learning about data mining in general is a good idea too. As I mentioned earlier, the *Advanced Analytics with Spark* book touches on that a little bit, but picking up a course such as *Statistics For Dummies* is probably a good place to start if you're totally new to that field. You can also look for courses on machine learning and data mining—they are probably the keywords you want to look for as well as data science is a more general term. There's a lot to learn.

I hope that this book has given you a good starting point on your journey toward a career as a data scientist. If you're already a data scientist or an engineer working at a large software company that has lots of big data to process, I hope you now have Spark as a new tool under your belt. Spark is a very easy, fast, and efficient way to mung large amounts of data on a cluster: if you don't have access to one, EMR gives you a good way to get one pretty cheaply. So, it's been a good ride, thanks for coming along with me.

Index

CPSIA information can be obtained
at www.ICGtesting.com
Printed in the USA
BVOW04s1548050817
490879BV00036B/126/P